Introducing
Psychopathology

SAGE has been part of the global academic community since 1965, supporting high quality research and learning that transforms society and our understanding of individuals, groups and cultures. SAGE is the independent, innovative, natural home for authors, editors and societies who share our commitment and passion for the social sciences.

Find out more at: **www.sagepublications.com**

Introducing
Psychopathology

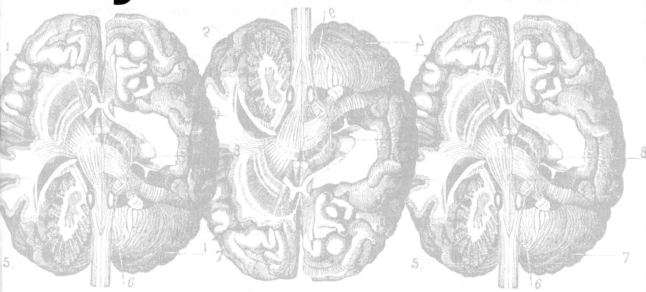

Betty **Rudd**

Los Angeles | London | New Delhi
Singapore | Washington DC

Los Angeles | London | New Delhi
Singapore | Washington DC

SAGE Publications Ltd
1 Oliver's Yard
55 City Road
London EC1Y 1SP

SAGE Publications Inc.
2455 Teller Road
Thousand Oaks, California 91320

SAGE Publications India Pvt Ltd
B 1/I 1 Mohan Cooperative Industrial Area
Mathura Road
New Delhi 110 044

SAGE Publications Asia-Pacific Pte Ltd
3 Church Street
#10-04 Samsung Hub
Singapore 049483

Editor: Kate Wharton
Editorial assistant: Laura Walmsley
Production editor: Rachel Burrows
Copyeditor: Helen Skelton
Proofreader: Fabienne Pedroletti Gray
Indexer: Martin Hargreaves
Marketing manager: Tamara Navaratnam
Typeset by: C&M Digitals (P) Ltd, Chennai, India
Printed and bound in Great Britain by Ashford Colour Press Ltd

MIX
Paper from responsible sources
FSC® C011748

Library of Congress Control Number: 2012954536

British Library Cataloguing in Publication data

A catalogue record for this book is available from the British Library

ISBN 978-1-4462-5290-1
ISBN 978-1-4462-5291-8 (pbk)

To my sister Mary, whose love is my huge pillar of support.

Contents

About the Author

Award-winning author Dr Betty Rudd currently practices as a Chartered Counselling Psychologist at Hygeia Health Centre in Sussex; she is a Doctoral Supervisor and Doctoral Examiner for British Universities, freelance author and inventor (of games for facilitating mental wellness) and Assessor and Co-ordinating Supervisor for trainees on the BPS QCoP Independent Route. Previously, Betty was Senior Lecturer on the Counselling Psychology Programme at the University of East London, and on the Board of Examiners for the BPS QCoP. She contributed to the government-endorsed document *Every Child Matters* and is named by the BPS as an expert in emotional intelligence and non-verbal communication. She has worked with children, teenagers and adults since the 1960s, for ten years under the NHS umbrella within a Community Adult Mental Health Service. In 2002, she retired as BPS DCoP Press Officer, in 2003 as BPS DCoP SCC Chair and in 2004 as an Ordinary Member of the DCoP committee. 'Who's Who in Research', 'Who's Who in Health' and 'Who's Who in the World' list Dr Betty Rudd for her outstanding contributions in her field of endeavour. For more information see www.emotionalliteracy.eu.

Author of the following books:

Talking is for Kids	*Body Mind Update*
Talking is for Us	*EQ Book*
Talking is for Teens	*Great Ways to De-stress*
Talking is for All	*Special Games*
Counsellor's Basics	*Help Your Child Develop Emotional Literacy*

Inventor of the following games:

EQ	*Handling Emotion*
Rainbow board game	*Problem Solving*
EI set of card games	*Relating*
Anger Management	*Responsibility*
Awareness	*Self-image*
Communication	*Stress Control*
Compassion	*Developing Life Skills*

Chapter publication:

'Emotional Intelligence' in *The Routledge International Handbook of Learning*, ed. Peter Jarvis and Mary Watts, 2011.

Preface

Present-day counsellors, counselling psychologists and psychotherapists are under growing pressure to provide evidence-based interventions for their clients within a limited set of therapy sessions ('clients' are referred to as 'patients' if within medical settings such as the National Health Service in the United Kingdom). These therapists are also expected to assess their client, identify purported mental disorders, offer effective interventions which can be backed up in court and deal with referring appropriately. In recent years, the number of sessions on offer has decreased, at least within the NHS in the UK.

My intention with this book is to help students, researchers and those in clinical practice easily understand the categorising of mental distress into specified sets of disorders. I include opportunities for critical debate, as well as information about what to do for mentally distressed clients, based on theory and evidence. In addition, I offer insights into assessments and referrals regarding individuals suffering from psychological problems.

Introducing Psychopathology is peppered with case vignettes. These are composites created to illustrate teaching and learning points. Due to ethical and confidentiality reasons, they do not represent real-life individuals in therapy.

The final part of this book contains an overview, in which research from other disciplines and how this can have a professional impact within the therapeutic field is perused and various highways of realistic hope are lit for future directions. I include clear pointers to where further relevant information can be found, in the hope of supporting trainees on their therapy courses.

Throughout, I have strived to write an interesting 'interactive' book because, during my student days, psychopathology books were boring to me so I did not want to read them. A few decades later, I humbly stand on the shoulders of the authors who wrote those texts in my endeavour to write a book with breadth and depth for trainees that is also a compelling read.

Acknowledgements

Good books are produced because mega-goals are broken into mini-steps. My deep thanks go to those who helped with actualising this work, whether personally known to me or not. Many are acknowledged in the references, others are credited here.

Kate Wharton, I thank you for each uplifting email every time I sent you chapters to read and for sending them to my anonymous reviewers whom I also thank for their sharp-minded feedback! I am further blessed that my commissioning editor, Alice Oven, sought me out because, like me, she cares that trainees learn in an exciting way. Alice, I appreciate you and your powerfully positive encouragement. When you asked me to write this book, I found various individuals for support in bringing the vision of this project into action, to whom I am profoundly and humbly thankful. My thanks go to the cover designer and the whole team at Sage who worked towards getting this book published. Harriet Garrod, when we first met, you were an uncertain doctoral trainee, now you are a confident and skilful doctor; thanks for happily sharing your expertise on assessing. Matthew Wilson, masterful water-sports instructor and educational psychologist, I am grateful to you for your passionate sharing of the implications regarding children being assessed and labelled. Artist and psychologist, JBR, thanks for your generous deliberations and emails on young people; find your influence in part of Chapter 3. William Bloom, you help me bloom; I am grateful to you for those amazing oases-of-light weekends in London and Glastonbury, joyously and generously sharing your thoughts and feelings on how you view the world and inner life, particularly on the necessity of self-reflection and the ripple effects this has. Empathic psychiatrist and gentle friend, Dr Bo Mills, thanks for so open-heartedly confirming aspects of psychiatry. Dearest, kind and knowledgeable medical doctor Louise Ma, I am so grateful to you for giving me such helpful feedback on that fifth chapter. Thanks Tracey Bruce and Annie Walker at Hygeia, your 'front of house' work enables me to have the space for writing, I have much to learn from your outstanding people skills and organisational abilities. Isabelmou, the amazing love you unleash buoys me up during my solitary writing times; thanks my darling. Thanks Marymou, for your pure love; I know that you have been, that you are and that you always will be there for me. Thanks Sophiemou, Mariamou, Benmou and Jasonmou, for letting me have an insight into (some of) your views. I love you! Stevemou, my thanks and love for your ongoing support. Thank you for your understanding, your encouragement, for sharing your opinion about every page and for your love.

Thanks to the thousands of young people and adults I have worked with since the 1960s. During those early days, you were the trailblazers for this book, although I did not know it then.

You, the reader – I may not know you but I thank you for purchasing this book. I hope you will absorb its principles and share its content with others who can benefit from it.

Abbreviations

ABA	applied behavioural analysis
ADHD	attention deficit hyperactivity disorder
APA	American Psychological Society
ASD	autistic spectrum disorders
ASDS	Asberger's Syndrome Diagnostic Scale
ASPD	anti-social personality disorder
AT	automatic thought
ATT	Appropriate Attribution Technique
AvPD	avoidant personality disorder
B	belief
BACP	British Association of Counselling and Psychotherapy
BDD	body dysmorphic disorder
BDI	Beck Depression Inventory
BMA	British Medical Association
BPD	borderline personality disorder
BPS	British Psychological Society
C	consequence
CBT	cognitive behaviour therapy
CD	conversion disorder
CoP	Counselling Psychology
CPD	continuing professional development
DRD	dopa-responsive dystonia genes
CSA	childhood sexual abuse
CV	curriculum vitae
DAPS	Detailed Assessment of Posttraumatic Stress
DBT	dialectical behaviour therapy
DRS-2	Dementia Rating Scale-2
DSH	deliberate self-harm
DSM	*Diagnostic and Statistical Manual*
DSPD	dangerous people with severe personality disorder
DTA	developmental trauma disorder
EMDR	eye-movement desensitisation and reprocessing

ERP	exposure response prevention
FI	family interventions
GAD	generalised anxiety disorder
GP	general practitioner
HCPC	Health and Care Professions Council
HCR-20	Historic Clinical Risk Management assessment tool
IAPT	Improving Access to Psychological Therapies
ICD-10	*The International Statistical Classification of Diseases and Related Health Problems*, 10th Revision
MgT	magnesium-L-threonate
MIT	Massachusetts Institute of Technology
NHS	National Health Service
NICE	National Institute for Health and Clinical Excellence
OCD	obsessive compulsive disorder
OCPD	obsessive compulsive personality disorder
PD	personality disorder
PTSD	post traumatic stress disorder
RCT	randomised control trial
REM	raid eye movement
RSVP	Risk of Sexual Violence Protocol
SA	sexual abuse
SAD	seasonal affective disorder
SPD	schizotypal personality disorder
THC	delta-9-tetrahydrocannabinol
UKCP	United Kingdom Council for Psychotherapy

1
Understanding Psychopathology

LEARNING OBJECTIVES FOR THIS CHAPTER

- Understand what *Introducing Psychopathology* is about
- Know the history behind the concept of psychopathology
- Discuss the philosophical underpinnings of psychopathology
- Have insight into the classification of mental disorders
- Realise that cultural and transcultural issues are involved in psychopathology

---

At the heart of counselling, psychotherapy and counselling psychology lies an understanding of mental distress. This is why knowledge of psychopathology is crucial for trainees entering these professions. Without it, they can get lost in a maze of psychobabble.

When I was a student, I wished for a book that explained mental disorders in a jargon-free, simple way. During my training, ploughing through the great third edition of the *Diagnostic and Statistical Manual for Mental Disorders* (APA, 1987) was a daunting task. What I needed was a simple introduction to psychopathology. I write the simply presented and jargon-free book I wish I had in the hope that it helps those who use (or will use) talking as a therapeutic 'tool' with their clients or patients.

Although having the ability to be a reflective practitioner is key (as I explain later in this chapter), without a breadth and depth of understanding how mental distress manifests in individuals, coupled with a knowledge from theory and research on how to facilitate these people to move in a desired direction, the therapeutic relationship is severely compromised; if indeed, it is present at all. Without such knowledge and understanding, therapists may unwittingly make matters worse. Bearing this in mind, *Introducing Psychopathology* specifically includes points to reflect on. There are teaching and learning features throughout and these are discussed further on.

You do not have to read this book in any particular order. Dip into it at any place. Each chapter can stand in its own right – if you want to find out about being depressed, just go to the chapter that deals with depression. Nevertheless, there is some logic to the order I have written the text. For instance, this chapter is the book's introduction. The one that follows deals with assessing and referring, because these tasks are normally necessary during a first appointment. Then there is a focus on children before the spotlight shines on adults, and finally I consider possible future avenues. Therefore, you can read *Introducing Psychopathology* from cover to cover for a more comprehensive picture.

WHAT IS PSYCHOPATHOLOGY?

Psychopathology derives from two Greek words: 'psyche' meaning 'soul', and 'pathos' meaning 'suffering'. Currently, 'psychopathology' is understood to mean the origin of mental disorders, how they develop and their symptoms. Traditionally, those suffering from mental disorders have usually been treated by the psychiatric profession, which adheres to the DSM-IV-TR (APA, 2002) or ICD-10 (WHO, 1992) for classifying mental disorders. It therefore follows that psychiatrists use the term 'psychopathology' more than people in other professions. Psychiatrists are medical doctors who then train in mental health and are able to treat with medication or/ and in whatever psychotherapy model they have trained in.

Within psychiatry, the term 'pathology' refers to disease. However, viewing mental problems as a disease is a contentious point. Psychotherapists, counselling psychologists and counsellors (who specialise in mind matters and are not medics), view apparent mental dysfunction as mental distress, not necessarily related to pathology. So, the term 'disorder' is used, rather than 'disease'. Other words for diagnosing distress within the mind remain: 'symptoms' meaning 'signs', 'aetiology' meaning 'cause', and 'prognosis' meaning 'expected outcome'.

HISTORY AND PHILOSOPHY

Historical and philosophical factors of psychopathology can easily take up a whole volume. This section offers a psychopathology foundation, which can be built on by looking up the related resources and references listed at the end of the chapter.

Historically, the concept of psychopathology is rooted in the medical tradition. This is where the terms 'diagnosis', 'symptoms', 'aetiology' and 'prognosis' come from (Murphy, 2010). Psychiatrists categorise severe mental distress into psychopathological disorders whose symptoms they can treat with prescribed drugs, and use the word 'patients'. Counselling psychologists, counsellors and psychotherapists favour the term 'clients' over 'patients' (because of the medical connotations of the word 'patients') and use talking, more than anything else, as a therapeutic 'tool'. They also prefer the concept of 'formulation' instead of 'diagnosis, symptoms, aetiology and prognosis'. Throughout this book, instead of repeating 'counselling psychologists, counsellors and psychotherapists', I use the word 'therapists', or 'talking-cures' to mean all three of these professions because although they may require different trainings, their overlap is substantial. But what are the historical roots of these professions?

Ancient Greece

Medical and talking-cure roots are embedded in the soil of ancient Greek philosophy. Indeed, the philosophy of the western world is rooted in ancient Greece, from which the mould of western-world thinking was wrought, influencing the way in which the west is. Therefore it follows that the source of my views grows from this mould, which shapes my world and consequently this book, because I was born, raised and live in the west. If I visit a non-western country, the cross-cultural differences may be too great for me to comprehend. I might think that I understand someone whose philosophical 'template' is embedded within a non-western philosophy, but I may, in my relative ignorance, misunderstand that person. For this reason, the philosophy focused on here relates to the western world. Nevertheless, as therapists in multicultural settings, we need to be aware of a client's culture and adapt appropriately.

It is possible to trace two fine philosophical threads stemming from the ancient Greek philosophers Plato and Aristotle (Plato's student) to the present day. The threads start together as one, with Plato.

The Platonic philosophical thread

Plato taught that humans comprise mind, body and spirit, that the latter is eternal and that there are universal truths outside of time and space, such as honesty and respect. Modern Rogerian counselling, with its basic values of honesty (congruence), compassion (empathy) and respect (unconditional positive regard) – neither judging nor psychopathologising – resonate with Plato's philosophy (Rogers, 1961, 1980). According to Plato, if mind, body and spirit are out of balance in individuals, distress or imbalance is created within them (for more on Plato, see Nails, 2006). This philosophical thread weaves its way into the seventeenth century.

Spinoza

Plato's philosophy influenced Spinoza, who was a seventeenth-century Jewish lens grinder, born in Holland. He stated that the notion of spirit, or God, is central and integral for the body and the mind and, like Plato, believed in an everlasting God. Spinoza philosophised that since our bodies and minds are part of the same divine essence of God, they must not contradict each other. His notion was that distress was not plausible with a harmonious body and mind, and upheld Plato's philosophy of honesty and respect (for more about Spinoza, see LeBuffe, 2010). This fine philosophical thread continued to weave its way, reaching the eighteenth century. At this time, in the UK, conditions for those with mental disorders were inhumane. Inmates in 'madhouses' such as Bedlam (also known as Bethlem and Bethlehem) were referred to as 'mad', 'insane' or 'lunatics'. They were locked up, practically all were naked, force-fed, iron-fettered and lived in disgusting conditions. But there came a change.

Madness cured

In 1700, a man named David Irish claimed to cure madness by offering mental asylum inmates warmth, nutritious food and drink, positive attention, comfort and care rather than having them manacled and living in filth (for more on Irish, see Hunter and Macalpine 1963). Underlying such humane acts is the assumption that all people deserve a basic amount of nurturing. Tension arose between the two philosophical threads, with purported mind-doctors 'pathologising' madness on the one hand and the move towards a more humane way of treating those in mental asylums on the other (Appignanesi, 2010). Indeed, the modern notion of formulation can be seen as having its genesis in the eighteenth century with the ideas of a great philosopher, Rousseau, who recognised that his formative years related to his 'nerves'.

Rousseau

During the eighteenth century, the thinking of Rousseau and the Romantic Movement exploded into the western world like a popping champagne cork. This movement aspired to merge reason with emotion and introduced the notion of the relationship between child and parent being important for sanity. It was Rousseau who reflected that adults suffer from mental distress (nerves) due to pain inflicted during their formative years. He claimed that human inequality is behind individual mental distress. His degeneration theory states that the people who have nothing to lose go back to their primitive and low brutish state, whereas those who can fulfil their potential are enabled to move towards gaining the ideal of perfection (for more on Rousseau see, for example, Farrel, 2006). Contemporary author Gerhardt expresses a similar idea. She illustrates how it is that the countries with the most inequality also have the most mental distress when compared with those with less inequality; she draws on a substantial amount of research findings that back up her theory (2010). This view adds to the tension between an approach to mental health using a medical model (with its focus on pathology) and one advocating talking-cures (which favour formulations).

Hegel

As history marched from the eighteenth to the nineteenth century, another great philosopher emerged, Hegel, who was immensely influenced by Rousseau's ideas. According to Hegel, philosophy is the best and absolute form of knowledge, derived dialectically, bringing together knowledge and experience (for more on Hegel see, for example, Stern, 2002). Talking therapies blossom from this stem. He was the forerunner of the existential school of psychotherapy, prizing the individual's experience and endeavouring to make sense of life; the very idea of psychopathology is anathema to this school and its philosophy.

Twentieth and twenty-first centuries

Existentialism eventually developed into Husserl's phenomenology (for more on Husserl see, for example, Smith, 2007), central to which is the describing of phenomena as they are experienced, rather than interpreting or theorising. It does not make a comfortable bedfellow with psychopathology. What is comfortable for phenomenologists is viewing the relationship between one human life and another. This view continues, flourishing into the current interest shown by many therapists that it is the interpersonal relationship which is of paramount importance for good mental health (Gerhardt, 2008; Rudd, 2008; Gilbert, 2010). Plato's philosophical thread, then, leads from ancient Greece through the Romantic Movement to modern times and the perspective that what happens to us as children has an effect on us as adults – and that we can do something about it (Dawson and Allenby, 2010). Growing numbers of twenty-first century authors support this perspective (for example, Read, Bentall and Mosher, 2004; Rudd, 2008; Gerhardt, 2010). Furthermore, if mental functioning becomes profoundly disturbed, some authors entwine the perspective of interacting with an important other in a relationship with that of pathology, thereby easing tension between the two philosophical threads (for example, Baldwin et al., 1982; Gerhardt, 2008).

By continuing to follow Plato's thread, we are led to emerging research showing that troubled minds, on the whole, are not diseased, and that talking with clients can be substantially helpful (Read, Bentall and Mosher, 2004; Lipton, 2008; Dawson and Allenby, 2010; McTaggart, 2011). Robust research such as that conducted by doctors Harriet, Macmillan and their team (2001) reveals that even lifelong suffering from psychopathological disorders or mental problems is not due to biological illness or disease, but to abuse in childhood. There is more information on this in Chapter 12.

So far, we have followed the thread from Plato in ancient Greece (who declared that the soul is in the pumping heart), to the present day; it therefore seems appropriate to now pick up the thread from Aristotle.

The Aristotelian philosophical thread

Aristotle disagreed with Plato, believing that the soul is in the head and not in the heart, that it dies in the body, and that only reason and rationality are eternal (for more on Aristotle see, for example, Halper, 2005). Due to this, the initial sturdy thread of ancient Greek philosophy split into two fine ones, which is where the tension between them starts. Following the thread from Aristotle, we again weave our way to the seventeenth century.

Locke and CBT

Seventeenth-century philosopher Locke said that mental distress results when we link our emotions to 'wrong' ideas (for more on Locke, see Grayling, 2005). This way of thinking can be seen in the modern approach of cognitive behaviour therapy (CBT) where certain thoughts of those who seek therapy are viewed as unreasonable and the therapist endeavours to teach the client to change these to reasonable ones, thereby influencing emotions. In other words: to change irrational ideas to rational thoughts and therefore impact on emotion. Within this model, the concept of psychopathology can nestle comfortably. Indeed, there is much literature linking CBT with psychopathological labels (for example, Butler, Melanie and Hackman, 2008; van Niekerk, 2009; Christensen and Griffiths, 2011; Kingdom and Turkington, 2005). What are these labels and how might they be grouped? This is deliberated further on.

No more demons

To continue following the Aristotelian thread from Locke, we reach the eighteenth century, where the idea of psychopathology took hold due to the notion that madness was a result of illness, rather than being possessed by the devil, and therefore not under the individual's control. So torturing, which went on previously to remove so-called demons, was stopped and the medical model, with its belief in pharmacology, was adopted, quickly becoming widespread even though much literature supports the perspective that psychological intervention has a powerful effect on individuals (for example, see Rudd, 2003; Gerhardt, 2008; Gilbert, 2010).

Nineteenth, twentieth and twenty-first centuries

The Aristotelian philosophical thread can be followed from the eighteenth, into the nineteenth century where, due to developments in medicine, theories of mental illness were expanded and bathed in medical descriptive language such as 'aetiology' and 'pathology'.

There was then a sea-change in the twentieth century with the closing down of mental asylums (in the UK) as a result of a move away from the disease model. This created space for an interpersonal approach to share the mental-health arena with the medical model. Consequently, tension between the two philosophical threads eased. Today, the mental-health arena continues to be shared, mainly by those who use formulation to look at psychological issues, with those using psychopathology.

HOW MENTAL PROBLEMS ARE ORGANISED

In terms of psychopathology, mental problems are labelled according to symptoms (for example, 'depression'), and theoretically organised by being chunked. Chunking forms categories, for ease of reference, as in the DSM-IV-TR (APA, 2002); an important book which can be, for therapists, what *Gray's Anatomy* is for medics (Gray, 1974). It is worth noting here that, at the time of writing, the DSM-V is soon due to be published (this is addressed later in the book).

I relate psychopathology to health services such as the NHS in the UK, since a substantial number of therapists work under the umbrella of the NHS and many work as independent practitioners, while others work on a voluntary basis or for corporations. In *Introducing Psychopathology* I discuss cultural and transcultural issues regarding psychopathology and underline medication, since it can have an impact on talking-cures. Prescribed medication can be cross-referenced with Chapters 8 and 9. Clients with diagnosed mental disorders who take prescribed drugs often wish to explore their use of medication with their therapeutic psychological counsellor, which should be achievable within the boundaries of the therapist's knowledge and experience (at the time of writing, therapists are not allowed to prescribe medication). I illustrate my point with a case vignette, further down.

Mental disorders

Depression, anxiety, bi-polar, attention deficit hyperactivity disorder (ADHD), autism spectrum disorders, bulimia nervosa, anorexia nervosa and schizophrenia as well as learning and developmental disorders such as autism, are embraced by the term 'mental disorders'. All of these are clustered under what is known as the Axis I category in DSM-IV-TR (APA, 2002). I define and discuss them in later chapters because they tend to be problems that therapists' clients say they suffer from.

Personality disorders and intellectual disabilities

There is a category for personality disorders and intellectual disabilities that includes borderline personality disorder (BPD), and mental retardation, for example, Down's Syndrome. This category is classified under Axis II in DSM-IV-TR (APA, 2002). Physical conditions a person is born with are not focussed on in this text because they are not an area that therapists are trained in. However, BPD is defined and discussed as individuals who can identify as suffering from this may be clients of those who use talking as a therapeutic tool.

Medical conditions and physical disorders

The category for acute medical conditions and physical disorders is classified under Axis III in DSM-IV-TR (APA, 2002). These conditions and disorders incorporate brain injury, medical and physical disorders which aggravate existing diseases or which include symptoms that are similar to other disorders. However, such problems are not fully deliberated on in this book because they are not normally included in the training of therapists.

Psychosocial and environmental factors contributing to disorders

Psychosocial and environmental factors contributing to disorders of the mind have their own category, classified under Axis IV in DSM-IV-TR (APA, 2002). I deliberate on such factors when discussing disorders. My reasoning is that they have either a positive or negative impact on mental health and therefore it is important to understand these issues.

Global assessment of functioning or children's global assessment scale

Classified under Axis V in DSM-IV-TR is a category for global assessment of functioning or children's global assessment scale (APA, 2002). Therapists must know about assessment. If, for example, a therapist is referred a client and the referral letter states that the client is suffering from obsessive compulsive disorder (OCD), the therapist should know about this condition and have the ability to assess for themselves, in order to ascertain whether they agree with the referrer or not. Knowing what to do about referrals, whether relating to a child or adult, is part of practising professionally.

A BIRD'S-EYE-VIEW OF *INTRODUCING PSYCHOPATHOLOGY*

Our journey through this book takes us via twelve stages. Every stage involves travelling through a different chapter. Thus, each chapter can be focused on either per week or month, depending on the course programme a student is on.

Chapter 1

The portal into our journey. Here we perceive the essence of the whole book. This stage puts psychopathology into perspective.

Chapter 2

Our route takes us into assessments and referrals. We see how mental distress is identified. We also perceive the limits of therapists' capabilities.

Chapter 3

Developmental mental problems is the next stage. Young people are highlighted here. In this way, we see issues that may arise at any time from pre-birth to late teens.

Chapter 4

We are a third of the way along our journey, travelling through the anxiety disorders. OCD, panic attacks and negative stress are included in this stage.

Chapter 5

Here, our journey takes us through diagnostic criteria for cognitive disorders. We also voyage through Alzheimer's and vascular disorders. For a more comprehensive view, we take a literary vantage point.

Chapter 6

Here, we travel through mood disorders. Self-harm and suicide are also visited. The difference between just feeling low and depression is spotlighted too.

Chapter 7

Next, our journey takes us to eating and sleeping disorders. For this stage, anorexia and bulimia nervosas are identified. Additionally, problems with over and under-sleeping are floodlit.

Chapter 8

Substance issues are addressed in this section. Substance dependency, commonly called 'addiction', is visited. Further, the concepts of compulsively using a substance or using it for social reasons are unpacked.

Chapter 9

We journey through psychotic disorders of schizophrenia, psychosis and psychotic problems. Factors associated with good and bad outcomes are looked at. We also look at signs and causes of such disorders.

Chapter 10

Somatic disorders are deliberated on at the tenth stage of our route. Body dysmorphia and hypochondriasis are covered. We 'discover' that a somatic disorder can also include pain.

Chapter 11

We voyage through the personality disorders. Here, we consider borderline, narcissistic, dependent, avoidant, paranoid, schizoid, schizotypal, antisocial, obsessive compulsive and histrionic disorders. Plus, relevant literature is perused.

Chapter 12

An overview of *Introducing Psychopathology* is our final stage, in which holistic approaches to mental health are also viewed. These include emotional literacy and the transpersonal concept. We exit our route via a tantalising glimpse of an amazing yet possible future direction.

ASPECTS OF LEARNING

Students have various ways of learning. For this reason, features I offer include all sorts of ways to learn. These are:

- Reflection points for pondering on, to aid independent thought while processing an understanding of the knowledge learnt.
- Case vignettes, for a fuller perspective of related disorders, helping to provide a deeper insight into the psychopathological areas discussed.
- An appropriate exercise for each chapter which can be used to self-test.
- A succinct summing up of every chapter's contents; this is handy for revision.
- A list of useful resources for the reader who wishes to delve deeper or broader into the issues discussed.

THE REFLECTIVE PRACTITIONER

Reflecting on what others say, as well as our own personal thoughts, is important for a therapist. For example, if told by your clinical supervisor to do something, reflect on it; you can decide whether you agree or not and then arrive at a (correct) decision. In this way, self-reflection links to self-management. There are many ways to self-reflect and we each have our own pet way. A few examples of self-reflective ways are: sitting still, lying in bed, or keeping a journal/diary. Whichever way we choose, '…we … need more … time, more reflection, more immersion … That doesn't mean we're retreating from the world, so much as we're moving into a deeper experience of it' (Williamson, 2008 p.155, ll.1–5). Being reflective is self-supervision. Therapists are not the only professionals who self-reflect. Priests, for example, have cloisters to walk around for their daily self-reflection.

We need to take daily time out to check in on ourselves compassionately, because we are human and so can be prone to pomposity about ourselves or to developing neuroses or to being overwhelmed. By reflecting, we can get back in touch with our highest values and deepen our own development, which has a ripple effect into our professional development (Bloom, 2011). Indeed, this ripple can influence the therapy model we decide to use with a client.

Although there are government-endorsed guidelines in NICE (2011) stating that specific therapy models are best used for particular disorders, there is mounting evidence that, irrespective of therapeutic approach, it is the relationship between the therapist and client that is of paramount importance (Davis, 2011; Ellis-Christensen, 2011; Krupnick et al., 2011). However, there is pressure and expectation, for instance in the UK within the NHS, to adhere to the NICE guidelines, apparently without question. This seems to be a way of standardising intervention programmes for psychopathological problems.

Psychopathology helps to identify and classify major mental distress. Nevertheless, if a purported disorder results from unbearable stress that has a detrimental effect in the mind of anyone experiencing the distress, is it really a disorder? Or, considering the stress, could it be viewed as a 'normal outcome', rather than a 'mental disorder'? For example, is it normal to dissociate while being tortured, or to stay connected and fully feel the agony? I know what I would rather do. Indeed, soldiers (in the UK) are taught to dissociate from their emotions (Danielson, 2007). Does this mean that all personnel within the British forces suffer from mental disorders? I do not think so!

Important questions arise, because if we are set up (or set ourselves up) to be experts in identifying mental disorders, there is an implication that we know what mental normality is. Yet, there is a paucity of literature defining this term (Seligman, 2011). We live in a poststructuralist or postmodernist society, where there is more than one truth. If we agree on this, then perhaps a patient labelled as psychotic (maybe because of seeing creatures or hearing voices that most others do not see or hear), has a more sensitive or expanded type of perception than most and is seeing what most are blind or deaf to. In some cultures, for example, Shamanic and Asian cultures (Lukoff, 2007), such a person might be seen as a visionary or spiritual leader. I am being contentious here in the hope of facilitating reflection and debate, as part of the learning experience. Throughout, I do this in various places.

CULTURAL AND TRANSCULTURAL ISSUES

Different disorders, as well as their prevalence in different countries and ethnicities, are involved in cross-cultural issues. It has been vehemently argued that both psychopathology itself and the DSM-IV-TR categories of mental disorders are 90 per cent culture-bound within the USA and the western world (Kleinman, 1997). Intriguingly, a good-enough research project was conducted in Ontario, Canada, where 142 adults aged between 22 and 26 years self-reported being born with very low birth-weight. Findings showed that a statistically significant number suffered as adults either from depression, anxiety or avoidant personality problems (Boyle et al., 2011). It could be useful to have further research conducted internationally to see whether such a correlation exists in other countries between low birth-weight and similar psychological problems in young adults. Societal and cultural factors are very important when it comes to mental health.

There is a gradual move away from disease models relating to mental distress (at least in the UK) and a movement towards explaining meanings, using the concept of formulation rather than diagnosing, while endeavouring to appreciate social and cultural aspects (Bentall, Boyle and Chadwisk, 2000). Consequently, there is a re-emerging of the tension between the psychiatric and psychological approaches, coming from the more contemporary comments on the notions of psychopathology from psychologists such as Bentall and his team who bring societal and cultural factors into relief (2000). An awareness of cross-cultural issues and ethnic diversity can help trainees realise that every town and social group has a different culture. For instance, those living in rural areas may cope differently to mental stresses than inner-city people. With this in mind, it is very important that the universality of psychopathology is not assumed, however tempting it might be when perusing findings from research.

PSYCHOPATHOLOGY RELATED TO THE HEALTH SERVICE AND INDEPENDENT PRACTICE

Within the UK, psychopathology is related to health services, either with those who work independently, for a charity, a private organisation or the National Health Service. Not just health service professionals, but anyone can have access to the NICE (2011) guidelines. Although seemingly prescriptive, they can be useful, particularly for trainees in placements when faced with clients, especially for the first time. However, it is important not to forget practice-based evidence.

Medication

Under the health services umbrella, clients seeing a therapist may also be prescribed medicine for a mental health disorder (see Chapters 8 and 9 for more on this). The case vignette below illustrates this point.

CASE VIGNETTE

Lucy, aged fifty-five, went to see a psychotherapist because she felt anxious. Her doctor had prescribed drugs, which she took diligently. The therapist noticed that Lucy's hands were shaking. During their initial meeting, Lucy said she did not know whether her hands shook because she felt anxious or because of her medication. The therapist looked up the medicine in a reference book and showed Lucy that a side effect is trembling hands. With her permission, he wrote to the doctor stating Lucy's concern about her hands shaking. Lucy's GP responded by changing the medication and gradually reducing it while she was supported by the therapist. Within a month, her hands stopped trembling and she was able to use psychological techniques for managing anxiety. In this case, the client's wish to explore medication was achieved within the boundaries of knowledge and experience of the therapist who liaised appropriately interprofessionally.

Points to ponder

- If much relevant research shows that the relationship is key in a therapeutic encounter, is it ethical to favour one theoretical model above all others?
- What are the implications of stating that specific symptoms point to a disorder, while we live in a twenty-first century postmodernist or poststructuralist society characterised by the idea that there is more than one truth?
- Is it important or not for therapists to belong to a professional organisation such as the UKCP, BPS, BACP or HCPC?
- If the study of psychopathology identifies mental disorder, how can we identify mental normality?

Exercise

(Answers are embedded in this chapter.)

1   What does 'psychopathology' mean?
2   Is body dysmorphia classified as a personality or somatoform disorder?
3   Is schizophrenia classified as a substance or psychotic disorder?
4   Is bulimia nervosa classified as a sleeping or eating disorder?
5   Is depression classified as a mood or cognitive disorder?
6   Is social phobia classified as an anxiety or developmental disorder?
7   Historically and philosophically, what are the roots of psychopathology embedded in?

CHAPTER SUMMARY

Psychopathology is the scientific study of mental disorders.

The history behind psychopathology is rooted in the medical model.

Philosophically, psychopathology stems from ancient Greece.

Within psychopathology, mental disorders are classified into categories of developmental, anxiety, cognitive, mood, eating, sleeping, substance, psychotic, somatoform and personality disorders.

LIST OF USEFUL RESOURCES

- Bergman, S.H. (1974) *Dialogical Philosophy from Kierkegaard to Buber* (Jerusalem, The Bialic Institute).
- Capobianco, R. (2010) *Engaging Heidegger* (Toronto, University of Toronto Press).
- Duncan, S.M. (2008) *The Proof of the External World: Cartesian Theism and the Possibility of Knowledge* (Cambridge, James Clarke and Company).
- Ellenberger, H.F. (1970) *The Discovery of the Unconscious: The History and Evolution of Dynamic Psychiatry* (New York, Basic Books).
- Freudental, G. (1977) *The Philosophy of Science* (Tel Aviv, Everyman's University).
- Joseph, S. (2001) *Psychopathology and Therapeutic Approaches: An Introduction* (London, Palgrave Macmillan).
- Mosley, A. (2007) *John Locke: Continuum Library of Educational Thought* (London, Continuum).
- Mansbach, A. (1998) *Existence and Meaning, Martin Heidegger on Man, Language and Art* (Jerusalem, The Magnes Press).
- Roth, L. (1951) *A Guide to the Study of Greek Philosophy* (Jerusalem, Rubin Mass).
- Roudinesco, E. (2008) *Philosophy in Turbulent Times* (New York, Columbia University Press).
- Stewart, G. (1993) *Understanding Mental Illness* (London, Mind).

RELEVANT WEBSITES

www.frontiersin.org/psychopathology

http://menshealth.about.com/od/conditions/a/eating_disorders.htm

www.myshrink.com/counseling-theory.php?t_id=87

www.radpsynet.org/journal/vol4-1/moreira.html

www.thesudentroom.co.uk/wiki/Revision:Psychopathology

REFERENCES

APA (1987) *Diagnostic and Statistical Manual of Mental Disorders* (Third Edition, revised) (Vancouver, American Psychiatric Association).

APA (2002) *DSM-IV-TR® Diagnostic and Statistical Manual of Mental Disorders* (Fourth Edition, revised) (Vancouver, American Psychiatric Association).

Appignanesi, L. (2010) *Mad, Bad and Sad* (London, Virago Press).

Baldwin, A.L., Cole, R.E., Baldwin, C.P., Fisher, L., Harder, D.W. and Kokes, R.F. (1982) 'The role of family interaction in mediating the effect of parental pathology upon the school functioning of the child', *Monographs of the Society for Research in Child Development*, 47, 5, p. 72.

Bentall, R. P., Boyle, M. H. and Chadwisk, P.D.J. (2000) *BPS Psychosis Report*, www.authorstream.com/Presentation/FunnyGuy-9087-abpsy-ppt-powerpoint/, accessed 19 September 2011.

Boyle, M.H., Miskovic, V., van Liesshout, R., Duncan, L., Schmidt, L.A., Hoult, L., Paneth, N. and Saigel, S. (2011) 'Psychopathology in young adults born at extremely low birth weight', *Psychopathology and Medicine*, 41, 8, pp. 1763–74.

Bloom, W. (2011) Personal communication, 9 November.

Butler, G., Melanie, F. and Hackman, A. (2008) *A Cognitive-Behavioural Therapy for Anxiety Disorders: Mastering Clinical Challenges* (Guides to Individualized Evidence-based Treatment) (New York, The Guilford Press).

Christensen, H. and Griffiths, K. (2011) *The Mood Gym: Overcoming Depression with CBT and Other Effective Therapies* (London, Vermilion).

Danielson, N. (2007) *Our Shell-shocked Soldiers*, www.ninadanielson.com/docs/ptsf.pdf, accessed 1 August 2011.

Davis, W. (2011) *Instroke, Empathy and the Therapeutic Relationship*, www.functionalanalysis.de/e107_files/downloads/Instroke,Empathy%20and%20theTherapeutic%20Relationship.pdf, accessed 19 December 2012.

Dawson, K. and Allenby, S. (2010) *Matrix Reimprinting Using EFT: Re-write Your Past, Transform Your Future* (London, Hay House).

Ellis-Christensen, T. (2011) *What is Talk Therapy?*, www.wisegeek.com/what-is-talk-therapy.htm, accessed 16 September 2011.

Farrel, J. (2006) *Paranoia and Modernity: Cervantes to Rousseau* (New York, Cornell University Press).

Gerhardt, S. (2008) *Why Love Matters* (Hove, Brunner-Routledge).

Gerhardt, S. (2010) *The Selfish Society* (London, Simon and Schuster).

Gilbert, P. (2010) *The Compassionate Mind* (London, Constable).

Gray, H. (1974) *Gray's Anatomy* (Philadelphia, Running Press Book Publishers)

Grayling, A.C. (2005) *Descartes: The Life and Times of a Genius* (New York, Walker).

Halper, E.C. (2005) *One and Many in Aristotle's Metaphysics, Volume 2, The Central Books* (Las Vegas, Parmenides).

Harriet, L., MacMillan, M.D., Fleming, J.E., Streiner, D.L., Lin, L., Boyle, M.H., Jamieson, E., Duku, E.K., Walsh, C.A., Maria, M.S.W., Wong, Y. and Beardslee, W.R. (2001) 'Childhood abuse and lifetime psychopathology in a community sample', *American Journal of Psychiatry*, 158, pp. 1878–83.

Hunter, R.A. and Macapline, I. (1963) *Three Hundred Years of Psychiatry 1535–1864* (Oxford, Oxford University Press).

Kingdom, D.G. and Turkington, D. (2005) *Cognitive Therapy for Schizophrenia* (New York, The Guildford Press).

(Continued)

(Continued)

Kleinman, A. (1997) 'Triumph or pyrrhic victory? The inclusion of culture in DSM-IV', *Harvard Review of Psychiatry*, 4, 6, pp. 342–4.

Krupnick, J.L., Stotsky, S.M., Elkin, I., Simmens, S., Moyer, J., Watkins, J. and Pilkonis, P.A. (2011) 'The role of the therapeutic alliance in psychotherapy and pharmacotherapy outcome: findings in the National Institute of Mental Health Treatment of Depression Collaborative Research Program', *Focus*, 4, pp. 269–77.

LeBuffe, M. (2010) *Spinoza and Human Freedom* (New York, Routledge).

Lipton, B. (2008) *The Biology of Belief* (London, Hay House).

Lukoff, D. (2007) 'Visionary spiritual experiences', *Southern Medical Journal*, 100, 6, pp. 635–41.

McTaggart, L. (2011) *The Bond* (London, Hay House).

Murphy, D. (2010) *Philosophy of Psychiatry*, www.plato-stanford.edu/entries/psychiatry/, accessed 24 September 2011.

Nails, D. (2006) *The Life of Plato of Athens* (Oxford, Blackwell).

NICE (2011) *National Institute for Health and Clinical Excellence*, www.nice.org.uk/action=by.Type&type=2&status=3, accessed 16 September 2011.

Read, J., Bentall, R. and Mosher, L. (eds) (2004) *Models of Madness: Psychological Approaches to Schizophrenia and Other Psychoses* (Hove, Brunner-Routledge).

Rogers, C. (1961) *On Becoming a Person: A Therapist's View of Psychotherapy* (London, Constable).

Rogers, C. (1980) *A Way of Being* (Boston, Houghton-Mifflin).

Rudd, B. (2003) *Body Mind Update, Resource for New Health Findings* (Haywards Heath, Hygeia Health).

Rudd, B. (2008) *Talking is for All: How Children and Teenagers Develop Emotional Literacy* (London, Sage).

Seligman, M. (2011) *Flourish: A New Understanding of Happiness and Well-Being – and How to Achieve Them* (Belgium, Hein Zegers).

Smith, D.W. (2007) *Husserl* (London, Routledge).

Stern, R. (2002) *Hegel and the Phenomenology of Spirit* (New York, Routledge).

van Niekerk, J. (2009) *Coping with Obsessive-Compulsive Disorder: A Step-by-Step Guide Using the Latest CBT Techniques* (Oxford, One World Publications).

WHO (1992) *ICD-10: The ICD-10 Classification of Mental and Behavioural Disorders: Clinical Descriptions and Diagnostic Guidelines* (Copenhagen, World Health Organization).

Williamson, M. (2008) *The Age of Miracles* (London, Hay House).

2

Assessment and Referrals

LEARNING OBJECTIVES FOR THIS CHAPTER

- Understand the importance of assessment
- Identify a client who is at risk
- Learn how to accept referrals
- Know when to refer on
- Communicate interprofessionally
- Realise strengths and weaknesses of classifying mental distress

---

Dealing with referrals and assessing, including risk assessment, are daily aspects of a therapist's life. In this chapter, I include sample assessment forms and referral letters to help students learn to manage these skills. I also aim to help trainee therapists understand the strengths and weaknesses of classification systems such as those in ICD-10 (WHO, 1992) and DSM-IV-TR (APA, 2002), which can be cross-referenced with Chapter 1. Knowing these systems, even if therapists do not agree with them, can help in communicating with other professionals who do classify mental distress.

ASSESSMENT

Assessing is a learnt skill, and a therapist's approach affects how a client is assessed. For example, if a therapist is psychodynamically orientated, assessment is different to that conducted by a CBT therapist. An assessment takes into account the sort of information which the agency that therapists work in wish to glean, as the assessment forms below show.

Before conducting assessments, there is one question to answer. What is the point of assessing clients? Unless you spot that you can work with your client's presenting problem you will be working in the dark, like a surgeon working with no lights on. To ascertain whether to accept a client, you need to assess what the client's problem is, so that you can determine if you can help or not and decide either what therapy model to use or who to refer your client on to.

It is not unusual for mental health agencies to embrace interdisciplinary teams whose members inter-refer and have their own standard assessment forms to use when seeing clients. On the following page is an initial assessment form used at a counselling agency for loss and bereavement, where most of the clients are referred via their GP.

By having this form filled in, a therapist can assess whether to refer a patient on, peek into the patient's history, spot the therapeutic goal, assess the best type of therapy to use and eventually evaluate goal achievement. This is one type of assessment form from a plethora. The one on page 17 can typically be used by an independent therapy service.

NHS AGENCY ADDRESS ...   AGENCY TELEPHONE NUMBER ...
BEREAVEMENT AND LOSS   ASSESSMENT FORM
PRIVATE AND CONFIDENTIAL
Patient's reference: AA1
Patient details:-
Surname ...   Forename(s) ...
Address ...
Date of birth ...   Telephone number ...
        ----*Keep the information above this line separate from the information below it.*----
Title ...   Place of birth ...
Occupation ...   Religion ...
Marital status ...   Number of children ...
Name and contact details of referrer (if different from GP) ...
Name of the patient's GP ...   GP's telephone number ...
GP's address ...
Has the patient received therapy before? ...   If so, when and what for? ...
Is the patient taking prescribed drugs? ...   If so, what for? ...
What medical treatment has the patient had (e.g. surgery)? ...
How tall is the patient? ...   What does the patient weigh? ...
Is the patient seeing any other professional regarding their reason for therapy? ...
What is the patient's reason for coming to therapy now? ...
When was the patient's loss? ...
Describe the patient's life before the loss ...
Describe the patient's life after the loss ...
Has the patient had other major losses and if so, what? ...
Is there anything else that the patient would like to talk about and if so, what? ...
What would the patient like to achieve by attending therapy? ...
How will the patient know when that goal has been achieved? ...
Does the patient have suicidal ideation? ...   Does the patient have a plan for
                                                suicide? ...
Does the patient wish to harm anyone? ...   Does the patient plan to harm
                                                anyone? ...
What are the patient's next of kin's name and contact details ...

Patient's reference: AA1

Patient's signature ...
Therapist's signature ...   Date ...

The two assessment forms, although similar in some ways such as the basic details of age and address, differ in that the one for the loss and bereavement agency focuses on loss. Being under the NHS umbrella, a succinct medical history is asked for. However, the second is more generic in its questions, providing a bird's-eye-view of a client's life, floodlighting the client's emotional arena. There are many assessment forms that are different from one another, depending on what is being assessed. Yet, two important questions are deemed necessary for risk assessment, specifically regarding suicide. These are: 'Have you thought of committing suicide?' and 'Do you have a plan for killing yourself?' If the answer to the first question is 'No', there is no need to

PRIVATE AND CONFIDENTIAL   INDEPENDENT THERAPY SERVICE

INITIAL ASSESSMENT

Reference: Z0Z

Client's full name and title …
Client's date of birth …
Client's full contact details …
      ----*Information above this line must be kept separately from the material below.*----
Permission to use client's contact details? …
Client's occupation … Client's religion … Client's marital status …
Number of children …   Birth place …
Name and contact details of referrer …
Name of client's GP … GP's telephone number …
GP's address …
Permission to contact client's GP? …
Has client received therapy before? … If so, when and what for? …
Is client seeing any other professional regarding their reason for coming here? …
What is client's reason for coming to this service? …
What would client like to achieve by attending this service? …
How will client know when that goal has been achieved? …
Does client have suicidal ideation? … Does client have a plan for suicide? …
Does client wish to harm anyone? … Does client have a plan to harm someone? …
Name and telephone number of the person that client feels closest to …
Permission to contact the person closest to client if necessary? …
Was there any type of abuse (including sexual) in client's family of origin? …
Is client taking any medication (whether prescribed or not)? …
Details of medication (if client is taking any) …
Is client addicted to anything and if so, what? …
Units of alcohol taken, per week? … Cigarettes smoked per week? …
Is client taking any drugs? … If so, which drugs? … How often? … What dosage? …
What is client's presenting problem? …
What was client's life like until the problem was identified (if under twenty years old)? …
What was life like during client's first twenty years of life? (if over twenty) …
What was client's life like between ages twenty and forty? (if over forty) …
What was client's life like between ages forty and sixty? (if under sixty) …
What was client's life like at age sixty-plus? (if over sixty) …
What is client's life like at present? …
Use the back of this form to show client's genogram (family tree with emotional relations)

Reference: Z0Z

Client's signature …
Therapist's signature …   Date …

CONTACT DETAILS OF THERAPY SERVICE

ask the second. Alarm bells ring though, if answers to both questions are 'Yes', as this indicates suicide risk.

RISK ASSESSMENT

An assessment form commonly used to assess depression and suicide risk is the Beck Depression Inventory (BDI; Beck, Steer and Brown, 1996). It is quick to use and can be self-scored. Training in administering the BDI and learning to interpret its score is not very time-consuming or difficult, making this 'test' appealing and handy. Consequently, many therapists use it as part of client assessment.

If it transpires at initial interview that a client has a history of violence and the therapist wants to know if there is a risk of repeated violence, then the Historic Clinical Risk Management assessment tool (HCR-20) can be used (Webster and Douglas, 1997; Ireland, Ireland and Birch, 2009). HCR-20 has twenty questions covering three areas: historical, such as previous violence; clinical, such as unresponsiveness to treatment; and risk management, such as stress.

For any client suspected of being a sex offender (or a potential sex offender), the Risk of Sexual Violence Protocol (RSVP) assessment tool can be used (Hart et al., 2003; Garrod, 2011). There is controversy around tests such as this one, because it is hard to pin down those who develop these types of tests to stating that their test is valid (that is, it tests what it sets out to test) and reliable (meaning that if different therapists use a specified test, they are more than likely to come to the same conclusions). However, because the RSVP claims to predict risk of violence by those who have already committed a sexual offence, it is useful, although limited. Both RSVP and HCR-20 tend to be used in forensic clinical settings, rather than in therapists' private consulting rooms.

DIFFERENT MODELS OF ASSESSMENT

Different strategies for assessing are growing. How is a therapist, in whatever setting, to choose one from the vast array? What seems important is that the mode of assessment is multidimensional, not just focusing on the individual, but also the client's family, life and culture. The key assessment strategy is the client's initial interview. A therapist's informal observation of a client should be twinned with the client's self-report. From this broad-based approach, a therapist can then focus more narrowly on specific aspects pertinent to the client, in order to identify the client's problem or psychological disorder. The therapist can then bring to bear relevant literature and research linked to the problem, in order to deal with the psychological disorder presented by using a relevant therapeutic model.

IDENTIFYING MENTAL DISTRESS

How can mental distress be spotted? Often, the client self-reports, and this is usually coupled with the initial interview. Sometimes, using an assessment form can help back up a therapist's interview assessment of clients. For example, if when seeing a child the therapist suspects Asperger's Syndrome, the Asperger's Syndrome Diagnostic Scale (ASDS) claims reliability and can be administered (Boggs, Gross and Gohm, 2006).

For attention deficit with and without hyperactivity in ages eight to eighteen years, the Clinical Assessment of Attention Deficit – Child (CAT-C) can be used (Arbor, 2011). This instrument consists of three forms: self-report, parent-report and teacher-report. The CAT-C claims strong validity and high reliability.

For a more overall assessment instrument when working with a teenager (aged twelve to eighteen years), the Adolescent Symptom Inventory-4 (ASI-4) can be utilised (Gadow and Sprafkin, 2011). The ASI-4 screens for the following: attention deficit hyperactivity disorder, conduct disorder, anti-social personality, separation anxiety, generalised anxiety, social phobia, depression, dysthymia, oppositional defiant disorder, obsessive-compulsive disorder, schizophrenia, schizoid personality, panic attack, specific phobia, bi-polar disorder, vocal tics, motor tics, anorexia, bulimia and drug use. ASI-4 is based on DSM-IV-TR (APA, 2002) and ICD-10 (WHO, 1992) symptom checklists and comprises two forms: one for the young person's teacher to complete and the other for a parent, or whoever is most familiar with the young person's behavioural and emotional functioning.

The following two tests are for use with adults:

1 The Dementia Rating Scale-2 (DRS-2; Mattis, Jurica and Leitten, 2011) is for assessing dementia. It mainly measures cognitive function. Changes in cognitive status can be tracked over time with this instrument. DRS-2 claims excellent reliability and validity.
2 The Detailed Assessment of Posttraumatic Stress (DAPS) for post-tramantic stress disorder (PTSD) (Briere, 2001) is understood to be a valid test, focusing on a particular trauma. What is useful about DAPS is that it can identify whether the trauma has resulted in other identifiable problems such as suicidal ideation or substance abuse.

There are many hundreds of instruments to choose from yet I do not identify the assessment items named above totally arbitrarily, but because they are either child, teen or adult tests.

(Note: to acquire any of the standardised assessment items above, the original publishers require evidence of qualification.)

First-glance logic

There is a burgeoning amount of information in the twenty-first century that states which treatments, based on evidence, are the most effective for psychological disorders (see for example Nathan and Gorman, 2002; SCP, 2010; NICE, 2011). Our initial logic tells us that it seems obvious to offer an evidence-based treatment for a psychological disorder. We may believe that in this way we do the best for our clients, because practice that is evidence-based is all about offering the care which a client or patient needs. Various investigations show that costly technology and complicated procedures do not necessarily improve the decisions that we therapists make (for example, see Fisher et al., 2003 and Sekhri et al., 2008). Basing clinical practice on a ground of evidence has been shown to work (see for example Norcross, 2002). Importantly, evidence can be empirical and practice-based (for support regarding practice-based evidence, see CORE, 2011). When considering which therapeutic approach to choose for a client, evidence-based practice should take into account the client's preferences. This seems obvious at first glance. However …

Things are not so simple

Research backing evidence-based practice is, on the whole, nomothetical. This means that it either shows overall patterns across samples of a population, or that its empirical evidence is based on group comparisons. When trying to match evidence deriving from such research to a single client in a particular setting, the match between therapeutic approach and the client may be problematic. So, practice-based evidence should not be ignored (CORE, 2011). Nevertheless, it is evidence-based practice that is currently favoured above practice-based (see for example Silverman and Hinshaw, 2008).

Look deeper

An assessment offers the evidence defining whether a therapeutic approach works or not! Looking deeper, it becomes clear that the way mental disorders are identified is through assessing, so the assessment process needs to be good enough if an evidence-base is chosen for an identified disorder.

What relevant literature says about assessment

Alarmingly, not much attention has been focussed on the evidence on which psychological assessments are based. However, authors Antony and Barlow (2010) have recently acknowledged that at the core of therapeutic practice, assessing and intervening are intertwined and tracked for evaluating the effects of therapy. They argue that this type of evidence-base is crucial for best clinical practice.

Strengths and weaknesses of classifying

Much can be said about classifying mental disorders. A strength of classification is that it can help therapists choose the best type of therapeutic approach for a client's disorder. Using a classification system can also help clients in understanding their problem and knowing what to do about it. Yet there are weaknesses too. For instance, being given a 'mental disorder' label may open a door for some to name the client 'mentally ill'. A label might also be unhelpful if it brings a sense of hopelessness or a belief that it is impossible to get better or change. Further, there may be clients who use the term 'mental disorder' as an excuse not to improve themselves, while other clients may find a label helpful because it enables them to understand that they are neither strange nor alone. Clearly, there are pros and cons to classifying mental distress, as discussed in Chapter 1.

In practice clients do not normally arrive as neat bundles that can be quickly classified with ease and fit into empirical research findings. Often, they present with co-morbidity (having more than one mental disorder), as researchers Brown, Campbell et al. (2001) identified with adult clients. Other researchers, such as Kazdin and Whitley (2006), discovered similar findings when they investigated children and adolescents. With this in mind, the therapist needs to formulate a hypothesis as part of a formulation before deciding which approach to take (Eells, 2007). What helps with assessing and formulating is being there with the client: collecting their history, observing them, interacting and being aware of co-lateral information, such as body language, the aroma of the client, cleanliness and personal appearance (Rudd, 2003). As this information is collated, therapists can formulate hypotheses and assess what the best approach might be (Eells, 2007).

If our knowledge, experience and understanding do not embrace how to deal effectively with our client's issue, we refer the client on. However, does it behove us to classify clients, using the DSM-IV-TR (APA, 2002) or ICD-10 (WHO, 1992), when referring them interprofessionally?

If clients are classified within such a system, the client is perhaps labelled for life. Yet if we do not classify a client within the DSM or ICD categorical system, we bypass an interprofessional short-hand method of explaining a client's problem. Either way, assessments and referrals are a necessary part of clinical practice.

REFERRALS

Knowing when to either refer a client on or accept a referral shows professionalism. For instance, if the client's presenting problem is outside the scope of your training, knowledge, understanding and experience, or you do not wish to work with the client or are unable to, then you must refer the client on. Similarly, if there are differences in personality between you and your client which cannot be resolved and interfere with therapeutic progress, or if a client presents with a problem that you are also grappling with, or you feel unable to bring your client's material to supervision, then refer on. Other reasons for referring are if you know the client personally, if you believe that your interventions are ineffective, or if a client thinks that they cannot disclose their problem to you. If you need help it is unprofessional not to ask for it, so ask sooner rather than later when it might be too late. It is not only trainees who refer on – the fully qualified do also. Making a referral shows professional competence and keeping the client's best interests at heart. So does keeping to the limits of confidentiality as provided by the law and a therapist's professional body such as the BACP or the BPS.

How to accept a referral

When receiving a referral, it can come as a letter. Below is an example of a referral letter a therapist might receive (in this case from a solicitor):

Referrer's contact details xxx
Date xxx

PRIVATE AND CONFIDENTIAL

Dear Mr Al Pilikian,

Mark Smith

Mr Mark Smith was involved in a car accident two years ago and suffers flashbacks. He has been diagnosed with PTSD and is seeking legal assistance to claim compensation. We refer him to you for six one-hour weekly sessions of CBT, for this problem, as previously agreed. His contact details are attached. Please telephone him so he can see you as soon as possible. We have informed Mr. Smith that you will be contacting him. If you have any questions, please contact us.

Yours sincerely,

Louise Braden
Mark Smith's solicitor

Having received a referral letter, therapists also write a return letter as a way of accepting a referral. This can be done by writing a 'thank you' letter on dated and headed notepaper. Here is an example to a medical doctor:

Dr Elizabeth Jones
Address: xxx
Date xxx

PRIVATE AND CONFIDENTIAL

Dear Dr Jones,

Re: Miss Beryl Bloggs
DoB: xxx
Address: xxx

Thank you for referring your above-named patient to me. I saw the child today, with her parents. My formulation is below (with the family's permission):

Beryl Bloggs and her parents present as a very organised family unit, neatly attired with flattened affect. The parents report having life 'under control'. Mother is a housewife and father works on an oil-rig for ten continuous weeks, coming home for two weeks before returning to work. Beryl seems unhappy, which manifests in excessive daily tantrums lasting approximately an hour each. Neither parent seems to play with her.

Further investigation revealed that the parents find the tantrums difficult to deal with, being a source of distress for the whole family. From my understanding, Beryl can benefit from weekly filial play therapy sessions, incorporating one or both parents.

Session 1: Educate the parent(s) about filial play therapy, stressing the importance of having uninterrupted time with firm boundaries. Session 2: Use filial play with Beryl, while parent(s) are in the session room, seeing how Beryl is contained within the boundaries explained to her so that she knows she has the choice of continuing with the child-centred play or stopping it. Session 3: Mother or father conduct the filial play with Beryl in my presence; by now the parent(s) are expected to know how to use the filial technique at home at least on a half-hourly uninterrupted weekly basis (mainly instigated by mother due to father's work schedule). Session 4: Follow-up one month after Session 3.

The outcome of filial play therapy is promising with four year olds. I expect rapid movement in a desired direction for Beryl and her family.

If you have any queries, please do not hesitate in contacting me.

Yours sincerely,
Betty K. Rudd, Ph.D., C.Psychol., Member HCPC

Cc the Bloggs family

Although GPs tend to be short of time, they appreciate a report of findings (sent with the client's permission). An example of this is the thumbnail formulation embedded in the above letter. It is not unusual also to send a copy to the client concerned, for the sake of transparency.

Here is an example of a 'thank you' note to a client's masseur:

Mr Adam Bunter
Address xxx
Date xxx

PRIVATE AND CONFIDENTIAL

Dear Adam,

Thank you for referring your client Mr Peter Blagowitz to my services.
He has booked an appointment with me.
I look forward to meeting him.

Kind regards,
Betty Rudd
HCPC member
Clinic contact details xxx

These two letters of thanks are similar in the way they say 'thank you', yet there are differences in that the one to the GP is formal and embraces an assessment report.

Writing a referral letter

Below is an example of a referral letter a therapist may write regarding a mentally distressed client with back pain:

Therapist's name and contact details xxx
Recipient's name and contact details xxx
Date xxx

PRIVATE AND CONFIDENTIAL

Dear Dr Faber,

Re: Mr Sebastian Papadopoullos
DoB: xxx
Address: xxx

My client, Sebastian Papadopoullos, complains of persistent back pain and shows interest in chiropractic treatment. I have given him your 'calling card'. With his permission, I am

(Continued)

(Continued)

writing you this referral letter, since you are his closest chiropractor. If you have any questions, please do not hesitate to contact me.

Yours sincerely,
Betty Rudd
C.Psychol.

Cc Sebastian Papadopoullos

This succinct referral letter honours confidentiality by not disclosing anything about the client's psychological problems. Importantly, it is written with the client's permission and uses the phrase, 'Private and confidential', and a copy is also sent to the client for the sake of transparency.

What relevant literature says about referrals

Practically nothing! When referring on, writing a referral letter is often necessary, while sending a note of thanks for a referral is a matter of etiquette, although not strictly necessary.

Knowing the limits of our capabilities

We need to understand the limits of our capabilities so that we ethically embrace competence and safety within our practice. We should know enough to assess when our capabilities are overstretched. We are, for instance, neither nutritionists nor medical doctors, therefore it is best to refer a client on to another if there is concern regarding nutrition, medication or anything else outside our professional area.

ETHICS, DILEMMAS AND THE LAW

Technically, it is primary health care practitioners who are legally allowed to diagnose when assessing. However, it is not uncommon for therapists to do so, perhaps due to workplace culture. The dilemma of diagnosis versus formulation is discussed in Chapter 1. Daily, therapists are faced with ethical dilemmas. For instance: Shall I help a client in extreme financial difficulty by giving money? (If 'yes' then there is a blurring of professional boundaries.) Shall I therap my friend's niece? (If 'No' or 'Yes', it will impact on our friendship.) Shall I accept a present from my client? (Some accept a present if it is worth less than five pounds. If an expensive present is accepted, problems can arise.) The professional body that the therapist belongs to will offer guidelines on such issues.

NOTE-TAKING AND FILING

Professional bodies also offer guidelines on note-taking and filing, which should be considered. In order to adhere to a standard of care, take notes of assessments and referrals. Remembering every client and not getting into a muddle is almost impossible without note-taking! 'Note-taking' means 'record-keeping'. Notes can be subpoenaed: this is when, by law, confidential client notes must be released (Zur, 2012). Hence, recording facts is important: clinically relevant information should be entered in the notes as well as a client's demographic information such as name and address. Hard-copy notes must be kept under lock and key, computer notes protected by a password and formulation updated in the notes. Records should be chronologically ordered and include a consideration of the approach which informs practice; they can include: a client consent form, communications (written and verbal) from and to other professionals and the client, and legible session notes understandable to others. A therapist's supervisor may ask how notes are taken and enquire how they are filed to assess whether these procedures are being conducted properly.

SUPERVISION

A necessity, before embarking on clinical work, is a clinical supervisor. Therapists need to assess whether it is possible to work with their supervisor – if not, another should be found. In practice, therapists are usually supervised either monthly or more often. The experience of being supervised can help therapists in exploring and developing their way of conducting therapy. If, for example, during clinical practice, a therapist experiences being 'stuck' within the therapeutic encounter, the process of supervision can help the therapist reframe the relevant problem, leading to enrichment of the therapeutic relationship. Supervision forms part of therapists' support network while aiding their professional development. Being supervised also abides by the codes of ethics and conduct of the professional organisations therapists belong to. Assessments and referrals can be discussed with supervisors, for the benefit of all concerned. However, most therapists and supervisors are not skilled in administering standardised psychometric assessment instruments. Remarkably, this is because psychometric assessment tools are not included in the majority of therapists' toolkits, the main reason being that test creators invent tests in separate locations to where therapists work, and report their innovations in journals aimed at other psychometricians, rather than therapists.

ESSENTIALS

- Assessment is both about you identifying clients' needs, ascertaining if you can work with them or whether to refer on, and clients assessing if they can work with you. Assessments help clients become clearer about their problems and the therapeutic direction they may follow.
- Clients come with much material, therefore the more you can put your own 'template' of how you see the world aside and endeavour to perceive the world through their 'template', the clearer they will be. Assessing is not only history-taking, it is a process in which the therapist feels empathic towards each client, is non-judgementally accepting of them and honest about the two-way working alliance, making boundaries and contract clear (for example, times of sessions, their length and cost).
- Direct questioning might sometimes be inappropriate if a client is not used to leading, so a therapist might let the client lead to see what and how they disclose.
- Whether clients lead or not, form-filling is required. Ethical and legal issues emerge when working with the severely mentally distressed. To minimise possible misunderstandings, write thank you letters for accepted referrals and refer on with a report if appropriate. Include in a report: the client's full name and contact details, assessment date, how the client presents in appearance and affect, and the presenting problem with a formulation, ending with your reasons for referring on.

Points to ponder

- How might you become aware of the limits to your professional capabilities?
- When might you use a classification system and why?
- When might you not use a classification system and why?
- A colleague tries to offer you some money for referring a client on to them – how would you deal with this situation?
- A client tries to offer you a gift because they experience your assessment as therapeutic – where might this lead if you do or do not accept the gift?
- If most therapists are not trained in evaluating the psychometric properties of standardised assessment instruments, how are they to keep their assessing skills sharpened?
- Since good communication skills are essential for dealing with assessing and referring, might it behove educational institutions to include communication skills in their therapy-training curriculum?
- Is it ethical that there are cost implications for some assessment tools, such as the much-used BDI?

Exercise

(Answers are embedded in this chapter.)

1   When would you refer a client on to another professional?
2   What is a weakness of using a classification system?
3   What is a strength of using a classification system?
4   How might you store notes on clients?
5   Why might you not see a client if you believe you can help that person?
6   Write your own assessment form with reasons for each question.
7   Create your own 'thank you' note to a psychiatrist who has referred a client to you.
8   Write a referral letter regarding a client you wish to refer on to another professional.
9   When must you release confidential client notes?

CHAPTER SUMMARY

Accepting and referring clients form part of therapists' practice.

Saying 'thank you' for referrals shows etiquette.

Referring on illustrates professionalism.

Positive and negative aspects of using classification systems are that it is convenient to use a shorthand method to describe a client's problem when communicating interprofessionally, but a client may be labelled for life.

LIST OF USEFUL RESOURCES

- Bea, S.M. and Tesar, G.E. (2002) 'A primer on referring patients for psychotherapy', *Cleveland Clinic Journal of Medicine*, 69, 2, pp. 113–27.
- Davey, G. (2008) *Psychopathology: Research, Assessment and Treatment in Clinical Psychology* (Chichester, Blackwell).
- Milner, J. and O'Byrne, P. (2003) *Assessment in Counselling* (Basingstoke, Palgrave Macmillan).
- Palmer, S. and McMahon, G. (eds) (1997) *Client Assessment* (London, Sage).
- Steinberg, D. (2000) *Letters from the Clinic: Letter Writing in Clinical Practice for Mental Health Professionals* (London, Routledge).

RELEVANT WEBSITES

http://apt.rcpsych.org/content/8/3/172.full

www.minddisorders.com/Flu-Inv/Historical-Clinical-Risk-Management-20.html#ixzz1b9Y3wfN7

www.thetherapyhour.co.uk/about-us/counselling-psychotherapy-assessment-form/

http://wiki.answers.com/Q/Evaluate_the_advantages_and_disadvantages_of_classifying_mental_disorders#ixzz1bKjuPi40

REFERENCES

Antony, M.M. and Barlow, D.H. (eds) (2010) *Handbook of Assessment and Treatment Planning for Psychological Disorders* (New York, The Guilford Press).

Arbor, A. (2011) *CAT- C –Clinical Assessment of Attention Deficit – Child*, http://annarbor.co.uk/index.php?main_page=index&cPath=249_139, accessed 24 October 2011.

APA (2002) *DSM-IV-TR® Diagnostic and Statistical Manual of Mental Disorders* (Fourth Edition, revised) (Vancouver, American Psychiatric Association).

Beck, A.T., Steer, R.A. and Brown G.K. (1996) *Manual for Beck Depression Inventory II (BDI-II)* (San Antonio Texas, Psychology Corporation),

Boggs, K.M., Gross, A.M. and Gohm, C.L. (2006) 'Validity of the Asperger's Syndrome Diagnostic Scale', *Journal of Developmental and Physical Disabilities*, 18, 2, pp. 163–82.

Briere, J. (2001) *Detailed Assessment of Posttraumatic Stress (DAPS)* (Odessa Florida, Psychological Assessment Resources).

Brown, T.A., Campbell, L.A., Lehman, C.L., Grisham, J.R. and Mancill, R.B. (2001) 'Current and lifetime co-morbidity of the DSM-IV anxiety and mood disorders in a large clinical sample', *Journal of Abnormal Psychology*, 110, pp. 585–9.

CORE (2011) www.coreims.co.uk/, accessed 17 November 2011.

(Continued)

(Continued)

Duijsens, I.J., Eurelings-Bontekoe, E.H.M. and Diekstra-Datec, R.F.W. (1995) *International Personality Disorder Examination (IPDE) DSM IV module* (Copenhagen, World Health Organization).

Eells, T.B. (ed.) (2007) *Handbook of Psychotherapy Case Formulation* (Second Edition) (New York, The Guilford Press).

Fisher, E.S., Wennberg, D.E., Stukel, T.A., Gottlieb, D.J., Lucas, F.L. and Pinder, E.L. (2003) 'The implications of regional variations in Medicate spending: Part 2. Health outcomes and satisfaction with care', *Annals of Internal Medicine*, 338, pp. 288–8.

Gadow, K.D. and Sprafkin, J. (2011) *Adolescent Symptom Inventory – 4 (ASI-4)* (California, Western Psychological Services), http://portal.wpspublish.com/portal/page?_pageid=53,69465&_dad=portal&_schema=PORTAL, accessed 24 October 2011.

Garrod, H. (2011) Personal communication, 6 October.

Hart, S., Kropp, P.R., Laws, D.R., Klaver, J., Logan, C. and Watt, K.A. (2003) *The Risk for Sexual Violence Protocol (RSVP): Structured Professional Guidelines for Assessing Risk of Sexual Violence* (Vancouver, The Institute Against Family Violence).

Ireland, J., Ireland, C.A. and Birch, P. (eds) (2009) *Violent and Sexual Offenders: Assessment, Treatment and Management* (Cullompton Devon, Willan).

Kazdin, A.E. and Whitley, M.K. (2006) 'Comorbidity, case complexity, and effects of evidence-based treatment for children referred for disruptive behaviour', *Journal of Consulting and Clinical Psychology*, 74, pp. 455–67.

Mattis, S., Jurica, P.J. and Leitten, C.L. (2011) *Dementia Rating Scale-2 (DRS-2)*, www.hogrefe.co.uk/dementia-rating-scale-2-drs-2.html, accessed 24 October 2011.

Nathan, P. and Gorman, J.M. (eds) (2002) *A Guide to Treatments that Work* (Second Edition) (Oxford, Oxford University Press).

NICE (2011) *National Institute for Health and Clinical Excellence: Published Clinical Guidelines,* www.nice.org.uk/, accessed 24 October 2011.

Norcross, J.C. (ed.) (2002) *Psychotherapy Relationships that Work: Therapist Contributions and Responsiveness to Clients* (New York, Oxford University Press).

Rudd, B. (2003) *Body Mind Update: Resource for New Health Findings* (Haywards Heath, Hygeia Health).

SCP (2010) *Society of Clinical Psychology: Research-supported Psychological Treatments*, www.psychology.sunysb.edu/eklonsky-/division12/, accessed 26 October 2011.

Sekhri, N., Feder, G.S., Junghans, C., Eldridge, S., Umaipalan, A. and Madhu, R. (2008) 'Incremental prognostic value of the exercise cardiogram in the initial assessment of patients with suspected angina: cohort study', *British Medical Journal*, 337, pp. 1272–5.

Silverman, W.K. and Hinshaw, S.P. (eds.) (2008) 'Special Issue: evidence-based psychological treatments for children and adolescents: a ten year update', *Journal of Child and Adolescent Psychology*, 37, 1, pp. 1–301.

WHO (1992) *ICD-10: The ICD-10 Classification of Mental and Behavioural Disorders: Clinical Descriptions and Diagnostic Guidelines* (Copenhagen, World Health Organization).

Webster, C.D. and Douglas, K.S. (1997) *HCR-20: Assessing Risk for Violence, Version 2* (British Columbia, Simon Fraser University).

Zur, O. (2012) *Subpoenas And How to Handle Them: Guidelines for Psychotherapists and Counselors*, www.zurinstitute.com/subpoena.html, accessed 17 October 2012.

3

Early Life Disorders Incorporating Developmental Psychopathology

---

LEARNING OBJECTIVES FOR THIS CHAPTER

- Spot childhood stress
- Know about ADHD symptoms
- Recognise autism
- Understand theories about stress, ADHD and autism
- Deliberate on empirically supported theories

Within mental health, developmental psychopathology embraces early life disorders. It is a way of understanding disordered behaviour within a framework of normal lifespan development. Initially, developmental psychopathology focussed on children (see Piaget, 1953). Only within approximately the last fifty years have developmentalists expanded their studies to include the lifespan (e.g. Erikson, 1979). This chapter spotlights children and teenagers.

DIAGNOSIS

Although psychiatrists diagnose, other professionals working with young people are expected to understand diagnostic terms such as 'autism', 'ADHD' and 'dyslexia'. However, as mentioned in the previous chapter, the impact of diagnoses is not necessarily straightforward. If children are diagnosed with, for example, 'dyslexia', will laziness tempt their teacher to think, 'these kids are dyslexic, that's why they can't read and write appropriately', rather than to work harder, or differently, to teach them to read and write better (Wilson, 2011)? Will they consider that perhaps it is because of stress that the young people seem to be falling behind?

STRESS

Some stress is normal. Every person can experience it, even foetuses. Although stress can be positive, the word 'stress' usually has negative connotations. What is childhood stress? If children feel overwhelmed, it means they are stressed. Stress can be traumatic.

Traumatic stress

A tremendously frightening event (or series of events) that a young person experiences or witnesses is classified as a 'traumatic stress', creating a traumatic stress response. (This can be cross-referenced with Chapter 4.) Signs can include horrific dreams, grumpiness, preoccupation with the stress-inducing event/s and bedwetting. These symptoms are normal and can disappear within weeks with support. If the trauma is perceived as life-threatening, post traumatic stress disorder (PTSD) may follow. Signs of PTSD include disturbed sleep, flashbacks and being startled easily. These interfere with enjoying life and can continue into adulthood. Utilising creative situations such as painting and allowing young people to talk without retraumatising can help prevent symptoms persevering.

Stress theories

Psychotherapist Sue Gerhardt (2010) states that stressed children acquire over-sensitive psyches; if feeling emotionally unsafe, they become defensive easily (2010). She says that if children are substantially hurt, it often leads to angry and resentful feelings, and that children with unmet needs eventually believe that their needs cannot be met. If children have profoundly painful experiences, being dependent or controlling and emotionally impoverished follows.

Forensic psychologist Beazley Richards (2011) explains that stress manifests for various reasons, such as feeling pressure to fit in with peers or parents divorcing. She describes symptoms of childhood stress, such as depression or antisocial behaviour, and offers information regarding what to do, for example, being emotionally available and communicating that you understand their emotions.

Sparrow, a medic, states that stress causes illness, that pre-natal stress affects development which can lead to ADHD, and that children can have a stress reaction if displaced, separated from any family member, if their routine is interrupted, if they are close to a dreadful event and continually reminded of it, or if their primary caregivers have mental health problems (Sparrow, 2007).

In a final example, psychologist Goleman (1991) argued that early childhood stress links to early puberty.

Where theories converge and differ

Theories overlap. Gerhardt's perspective that childhood stress is caused by unmet needs, shame and substantial hurt converges with Richards' of stressed children feeling overwhelmed, experiencing extreme fright or being pressurised to fit in. Gerhardt's linking of stress with shame also overlaps with Goleman's and Sparrow's on social stress. Further, Sparrow's theory converges with Goleman's and Richards' in areas of separation from a family member, parents divorcing and lack of parental coping skills.

Each theory does not identify identical risk factors for childhood stress, however. On one hand, Sparrow links a stressed pre-natal mother to problems in a child's later life, and childhood stress with interrupted routines or displaced culture. On another, only Goleman theorised the link between childhood stress and onset of early puberty.

Stress research

Gerhardt's investigations identifying risk factors for stress back up her theory. These are:

- low income
- bad housing
- ambivalent parents
- parental mental health problems
- poor attachment to caregiver/s
- profound hurt
- unmet needs
- poor education.

Research by Kaufman, Yand and Douglas-Palumberi (2006), offers solid grounding for Sparrow's theory that stress leads to illness. Lieberman and colleagues' (2005) research also supports Sparrow's theory by showing that mental distress and a change in the physical conditions a child is used to can result in stress reactions. Additional research (Diego, Jones and Field, 2006) supports Sparrow's theory that pre-natal stress affects development. Sparrow's declaration that young people's problems with behaviour and attention relate to mothers' stress during pregnancy is further supported by other researchers who link maternal distress to ADHD in young people (for example, van den Bergh and Marcoen, 2004). O'Connor's (2011) work similarly supports Sparrow's theory, but also offers hope by showing that although a stressed pregnant woman puts her unborn infant at risk of later-life cognitive problems, it is possible for her nurture to protect against this.

And what about Goleman's hypothesis? His statement that early puberty is linked to early stress seemed outrageous when he made it – his peers did not accept it. However, approximately two decades later, research supports his theory (Shriver, 2007).

Stress causes

Children become stressed as a result of numerous causes, for example:

- parents separating
- over-structured time
- believing they must fit in with peers
- hearing adverse news
- seeing disturbing images
- abuse
- neglect
- trauma (see the section in this chapter on traumatic stress).

Signs

Symptoms in children can include:

- short-temperedness
- persistent worrying

- withdrawal
- change in sleeping and eating patterns
- clingyness
- tearfulness.

Additional symptoms in teenagers can include:

- suddenly changing friends
- hostility
- avoiding parents (APA, 2011).

Prevalence

At the time of writing, incidence of stressed young people is reported to be at an all-time high in the UK (Walsh, 2011). It is not easy to identify factors contributing to this rise.

Interventions

Ways of intervening are multiple, for instance using local mental health services, accessing an evidentially effective family support programme or telephoning a helpline offering emotional support (Walsh, 2011). The staggering annual cost of mental health problems in the UK is over 100 billion pounds (Meltzer, Gatward and Corbin, 2003). A statement by the Royal College of Psychiatrists (2010) argues that if a fraction of this was spent on early intervention, a significant amount of expense could be prevented. Indeed, studies show that evidence-based parental interventions boost better mental health in parents while reducing the possibility of a lifetime's mental distress and physical illness in children (Family Lives, 2011).

Outcome

Stress can be toxic. If not appropriately dealt with in childhood, it can impact on eventual adult health (Anda et al., 2002). However, maltreatment (a cause of toxic stress) can be stopped and prevented with support that shows deep understanding and provides strategies to strengthen coping skills (Daro and McCurdy, 2007).

In practice

When seeing stressed children and young people, it is important also to work with their caregivers and offer overall support for wellbeing. Drawing and naming the emotions they are feeling, listening in an accepting, non-judgemental way, distinguishing between the behaviour and the person, and facilitating them to think things through can be helpful. Crucially, therapists should also be well supported in order to ensure they deal with their own stress adequately and are fit to practice; being supervised helps therapists with such issues.

STRESS CASE VIGNETTE

Sixteen-year-old Jacob's exam stress seemed to be exacerbated by what he described as his 'raging hormones'. He said that all he wanted was to go out with friends. Yet, he longed to pass his examinations that were close ahead. Jacob went out every evening, returning home in the early hours. He believed that his parents were nosey and dictatorial. Consequently, he had little to do with them. Jacob felt estranged from his family, tired and sad. Talking to his therapist helped because she was compassionate, endeavoured to understand him and did not try 'fixing' him. During therapy, he realised that he and his parents needed to communicate. One family session was conducted where the parents realised the impact they had on Jacob. They communicated their empathy to him, which had a positive effect. Jacob understood that he could choose to spend less time with friends and more time with his family by perhaps eating a meal together. He slept earlier and created a revision programme, enabling his survival of both his exams and 'raging hormones'. He and his parents enjoyed their weekly family meal. Getting more sleep at night meant that he was awake during lessons. Jacob soon felt reconnected with his family, which dissolved his ongoing sadness. He paced his social life, which enabled him to revise. Jacob's therapist received a card a few months after therapy ended, stating that he had passed most of his exams.

Jacob did not feel the need for therapy in later life. The therapist offered him 'tools for life' which he used. (This can be cross-referenced with Chapter 12.) Fortunately, Jacob did not suffer from developmental trauma disorder (DTD; see below).

DEVELOPMENTAL TRAUMA DISORDER

DTA is about being chronically or repeatedly exposed to inter-relational trauma, such as abandonment, assault or coercion. Children experiencing these can feel ashamed, frightened and resigned. These experiences are detrimental: behaviourally, young people may self-harm; cognitively, their thinking might become confused; relationally, they may cause disruption in the family, make wrong choices regarding their life-course and hate themselves. Professor of Psychiatry, van der Kolk, shows that individuals experiencing overwhelming distress can enter a fantasy world during trauma (van der Kolk et al., 2007). They may dissociate and, unfortunately, traumatic events may 'return' and 'haunt' in nightmares, flashbacks and physical sensations. Children can have difficulty explaining these, which may be related to childhood sexual abuse. This difficulty in communication is, however, different from that seen in autistic spectrum disorder (ASD; see below). DTA should not be confused with the cognitive disorders in Chapter 5.

AUTISTIC SPECTRUM DISORDER

Communication difficulties, restricted and repetitive behaviour and social impairments characterise ASD. Autism is at its severe end. Asperger syndrome, pervasive developmental disorder not otherwise specified (PDD-NOS) and childhood disintegrative disorder, are other, milder conditions along the ASD spectrum.

Although nobody suggests a cure, studies have shown that children with autism can be helped if, for example, CBT techniques are used to teach social skills (Reichow et.al., 2011). Involving the parents and keeping the child's school informed about how to be supportive also help. However, it is applied behavioural analysis (ABA) that is often used to help children with autism (see below).

What is autism?

Autism is a neurodevelopment disorder (Ashwood, Wills and van de Water, 2006). This means that there is impaired growth in the brain (or nervous system). Such a neuronal problem affects emotions, memory and the ability to learn, becoming more apparent as the affected child grows.

Theory and research

Researchers have not found what causes ASD, although they have identified some genes associated with it (Ashwood, Wills and van de Water, 2006). Certain evidence suggests that individuals suffering ASD are more frequently found in families where there are emotional disorders, however, more research is needed either to support or refute this (NINDS, 2011).

Another theory is that parental factors cause autism. Although this was refuted, more recently it has returned with studies suggesting that during early pregnancy, a mother causing stress to her foetus (by, for example, smoking) can give birth to an offspring who will suffer autism or schizophrenia (Forsloff, 2009).

A pioneer approach developed in order to treat children diagnosed with autism is Dr Lovaas's ABA theory, which teaches children techniques for adapting their behaviour to fit in with mainstream society (1998). Her work has been criticised in four main areas:

1 It stops children attending school.
2 She has not updated the theory.
3 It ensures children fail, by saying 'no' to them.
4 It uses discrete trial techniques, teaching the child skills in a 'contrived' area such as the home, rather than a 'natural' environment such as school.

However each criticism has a respective counter-argument:

1 Children are first taught skills in discrete trial techniques, so that they can eventually learn to use them in a wider environment.
2 The programme changes annually after scientific evaluation.
3 Rarely is a child told 'no' because instruction is set up so that the child mostly succeeds, however, saying 'no' to incorrect responses helps keep behavioural boundaries intact; instructors ensure that key to the programme is the child's motivation to learn and that they are 80 per cent successful.
4 When basic skills in the programme are mastered, later learning teaches all skills in a more natural environment.

Signs

Early symptoms of ASD are that the child does not babble or point by twelve months, does not say a word by sixteen months, does not make two-word phrases by age two and has repressed language by three years. Children are unresponsive socially, excessively line up objects and do not seek eye contact. They do not seem to want conversation, lack social skills and are unresponsive to their name. Later indicators include impaired conversing ability, little creative play, repetitive language, inflexibly repeating routines, no empathy and restricted focused interest. Other possible symptoms are depression during adolescence, behavioural problems such as head-banging, potential seizure-like activity in the brain (perhaps the development of epilepsy), overall unresponsiveness to humans or understanding of others' emotions, abusive behaviour such as biting, a disregard of others' interests and sometimes speaking in a sing-song voice.

Prevalence

Boys suffer from ASD four times more than girls and six children from every 1,000 are diagnosed with it (Reichow et al., 2011). Autism is found across every socio-economic group, in all age ranges and all ethnicities (NINDS, 2011).

Intervention and practice

Therapeutic interventions dealing with specific symptoms on an individual basis help (see for example, Breunlin, Pinsof and Russell, 2011 and Feucht, Ogata and Lucas, 2010). Those with ASD need support throughout their developmental years; within a supportive environment, many grow into adults who are able to earn their living. Finding any evidence-based intervention programme for a child with autism is difficult, so interventions that can be found are often controversial (apart perhaps from evidentially effective ABA, previously discussed). As a result, therapists should be wary of following the latest therapy fashion. A team effort is useful, for instance, dietary interventions from a nutritionist, anti-convulsant drugs from a medic (for treating seizures) and ABA from a trained therapist.

AUTISM CASE VIGNETTE

A Lovaas-based programme was followed for a five year old with autism. The trained therapist spent forty hours weekly working intensively with little Alexander in the family home. Parents were also taught ABA. Alexander practiced new skills. Eventually he gained enough skills to be gradually introduced to a classroom and was able to benefit by being in a school, accompanied by his ABA instructor who encouraged interaction with others and ensured that he was able to cope with the school routine. Eventually, his instructor was carefully phased out once Alexander could attend school full time.

Intriguingly, there is a programme for helping children with high-functioning autism, named Lego Club (de la Cuesta, 2011). This offers a structured approach to building with Lego. Investigative outcomes showed that after six months of attending Lego Club twice-weekly significant improvement in social competence, communication skills and maladaptive behaviour was found in children who were on the programme, when compared with control groups. A three-year follow-up continued showing significant improvement. The groups at Lego Club were conducted so that one child described the instructions, another constructed with Lego and a third found the correct pieces. All co-operated for Lego-building to happen. Further rigorous research is needed for exploring the effectiveness of similar approaches with groups of children.

ADHD

There are a few similarities between autism and attention deficit hyperactivity disorder (ADHD). They share features such as behaving thoughtlessly and relationship difficulties. Young people with ADHD have difficulty concentrating, become frustrated or bored quickly, are impulsive and tend to move much.

Causes

Although precise causes of ADHD are unknown, there are suspected contributing factors:

- problematic brain function – an imbalance in the brain chemicals (called neurotransmitters) that help brain cells intercommunicate might be a reason for the symptoms of ADHD developing
- heredity – ADHD sometimes runs in families
- underactive brain area – brain areas controlling attention are less active in those with ADHD
- toxin exposure in early childhood (for example, lead) can affect brain development, leading to ADHD
- infection, substance abuse (for example, alcohol or tobacco) and inadequate nutrition can affect the baby's developing brain
- brain injury may trigger ADHD.

Theories

The social construct theory purports that ADHD is not pathological, but rather is a socially constructed explanation of behaviours that are not society's norms (Parens and Johnston, 2009). It posits that within western society, pressure on parents makes them stressed, which has a domino effect on their children who then manifest with ADHD symptoms. Therefore, a child displaying ADHD signs is within the spectrum of normal behaviour, rather than dysfunctional or pathological. This theory also takes the view that some parents, who have not succeeded in their parental responsibilities and have children with ADHD symptoms, use the ADHD label to absolve themselves of guilt or failure (Timini and Taylor, 2004). Hence, society values passive citizens but some are active on the continuum of active-passive; it may then suit society to say that the active individuals 'have problems'. A follow-on from this is that blame is thereby taken away from the ones 'creating the problems'.

Another perspective, Barkley's ADHD theory, states that children lack self-control and that other related problems cascade from this (Barkley, 2005). These theories converge because neither views ADHD as pathological, but differ where Barkley sees the problem arising from the individual rather than the surrounding culture.

Certain studies illustrate neurological differences between those with ADHD symptoms and those without (for example, Coccaro, Hirsch and Stein, 2007). Some authors theorise that ADHD is due to a brain problem (for example, Dougherty et al., 1999). However, neurological differences may not be the cause, but may be the effect; for instance, of taking medication to pacify activity.

Research

Research shows that the diagnosis of ADHD by medical doctors is not an adequate way of identifying who needs help (Thapar and Thapar, 2003). Also of concern is that research shows that children with ADHD indulge more in crime as adults when compared with children without ADHD (Fletcher and Wolfe, 2009). Finances are needed to fund further research into the impact of having a child with ADHD in a family and in order to provide good quality education and appropriate health care.

Signs

Symptoms are categorised three-fold: impulsivity, inattentiveness and hyperactivity.

1 Impulsivity:

- blurts an answer out without listening to the whole question
- interrupts others
- has problems turn-taking.

2 Inattentiveness:

- seems to not listen
- is forgetful
- makes careless mistakes
- lacks consideration
- daydreams a lot
- does not finish tasks or follow instructions
- often loses things
- experiences difficulties with everyday activities
- is averse to continuous effort or sitting still.

3 Hyperactivity:

- is restless
- has difficulty with quiet play
- fidgets
- talks a lot
- does not sit as expected.

These symptoms can make it difficult for families and schools to cope.

Prevalence

Reportedly, incidence of ADHD in eighteen year olds is a global average of 5.29 per cent (Polanczyk et al., 2007) This figure varies depending on location (Bird, 2002). In North America and Europe there is significantly larger prevalence than in the Middle East, Oceana, Asia and South America (Faraone et al., 2003). Further, investigations show that there are significantly more young people with ADHD in North America than in Europe (Timini and Taylor, 2004). These varying results may be because of different methods used for data collection, and could illustrate a need for the World Health Organization to standardise worldwide epidemiological studies so that comparable data becomes available.

Intervention

Interventions should be targeted at the three problem areas. The following can help:

- ensure that homework is done in a quiet place
- teach social skills in a group
- be specific, for example, say 'Don't hit', rather than, 'Be good'
- ensure there is proper nutrition and a good breakfast daily
- allow the child to be active (sitting still for a long time is difficult)
- sit the child close to the teacher
- speak to the child face-to-face
- have a structured timetable
- watch the child continuously (so that impulse can be controlled)
- limit television
- restrict computer use
- reduce stimulus of sight, sound and people
- diminish stress
- ensure adequate sleep.

Outcome and practice

A programme called Response-to-Intervention (RIT; Wright, 2011) shows promise. Children on the programme have catch-up time with peers in relation to school work, and it has been found that those taught reading in small groups, using a variety of methods, learn quicker than those taught on a one-to-one basis.

Unfortunately, some young people are wrongly diagnosed with ADHD when they could more accurately be described as having developmental trauma disorder (Levin, 2009), as discussed above.

CHILDHOOD SEXUAL ABUSE

In the USA, 25 per cent of women who are identified as suffering from a psychopathological disorder, and 16 per cent of men, reported being subjected to childhood sexual abuse

ADHD CASE VIGNETTE

Eleven-year-old Franceska was two years behind with reading skills. In class, she felt unable to sit still, was bored and distracted. At home, her behaviour was chaotic. A neurologist found too much slow brainwave activity in her brain and taught Franceska to change her brainwave activity using computer software (a video game). A psychotherapist helped her self-esteem improve and gave Franceska's parents education in parenting sessions. A nutritionist advised the family on meals. Franceska's parents liaised with her teachers to develop a workable educational plan. Within six months, Franceska's reading skills improved to that of an average ten year old. She was able to achieve her goals, one small step at a time.

Currently in the UK, the government wants schools to be all-inclusive. However, Franceska's family found that she was happier at a special school for children with ADHD.

(Dube et al., 2005). These figures testify to the toxicity of such an experience. (See also Chapter 4.) Children who reported sexual abuse also reported other adverse childhood experiences (Dube et al., 2005).

Studies have found that adults who reported being sexually abused as children attempted suicide twice as much as those who were abused in other ways (Dube et al., 2005). In addition, it has been found that there is significant risk of males being involved in teenage pregnancy if they were sexually abused as children (Anda et. al., 2001), that women were more likely to have a child before the age of twenty (Dietz et al., 1999), and that adults who experienced CSA were more likely to have marital problems when compared with those who did not (Dube et al., 2002). Many people who have been sexually abused become depressed (see also Chapter 6).

CONFUSION BETWEEN COGNITIVE AND CHILDHOOD NEUROLOGICAL DISORDERS

Children and young people suffering from symptoms of depression or psychosis can show signs of childhood neurological disorders. Potentially, this is confusing because therapists could muddle a psychological problem with a neurological one (neurology is an enormous topic dealing with anything concerning the brain or nerves in the body). For example, staring into space may or may not indicate the child is suffering from depression, seizures might or might not be epilepsy, seeing spots in front of the eyes may or may not indicate the child is suffering from psychosis), while unresponsiveness could or could not be a result of a brain tumour. In such situations, therapists should refer to neurologists (see also Chapter 5).

AGE

How old a child is when displaying particular behaviours can determine whether there is a problem. For instance, it is normal for two year olds to have tantrums but not nine year olds.

GENDER

A school only allowing boys to join a football club and girls to join a dance class influences stereotypical gender-role behaviours in pupils. Similarly, a parent saying, 'Boys don't cry' or 'Girls don't get angry' can cause problems in a child's life by limiting their available choices and creating distress, as suppressing emotion is unhealthy. Certain research links emotional suppression to PTSD and OCD, irrespective of gender (Salters-Pedneault, 2010). (For PTSD and OCD see Chapter 4.) Culture also influences gender roles.

CULTURE

What is learned and shared between individuals in their environment can be described as culture. Although culture shapes children's psychological make-up, the perspective of psychopathology is that children are not passive. Rather, they interpret their experiences. Consequently, each child experiences culture differently because the dynamics of their experiences are unique to them. Clustering race, colour, gender or religion is meaningless – there is more to culture than these aspects due to independent variables such as family income and minority groups. It is interesting, for instance, to note that enormous variance has been found in the numbers of children suffering from autism in Sweden: Swedish-born boys with Ugandan mothers (a minority group) have been found to be more at risk of being diagnosed as autistic as they are 200 times more likely to display signs of autism than those born in the Swedish general population (Martin, Volkmar and Lewis, 2007).

CONCERN

Within the last dozen years in England the use of methylphenidate-based drugs, such as Ritalin, for treating children with behavioural problems increased by over 600 per cent (McFadden, 2011). Over 600,000 prescriptions were issued in 2010. This is concerning because although the government's policy is that no child under six years should be issued such a prescription, we do not know whether this policy is followed – anecdotally, it seems that it is not (McFadden, 2011). Research is needed to ascertain the long-term effects of taking drugs compared with non-drug alternatives. Such research could support the use of other theoretical models, contribute to accumulated epistemology and inter-relate with what can otherwise just be separate pieces of speculation.

Points to ponder

- Both environmental and biological factors impact on children and young people suffering early life disorders.
- Assuming that some stress is necessary and other stress is detrimental, how can we distinguish between them?
- Theory guides research processes and emerges from practice, so what argument is there for using non-research-based interventions?
- Although is it usually adults who care for children, too many children currently care for a parent and this can create negative stress in a child. How might such a situation be relieved or alleviated?

- A child suffering from depression or psychosis can show signs of neurological disorders – in such cases, what should a therapist do?
- The British psychoanalyst John Bowlby (1907–1990) noticed that infants manifested with attachment behaviours (for example, crying and seeking) if separated from their primary attachment figure (such as their mother) and therefore theorised that the ones more likely to survive healthily were those who could maintain proximity because of their attachment behaviours. If, as some theorise (Fraley, 2012), adults find partners who mirror the attachment pattern of the infant/caregiver relationship – feeling either secure or insecure – where does free will fit in and how might therapy help?

Exercise

(Answers are embedded in this chapter.)

1 What causes childhood stress?
2 In what ways can children with ADHD be helped?
3 How can autism be spotted?
4 Why is it important to support theories with research?

CHAPTER SUMMARY

There is much speculation about developmental psychopathology, which initially spotlighted young people, but which more recently has focussed on disordered behaviour within a framework of normal development throughout life.

A child with distressed parents, mental health problems, or who is displaced, is likely to be stressed.

Autism is distinguished by impairment in relating with others.

If children have substantial problems concentrating and being still for the amount of time that is appropriate for their age, they have signs of ADHD.

Research supporting theory is important because it increases accumulated knowledge and inter-relates with what could otherwise only be discreet bits of information; it can also justify why a therapist uses a particular approach.

LIST OF USEFUL RESOURCES

- Berk, L.E. (2011) *Study Guide for Infants, Children and Adolescents* (Fourth Edition) (Harlow, Pearson Education).
- Hendrick, H. (2007) 'Optimism and hope vs anxiety and narcissism: some thoughts on children's welfare yesterday and today', *History of Education*, 26, 6, pp. 747–68.

(Continued)

(Continued)

- Rudd, B. (2008) *Developing Life Skills* (card games for ages 8 to 12 years) (Milton Keynes, Speechmark).
- Rudd, B. (2009) *Talking is for All* (London, Sage).
- Rudd, B. (2009) *Help Your Child Develop Emotional Literacy* (New York, Continuum).
- Rudd, B. (2011) *Special Games* (Nottingham, LDA).
- Slater, A. and Bremner, B. (2011) *An Introduction to Developmental Psychology* (Chichester, John Wiley and Sons).

RELEVANT WEBSITES

www.cdc.gov/nccdphp/ace/index.htm

www.developingchild.net

www.lifepositive.com/mind/psychology/depression/depression.asp

REFERENCES

Anda, R.F., Felitti, V.J., Chapman, D.P., Croft, J.B., Williamson, D.F. and Santelli, J.S. (2001) 'Abused boys, battered mothers, and male involvement in teen pregnancy', *Paediatrics*, 107, 2, p. E19.

Anda, R.F., Whitfield, C.L., Felitti, V.J., Chapman, D., Ewards, V.J. and Dube, S.R. (2002) 'Adverse childhood experiences, alcoholic parents, and later risk of alcoholism and depression', *Psychiatric Services*, 53, 8, pp. 1001–9.

APA (2011) www.apa.org/helpcenter/stress-children.aspx, accessed 30 November 2011

Ashwood, P., Wills, S. and van de Water, J. (2006) 'The immune system in autism: a new frontier for autism research', *Journal of Leukocyte Biology*, 80, pp. 1–15.

Barkley, R.A. (2005) *ADHD and the Nature of Self-Control* (New York, Guilford Press).

Bird, H.R. (2002) *The Diagnostic Classification, Epidemiology and Cross-cultural Validity in Attention Deficit/Hyperactivity Disorder: State of the Science: Best Practice* (Kingston New Jersey, Civic Research Institute).

Breunlin, D.C., Pinsof, W. and Russell, W.P. (2011) 'Integrative problem-centered meta-frameworks therapy 1', *Core Concepts and Hypothesizing*, 50, 3, pp. 293–313.

Centers for Disease Control and Prevention (2003) 'First reports evaluating the effectiveness of strategies for preventing violence visitation and firearms laws. Findings from the Task Force on Community Services', *Morbidity and Mortality Weekly Report*, 52, RR-14, pp. 1–9.

Coccaro, E.F., Hirsch, S.L. and Stein, M.A. (2007) 'Plasma homovanillic acid correlates inversely with history of learning problems in healthy volunteer and personality disordered subjects', *Psychiatry research,* 149, 1–3, pp. 297–302.

Daro, D. and McCurdy, K. (2007) 'Interventions to prevent child maltreatment', in Doll, L., Bonzo, S., Sleet, D., Mercy, J. and Hass, E. (eds) *Handbook of Injury and Violence Prevention* (New York, Springer) pp. 137–56.

de la Cuesta, (2011) 'Using Lego® to help children with high functioning autism spectrum disorders', *Assessment and Development Matters*, 3, 4, pp. 24–5.

Diego, M.A., Jones, N.A. and Field, T. (2006) 'Maternal psychological distress, pre-natal cortisol, and fetal weight', *Psychosomatic Medicine,* 68, 5, pp. 747–53.

Dietz, P.M., Spitz, A.M., Anda, R.F., Williamson, D.F. and Santelli, J.S. (1999) 'Unintended pregnancy among adult women exposed to abuse or household dysfunction during their childhood', *Journal of the American Medical Association*, 282, 14, pp. 1359–64.

Dube, S.R., Anda, R.F., Whitfield, C.L., Brown, D.W., Felitti, D.J., Dong, M. and Giles, W.H. (2005) 'Long term consequences of childhood sexual abuse by gender of victim', *American Journal of Preventive Medicine*, 28, 5, pp. 430–8.

Dougherty, D.D., Bobab, A.A., Spencer, T.J., Rauch, S.L., Madras, B.K. and Fischman, A.J. (1999) 'Dopamine transporter density in patients with attention deficit hyperactivity disorder', *Lancet*, 354, 9196, pp. 2132–3.

Dube, S.R., Anda, R.F., Felitti, D.J., Edwards, V.J., Williamson, D.F. (2002) 'Exposure to abuse, neglect and household dysfunction among adults who witnessed intimate partner violence as children: implications for health and social services', *Violence*, 18, 2, pp. 166–85.

Erikson, E.H. (1979) *Dimensions of a New Identity: The Jefferson Lectures in the Humanities* (London, W.W. Norton).

Family Lives (2011) *Families Matter Report* (London, Family Lives).

Faraone, S.V., Sergeant, J., Gillberg, C. and Brederman, J. (2003) 'The world wide prevalence of ADHD: Is it an American condition?', *World Psychiatry*, 2, pp. 104–13.

Feucht, S., Ogata, B. and Lucas, B. (2010) 'Nutrition concerns for children with autism spectrum disorders', *Nutrition Focus*, 25, 4, pp. 1–13.

Fletcher, J. and Wolfe, B. (2009) 'Long-term consequences of childhood ADHD on criminal activities', *Journal of Mental Health Policy and Economics*, 12, pp. 119–38.

Forsloff, C. (2009) *Schizophrenia, Autism Links Brings Specter of Parental Fault*, http://digitaljournal.com/article/266199, accessed 07 December 2011.

Fraley, C. (2012) *A Brief Overview of Adult Attachment Theory and Research*, http://internal.psychology.illinois.edu/~rcfraley/attachment.htm, accessed 19 October 2012.

Gerhardt, S. (2010) *The Selfish Society* (London, Simon and Schuster).

Goleman, D. (1991) 'Theory links early puberty to childhood stress', *New York Times*, 30 July.

Kaufman, J., Yand, B.Z. and Douglas-Palumberi, H. (2006) 'Brain-derived neurotropic factor – 5-HTTLPR gene interactions and environment modifiers of depression in children', *Biology and Psychiatry*, 59, 8, pp. 673–80.

Levin, E.C. (2009) 'The challenges of treating developmental trauma disorder in a residential agency for youth', *Journal of The American Academy of Psychoanalysis and Dynamic Psychiatry*, 37, 3, pp. 519–38.

Lieberman, A., Padron, E., van Horn, P. and Harris, W. (2005) 'Angels in the nursery: The inter-generational transmission of benevolent parental influences', *Infant Mental Health Journal*, 26, 6, pp. 504–20.

(Continued)

(Continued)

Lovaas, I. (1998) *Myths About the Lovaas Model*, www.lovaas.com, accessed 08 December 2011.

Meltzer H., Gatward, R. and Corbin, T. (2003) *Persistence, Onset, Risk Factors and Outcomes of Childhood Mental Disorders* (London, Office for National Statistics).

Martin, A., Volkmar, F.R. and Lewis, M. (2007) *Lewis's Child and Adolescent Psychiatry: A Comprehensive Textbook* (Philadelphia, Lippincott Williams and Wilkins).

McFadden, P. (2011) *EPNET home page*, www.jiscalmail.ac.uk, accessed 25 October 2011.

NINDS (2011) *Autism Fact Sheet,* National Institute of Neurological Disorders and Stroke, www.ninds.nih.gov/disorders/autism/detail_autism.htm, accessed 07 December 2011.

O'Connor, T. (2011) *Stress in Womb can Alter Life Later*, www.lifescience.com/10633-stress, accessed 30 November 2011.

Parens, E. and Johnston, J. (2009) 'Facts, values and attention-deficit hyperactivity disorder (ADHD) an update on the controversies', *Child and Adolescent Psychiatry in Mental Health*, 3, 1, doi: 10.1186/1753-2000-3-1 www.capmh.com/content, accessed 27 January 2013.

Piaget, J. (1953) *The Origin of Intelligence in the Child* (New York, Routledge and Kegan Paul).

Polanczyk, G., de Lima M.S., Horta, B.L., Bicderman, J. and Rohde, L.A. (2007) 'The worldwide prevalence of ADHD: a systematic review and metaregression analysis', *American Journal of Psychiatry*, 164, 6, pp. 942–8.

Reichow, B., Doehring, P., Cicchetti, D.V. and Volkmar, F.R. (eds) (2011) *Evidence-Based Practices and Treatments for Children with Autism* (New York, Springer).

Richards, J.B. (2011) Personal communication, 21 November 2011.

Royal College of Psychiatrists (2010) *No Health Without Public Mental Health: The Case for Action, Position Statement (PS4/2010)* (London, Royal College of Psychiatrists).

Salters-Pedneault, K. (2010) *Suppressing Emotions – Why Suppressing Emotions Doesn't Work*, http:bpd.about.com/od/livingwithbpd/a/suppress.htm, accessed 28 November 2011.

Shriver, E.K. (2007) *Precocious Puberty*, National Institute of Child and Health Development, www.nih.gov, accessed 26 November 2011.

Sparrow, J.D. (2007) 'Understanding stress in children', *Paediatric Annals*, 36, 4, pp. 187–93.

Thapar A.K. and Thapar A. (2003) 'Attention-deficit hyperactivity disorder', *British Journal of General Practice*, 53, 488, pp. 225–30.

Timini, S. and Taylor, E. (2004) 'Samini Timini and Eric Taylor in Debate: ADHD is best understood as a cultural construct', *The British Journal of Psychiatry*, 184, pp. 8–9.

van den Bergh, B.R. and Marcoen, A. (2004) 'High antenatal anxiety is related to ADHD symptoms, externalizing problems, and anxiety in 8- and 9-year-olds', *Child Development*, 75, 4, pp. 1085–97.

van der Kolk, B., Roth, S., Pelcovitz, D., Sunday, S. and Spinazzola, J. (2007) 'Disorders of extreme stress: the empirical foundation of a complex adaptation to trauma', *Journal of Traumatic Stress*, 18, 5, pp. 389–99.

Walsh, S. (2011) http://familylives.org.uk/press-pr/statements/family-stress-levels-record-new-high, accessed 30 November 2011.

Wilson, M. (2011) Personal communication, 23 October 2011.

Wright, J. (2011) *RTI*, www.jimwrightonline.com/php/rti/rti_wire.php, accessed December 2011.

4

Anxiety Disorders and Sexual Abuse

LEARNING OBJECTIVES FOR THIS CHAPTER

- Know what is meant by 'anxiety conditions'
- Understand the physiology of stress
- Identify a phobia, obsessive compulsive disorder, post traumatic stress disorder, generalised anxiety disorder and panic attack
- Learn about survivors of sexual abuse
- Apply knowledge to practice

Some of us know what makes us anxious, while some of us do not. One stressful situation on top of another, such as suffering repeated sexual abuse (SA), can build up the pressure of feeling anxious. Feelings of anxiety can stop us from facing our fears, and therefore prevent us from living life more fully. When anxious, we may think of many dangerous things that might happen. Not everyone, however, who has experienced stressful times suffers from an anxiety problem.

ANXIETY

The core of anxiety problems is a sense of being engulfed by worry and attempting to avoid that sense. Worrying about certain situations can have the function of keeping us safe, for example, 'I must watch the chips frying 'cos if I don't, then I'll have a chip-pan fire'. But if worry is so persistent that it acts as a chain, binding us from freely living our day-to-day lives, then problems arise. For example, our sympathetic nervous system may boost its activity by pumping up our heart-rate, increasing muscular tension and producing more moisture in our body, resulting in more mucus, sweat, a desire to urinate and have diarrhoea, as well as a feeling of nausea. When this happens regularly, an anxiety problem may be present. There are a number of recognised anxiety disorders, including five main ones: generalised anxiety disorder (GAD), phobias, obsessive compulsive disorder (OCD), panic disorder and post traumatic stress disorder (PTSD). Although there is agreement that anxiety manifests in different ways, there is no agreement why. Anxiety and stress are enmeshed.

To deal with stress, we have an in-built alarm system protecting us from danger, known as the fight-or-flight response (Friedman and Silver, 2007). This increases adrenaline, raises blood pressure and brings more oxygen to our limbs for either fighting or running away. Unfortunately, when stress accumulates, the fight-or-flight response can 'get stuck', causing continuing anxiety. Symptoms of high anxiety include disturbed thoughts, feeling panicky or being phobic. Healthy ways of releasing stress help us deal with anxiety (Ulrich, 2000).

There are three main theories of anxiety: behavioural, cognitive and biological. The behavioural understanding stems from animal experiments: it has been found, for example, that if a certain situation an animal experiences is coupled with a fear-inducing event, the animal can become afraid of the situation. However, animal conditioning cannot satisfactorily be transposed onto humans. Another behavioural observation is that phobias may be learnt; it is not uncommon for parents and their children to have the same phobia (Schaefer, 1987). Yet, not all who have parents with a phobia develop phobic-like symptoms. Clearly, the behavioural theory is flawed (see Sikazwe, 2009).

The cognitive perspective is that cognition malfunctions have the effect of producing dysfunctional behaviour and inappropriate emotions. For example, a person may not go out because they think that anyone who looks at them will judge them negatively; this thought scares the person into staying in. The theory leads on to suggest that a change in cognition will therefore have a knock-on effect on behaviour and emotion (Beck and Emery, 1985).

The biological view is that anxious people's hormone levels are outside the normal range, causing stress. For example, they have abnormally high cortisol levels (normally, cortisol rises when stressed), which then causes stress (Maglione-Garves, Kravitz and Schneider, 2005). This can manifest as ongoing anxiety.

GENERALISED ANXIETY DISORDER

Individuals who feel anxious most of the time without knowing why, may be suffering from GAD. If so, they may feel pessimistic, have an unrealistic view of problems and keep worrying. Over a period of at least six months, most days are spent feeling anxious or worrying, which interferes with daily living; for example, missing some days from work.

GAD signs

These include:

- nausea
- fatigue
- shaking
- easy startle-response
- tension
- sleeping problems.

A full list of symptoms can be found in the DSM-IV-TR (APA, 2002).

GAD causes

Not all reasons for having GAD are known but family, stress, environment and brain chemistry may contribute (PsychCentral, 2013). For instance, sufferers may have learnt to be anxious because someone in their family was a worrier, or a stressful event may have happened in their environment that caused trauma. During stressful times, GAD tends to worsen. Further, abnormal levels of certain neurotransmitters (particular chemical messengers which aid in transferring information from nerve cell to nerve cell) in the brain are associated with GAD (University of Maryland Medical Center, 2011).

GAD prevalence, intervention and outcome

Approximately twice as many women as men report GAD symptoms. Although there is no 'cure' as such the majority of sufferers do glean relief from appropriate intervention. As a result of the NICE (2012) guidelines, GAD is often treated with a combination of cognitive behaviour therapy (CBT) and medication, usually in the form of benzodiazapines (tranquilisers) that help with calming down and relaxing. CBT helps the sufferer learn to spot the thoughts and actions that trigger their anxiety, and change them. CBT also helps people learn to look at worries more realistically. Stress-management techniques such as relaxation or meditation are helpful too, in relieving the tension that accompanies stressful feelings and thoughts. Additionally, factors of good nutrition, keeping well hydrated (with water) and daily movement such as regular exercise can lessen symptoms (indeed, they do so on the whole for stress as well as anxiety but these aspects of symptom-reduction are not usually embraced within a therapist's training). Interestingly, a good-enough outcome study by researcher Anestis (2010) found that group CBT was better for GAD than any other intervention, including one-to-one CBT, medication and psychodynamic therapy.

GAD in practice

This disorder often starts in childhood, but as evident from much clinical practice, onset can come during early adulthood. Many do not seek therapy, perhaps believing that feeling the anxiety they do is part of 'normal' life. Sometimes, due to loving concern (or familial irritation!) a family member will endeavour to refer the sufferer for therapy. Often a sufferer is not attended to until the weight of worry develops into extreme anxiety, interfering significantly with their day-to-day life. So, therapists may not see sufferers of GAD until years after its emergence, when it has intensified and daily life is majorly hampered.

GAD CASE VIGNETTE

Albert, a wealthy supermarket owner in his early forties, was referred for therapy by his chiropractor. He complained of back pain due to muscle tension, headaches that kept him awake nightly and financial worries. He thought, 'If something happens to me and I become ill or have an accident and cannot work, or I die, my wife and kids will suffer'. He also worried that people might stop using his supermarket and thought of the worst scenarios that might happen to him. Albert suffered from high blood pressure and palpitations; his feelings of anxiety meant that he missed some deadlines

(Continued)

(Continued)

related to work, such as not doing his accounts on time. Albert and his therapist co-created this formulation:

- He did not feel financially secure (an external factor because Albert's money depended on customers buying products from his supermarket).
- He felt nervous about not being able to provide for his family, becoming ill or dying early, or being unable to care for himself, with the consequence that his family would suffer because he was not a good enough family man (internal factors because of his pessimism, thinking that the worst will happen).
- His irrational thinking was spotted (for example, 'I'm not a good family man').
- His physical symptoms were identified (for example, fatigue and tension).
- His ways of coping in order to avoid a corrective course were recognised (for example, increased use of primary health care services, working longer hours and his need for reassurance from his spouse and a few favourite customers that they were loyal to him).
- It was recognised that the consequence of his avoidant actions was temporary relief.

With Albert's co-operation, his therapist used exposure response prevention (ERP).

- The therapist and Albert highlighted all of his fears and for each one, he was taught specific coping skills.
- They used the therapy sessions collaboratively, so that therapy supported Albert in removing hindrances to his goals.
- From the therapist, Albert learnt to reduce anxiety; this exterminated unwanted symptoms.

A reduction in Albert's use of primary health care services and a more appropriate use of them was one of the outcomes of therapy. Also, he and his accountant created a plan that he could stick to so that his accounts were done in a timely way, and a well-balanced work/home time-management plan was worked out between Albert and his wife. With such a reduction in worry, his blood pressure normalised and his sleeping pattern became good enough, due to the elimination of headaches. Albert continues to use his newly learnt healthy coping strategies for keeping symptoms of anxiety well managed.

GAD research and theory

Emergent research findings reveal that the experience of childhood abuse is a high indicator of later anxiety. For example, a research team headed by Shackman (2007) found that abused children were more sensitive to picking up emotional cues of anger, when compared with non-abused children. The team used research methods such as brain-imaging to collect data. On sensing anger in others (by, for example, hearing a recording of adult voices with emotional content), the abused children involuntarily became highly anxious while the non-abused did not. (This links with Chapter 3.) From this, it seems logical to theorise that the way of processing which abused children learn regarding fear-provoking factors can continue into adult life, deepening the way their personal worldviews are shaped, thereby leading them to become more sensitive to environmental factors that can provoke fear and consequently leading them to suffer from anxiety, such as GAD, during adulthood.

Others, such as authors Mineka and Zinberg (2006), support this view by offering a scholarly argument that learning theory offers a foundation for viewing the course and development of anxiety disorders. They illustrate that by keeping in mind people's histories of learning, it is possible to see how the outcomes of stressful experiences vary in individuals and may indicate whether any anxiety problems persist. Work such as that of therapist Gerhardt also supports this perspective (2004). Further research and theory strongly imply that GAD is linked to an impaired quality of life due to feeling distressed and avoiding certain situations for fear of exacerbating the emotional distress (Michelson et al., 2011).

PHOBIAS

'Phobia' is the Greek word for 'fear'. If there is extreme fear of a situation or thing, a phobia is present. There are many phobias – a person can be phobic about anything, for example: agoraphobia (fear of public or open spaces), bird phobia, dog phobia, spider phobia or social phobia. Therapists may see clients with a phobia practically daily.

Agoraphobia

This is one of the more common phobias. It is characterised by extreme unrealistic fear of being 'trapped' in public places. Commonly, sufferers stay at home.

Agoraphobia prevalence, intervention, signs and outcome

Just as with GAD, women are reportedly twice as likely to suffer agoraphobia than men (Phobics-Awareness, 2012). Initial incidence of agoraphobia is identified mainly between 25 to 35 years of age; onset, however, can be later, for example, after menopause. Signs include feeling shaky, sweaty, nauseous, having palpitations and physical pains (a comprehensive list of symptoms can be found in DSM-IV (APA, 2002)). In order not to experience the symptoms, sufferers avoid going out – agoraphobia is therefore disabling. CBT seems to be the intervention most commonly offered. One outcome study revealed that on completion of a CBT programme, between 75 and 95 per cent of sufferers showed improvement (Leahy and Holland, 2000).

Agoraphobia theory, research and practice

There is a limited availability of theories and research which are good-enough (Wittchen et al., 2010), but when looking at practice it seems that once the therapeutic relationship is grounded in safety and trust, degrees of anxiety can be raised, followed by calm states, so that emotional management (affect regulation) can be developed. The therapist can help the client integrate new knowledge with physical and emotional experiences within the safety of sessions. Then, a way of processing and managing novel experiences outside the therapeutic arena can be developed, helping to relieve the symptoms of agoraphobia.

Social phobia

The terms 'social phobia' and 'social anxiety' are interchangeable. Social phobia is intense worry relating to facing social situations, mainly due to the fear of being judged negatively by others. This can be described as extreme shyness.

Social phobia theory and research

A major theory is that irrational thoughts trigger anxious feelings, which fuel social phobia and which in turn affects behaviour (Abramowitz et al., 2009). Therapists can help clients change irrational thoughts to more realistic ones, which has a domino effect on their emotions and behaviour. Negative experiences in social situations may be a cause, and certain research links social phobia with low self-esteem (see Vassilopoulos, 2005). Low self-esteem can manifest as shyness.

Social phobia signs, prevalence and intervention

Shyness can appear as part of normal child development, and is often undetected; most outgrow it before adulthood. Signs of social phobia fall into three areas:

1 Behavioural:

- avoiding social situations so much that it reduces life-quality
- believing that they have to take a friend with them if they go anywhere
- trying to hide or staying in the background so that others will not notice them
- sometimes using alcohol before interacting socially, as a way of coping.

2 Emotional:

- nervousness over self-humiliation due to their own actions
- having tremendous fear of particular social situations
- feeling extremely self-conscious in even 'ordinary' social situations
- going to tremendous lengths to avoid these social situations
- experiencing anxiety even thinking about the social situations
- fearing being looked at and judged
- fearing that others will see their nervousness.

3 Physical:

- blushing
- sweating
- shaking
- panting
- feeling faint.

Clearly, extreme social anxiety can result in reduced life-quality because sufferers would rather stay home alone indefinitely than meet someone for interaction. This may mean not grasping educational opportunities and no enjoyment of a social life.

After depression and substance abuse, social phobia is the most common mental health problem, with approximately one in fifty-one people of the population in the USA, and 1,174,400 individuals in the UK, suffering (Peterson, 2009). It is the most common of all the anxiety disorders; hence its fuller description here. As with anxiety disorders overall, the incidence of suffering social phobia is reportedly greater in women than men. Intervention is often CBT as a result of the guidelines set by NICE (2012). This incorporates: identifying irrational thoughts in order to analyse and challenge them; learning to control breathing using relaxation techniques; facing fears in a step-by-step way (with the least fear-inducing faced first and the most, last); learning to be patient; and developing techniques to remain calm, be assertive, help others (for example, offering to take a neighbour's dog for regular walks), develop communication skills, expand emotional literacy, drink alcohol in moderation and have enough sleep (Bernstein, 2011).

Social phobia expected outcome

Using CBT alone is often enough because the following outcomes can be expected (Priyamvada et al., 2009):

- a change of irrational thoughts to rational ones
- stopping avoiding social situations
- learning to react differently
- symptom-reduction as a result of graded exposure to anxiety-provoking experiences
- self-soothing as a result of the use of relaxation techniques.

Medication alongside CBT may also be used if CBT alone is unsuccessful.

Social phobia in practice

As therapists, when seeing clients with social phobia it is not unusual to experience them as looking at the wall away from us while we are speaking to them. As they feel safer within the therapeutic relationship, they often begin to be able to look at us – one fleeting glance to begin with then, gradually, in a more socially acceptable or 'normal' way.

SOCIAL PHOBIA CASE VIGNETTE

Sundai missed her first day of a cookery course because she was too nervous to face new classmates and a new teacher. She went for therapy to help overcome her fear of meeting people. Early during therapy, the therapist helped Sundai identify her automatic irrational negative thoughts such as 'Everyone'll think I'm stupid, I'll look like an idiot and make myself look ridiculous'. He helped her replace such thoughts with more realistic ones. To help her cope, the therapist also gave Sundai homework: listen to others; look at others; do not keep talking but let others have the chance to talk. (She had a friend who supported her in practising the homework.)

The therapist taught Sundai breath-control, which included how to slow down her breathing in order to reduce anxiety (hyperventilating causes symptoms of anxiety since it disturbs the carbon dioxide and oxygen balance in the body). Additionally, Sundai used relaxation techniques such as physical relaxation.

Next, Sundai was enabled to face social situations, rather than avoid them, by first facing her smallest fear before building up gradually to face more challenging ones.

Approximately mid-therapy, with her therapist's encouragement, Sundai volunteered to go shopping for her elderly neighbour, an activity she enjoyed.

By the end of therapy, Sundai changed her lifestyle to a healthier one by reducing her caffeine intake, limiting her alcoholic drinking to moderate consumption, getting enough sleep, eating nutritiously (on the whole) and drinking adequate amounts of water. She had learnt to control her physical symptoms of social anxiety, challenge her irrational negative thoughts and, in a step-wise way, face social situations.

The psychopathological perspective of social phobia seems contentious, because a person may not have a disorder, but rather might just feel anxious due to being within a social situation without being phobic. Differences along a continuum of shyness, feeling anxious in a social situation and social phobia are difficult to demarcate. Of concern is that social phobia might be confused with paranoia; therapists can use tests to assess whether there is a disorder of paranoia or social phobia (see Chapter 2). To an onlooker, one person suffering from agoraphobia and another from social phobia can seem as if they have the same problem. Although there can be co-morbidity with agoraphobia and social phobia, armed with knowledge and understanding from theory, research and clinical practice, it is apparent that the two phobias are different, although both come under the umbrella of 'anxiety disorders'.

OCD

Irrational thinking and repeated compulsive actions characterise OCD. Most sufferers experience both, though some only experience the obsessive thoughts and others only the compulsive actions.

OCD signs and prevalence

Repeated unwanted thoughts and behaviours that interfere with daily living define OCD. Sometimes the obsessive ways of thinking are not as strong as at other times. The thoughts instil a feeling of anxiety in the person having them, so to rid themselves of the anxious feelings, they behave in certain ways according to their own 'rules', performing ritualised, compulsive behaviour. For a while after the behaviour is performed, the anxious feelings disappear; the unwanted thoughts and feelings then return, therefore the behaviour is repeated.

Obsessions and compulsions that are minor, such as checking once if the back door is locked or that the oven is turned off, are not problematic. When obsessions and/or compulsions interfere with daily life, however, then OCD can be diagnosed. It is not uncommon to try to hide OCD because of feeling shame. Most onset of OCD is before the age of twenty-five. Reportedly, 2.3 per cent of people between eighteen and fifty-four years have OCD (Fireman et al., 2001).

OCD theory and research

A theory is yet to be found that explains the causes of OCD adequately (Wilson and Veale, 2005). Some believe it is due to early childhood experiences; others that it is learnt from parents or that there is lack of a brain chemical (serotonin), though there is much disagreement on this biological explanation. Research shows that the most common obsessive thoughts are sexual, blasphemous or aggressive and that the most common compulsive actions are washing or checking, such as washing hands twenty times or checking emails ten times before sending (Bling, 2005).

Intervention for OCD

The bad news is that cure is not instant. The good news is that ERP, in a graded way, for example repeatedly touching a door handle and then not washing hands if contamination by 'bad germs' is feared, helps in wiping away symptoms. CBT is also often used for OCD. NICE (2012) recommends a stepped model:

Step 1: CBT (up to ten hours).

Step 2: If Step 1 is unsuccessful, Step 2 is to provide more CBT either with or without medication which tends to be anti-depressants (such as fluoxetine, the trade name of which is Prozac). Unfortunately, drugs can have detrimental side effects.

Step 3: If Step 2 does not work, Step 3 provides further CBT and medication plus additional specialist support. When all else is unsuccessful, but only with consent from the patient, neurosurgery may be performed, though this is rare.

CBT can be provided by the NHS, but the waiting list can be very long. Independent therapists do not tend to have long waiting lists.

Other forms of help are also available, for example, self-help groups, action plans for coping with stressful situations and relaxation techniques. Information on finding help can be obtained from local GPs. They often display leaflets about OCD (and other anxiety disorders) in their waiting rooms.

OCD expected outcome

Family and friends can help by accepting the person's emotions. Results from investigations show that in the region of 83 per cent of people who complete a CBT programme for OCD improve long-term (see, for example, Keeley et al., 2008), and that the relapse rate is low.

CBT is the most researched model relating to OCD, offering a substantial evidence-base (O'Kearney et al., 2010). This does not mean that other therapeutic approaches do not work, but that more research is needed for an evidence-base to support different models.

OCD CASE VIGNETTE

Min was referred to her current therapist by a colleague who had unsuccessfully endeavoured to find the cause of Min's OCD. Unfortunately her OCD had become worse. Due to the number thirty-seven (for example, walking around her car thirty-seven times), she arrived late for her first session with the therapist. The therapist decided not to focus on the reason for Min's OCD, but on alleviating symptoms that caused her distress and interfered with her daily life. She had much insight into her problem and was highly motivated to overcome it. With Min's informed consent, CBT was chosen as the therapeutic model not only because of its base of evidence for OCD but also because the therapist was well trained in it.

Min was afraid to open her car door and enter the car unless she first walked around it thirty-seven times. There was something about this number but she did not know what, although she used it repeatedly throughout each day, for example, stepping thirty-seven times in and out of her front door, and turning the light on and off in her hall thirty-seven times. It is because of the number thirty-seven that she was usually late getting into work or arrived very late for social occasions; indeed, she often did not manage even to attend them. If she did not do what she felt compelled to do thirty-seven times, she thought that something dreadful would happen.

(Continued)

(Continued)

Her therapist was highly skilled in using ERP. Min voluntarily and deliberately was exposed to her fear, first in her imagination in the safety of the therapy room. The therapist talked her through visualising not going around her car but getting into it, driving off and being safe. After each visit to the therapist, she was given homework, which she followed, using a number less than thirty-seven during her rituals and gradually reducing the number in her daily life. Concurrently, Min suffered less and less anxiety from her obsessive thoughts. She continued faithfully working through her homework assignments, with the support of her family. The therapist also suggested a self-help book to help Min, keeping a diary of her thoughts, actions and emotions. By the end of her CBT course, Min improved substantially, functioning well enough in her work and social life.

OCD in practice

A form of evidence-based practice for OCD sufferers was created by therapists Fairfax and Barfield (2010). They conducted therapy groups that used a combination of techniques such as socialisation and mindfulness. Mixed methodology (quantitative and qualitative) was used to measure outcome and discover findings, which revealed that participants were positive in attitude (rather than continuing to be OCD sufferers). Such practice-based evidence can be used for future evidence-based practice.

PANIC

Panic disorder is characterised by panic attacks. If feeling as if something dreadful and unexpected is about to happen while experiencing extreme fear, then panic disorder can be identified. Its hallmark is unexpected, repeated panic attacks.

Panic theory and research

Panic attacks include sensations in the body such as palpitations, thoughts such as 'I'm having a heart attack' and emotions such as fear. If the person is also suffering from PTSD, a panic attack can worsen it (Hinton et al., 2008). Additionally, co-morbidity between panic disorder, agoraphobia and irritable bowel syndrome is high (Gros et al., 2011). Unfortunately, there is a paucity of investigations about whether those suffering from panic disorder experience the perceived catastrophes they are afraid of, such as fainting (Green et al., 2007). Interestingly, a smaller amygdala is associated with panic disorder (Hayano et al., 2009).

Recent research shows a link between the use of cocaine and experiencing panic attacks (for example, Alvarado, Storr and Anthony, 2010). Using standardised interviews with 1,692 young adults, researchers Alvarado and team found that a significant number who used cocaine experienced panic attack-like symptoms at least once in their lives.

Panic risk factors prevalence and causes

Genetics may influence who is susceptible to panic disorder. Some twin studies show that if one twin suffers from panic attacks, the other is 40 per cent more likely also to suffer than a non-twin. However, the problem more often occurs in those without a family history of it. Just as with agoraphobia, twice as many women than men report panic disorder. Exact causes are unknown. Usually, signs of the problem manifest in individuals between the ages of twenty-five and thirty years. The prevalence of panic attacks in the UK is 1.7 per cent of the population (Skapinakis et al., 2010).

Panic signs

This disorder is characterised by a variety of symptoms (Kircanski et al., 2009). They include:

- a sudden inexplicable change in body temperature
- a rapid heartbeat
- feeling choked
- nausea
- shaking
- dizziness
- chest discomfort
- fear of death.

Panic attack onset is sudden, usually reaching a climax after fifteen minutes, though symptoms may persevere for an hour. The episode might be mistaken as a heart attack. It is difficult to predict when a panic attack may happen and not easy to pin-point its trigger.

Panic remedy

The aim of intervention is to support those with panic disorder to function well in their daily living. A combination of prescribed drugs and CBT is often recommended (Stein et al., 2009). The following can also help:

- nutritious diet
- regular exercise
- adequate sleep (Life Extension, 2012).

although these are generally beneficial for most health problems.

Panic expected outcome

Most sufferers improve after adhering to an appropriate intervention programme, but a significant number are more likely to drop out of a treatment programme if suffering from panic attacks compared with those suffering with another anxiety disorder (Santana and Fontenelle, 2011).

In some, it can be a long-lasting problem, despite conventional treatment. A further complication may be agoraphobia; if a person who suffers a panic attack fears visiting places in case they have another one, this can severely restrict their movements regarding going out and also interfere with their feelings of self-worth, socialising and working. If prone to panic attacks, it is suggested that certain products are avoided, such as alcohol, cocaine or caffeine as they may trigger or worsen an attack (see Mind, 2012).

PANIC DISORDER CASE VIGNETTE

Lyndsey finished her course of medicine for panic, but the panic attacks returned after the medication stopped. She sought support from a therapist who used a CBT treatment manual in tandem with the therapy sessions. After eleven weekly therapy sessions of fifty minutes each, which mainly focussed on managing anxiety, Lyndsey was free of panic attacks and continued being panic-free at her six-month follow-up session. This is what happened during the therapeutic process:

Approximately four weeks into the therapy sessions, once trust and a good working alliance was established between Lyndsey and her therapist, Lyndsey experienced much delight, which meant a great deal to her because she was able to do things she could not do before, such as going to the cinema or ten-pin bowling with friends. She rapidly improved.

Doing her 'homework', set weekly by the therapist (with Lyndsey's input), took less than half an hour a day. She was encouraged by her therapist to keep doing the 'homework', and in this way, Lyndsey's confidence was boosted.

One of the first things that occurred during therapy was that Lyndsey became aware of the reason for her panic attacks. During therapy, she was taught to breath in a different way, in order to decrease her panic and anxious feelings. How to handle her panic thoughts was another skill that Lyndsey learnt. Gradually, over the eleven weeks, on a daily basis, Lyndsey tested her newly learnt abilities, initially in low-anxiety situations then, in a step-by-step way, in higher anxiety situations. Through this desensitisation process, Lyndsey was able to eventually expose herself to previously anxiety-provoking situations armed with the ability of handling any panic attack or feeling of anxiety, if it ever re-arose.

Panic disorder in practice

Experiencing a panic attack is extremely stressful. It is important for a therapist not to be alarmed if a client has a panic attack during therapy. If this happens, some therapists encourage clients to breath into cupped hands. Others talk the client through relaxed 'belly-breathing', continually reassuring the client and role-modelling the breathing, until the panic attack finishes.

STRESS

What happens to our body when something upsets its balance is stress. The body produces stress hormones such as cortisol and adrenaline, which prepare us to act in an emergency. This can be good: for example making us study for an examination when we would rather have a drink with friends. But too much stress is harmful and can destroy our health, interfere with relationships and be detrimental to our productivity.

Cognitively, stress can affect us in these ways:

- worry
- forgetfulness
- pessimism.

Emotionally, stress can make us:

- irritable
- lonely
- miserable.

Physically, stress can cause:

- illness
- palpitations
- nausea.

Behaviourally, stress can affect us in these ways:

- a change in appetite
- a change in sleeping pattern
- using drugs to relax, for example alcohol or nicotine.

The following can act as buffers against negative stress:

- social support (from friends and family)
- believing that we can influence events (rather than feeling events are uncontrollable)
- optimism (most of the time)
- self-soothing (healthily, such as having a rest but not as a result of a drunken stupor)
- preparing for stressful situations (knowing how quickly and easily to use stress-busting techniques).

The following can be reasons for being stressed:

- relationships (such as a choosing a 'toxic' partner)
- finances (such as becoming bankrupt)
- work (such as being fired from a job)
- major life events (such as a death in the family)
- perfectionism (such as not finishing anything due to wanting perfection)
- unrealistic expectations (such as buying a lottery ticket daily, expecting to win).

What is stressful for one is not stressful for another. For example, giving a talk may be experienced as eustress (positive stress) in one person and distress (negative stress) in another; or asking for heating to be turned on in a restaurant may be too stressful for one person but not a problem for another. Experiencing prolonged distress (chronic stress) is dangerous. Chronic stress can:

- raise blood pressure
- lower immunity
- increase the risk of heart attack
- increase the risk of stroke
- increase the risk of depression
- increase the risk of anxiety
- increase the risk of digestive problems
- increase the risk of skin problems.

The following can help manage stress:

- relaxing
- deep breathing
- developing calming abilities that can be used when under pressure.

Stress in adults is in some ways different to stress in a child because a juvenile's developing brain is very different from that of an adult. Research findings reveal that memories in juveniles are not well imprinted, which makes things easier to forget, while in adults memories are well-imprinted, making things harder to forget (Gundelfinger et al., 2010). For instance, it is not unusual for children to forget what their mother was like (if she has died) unless they see her picture and she is often spoken about. Not remembering her can be very stressful. If an adult's mother dies, the person can remember her, so the stress is not likely to be the same as the children's. Some who experienced stress also suffer from PTSD (see also Chapter 3).

PTSD

This is characterised by severe anxiety following a traumatic event or overpoweringly stressful situations. It results from an unusual experience in life, often where one's life is in danger, or someone else's is and this is witnessed. PTSD can result from experiences such as rape, or any assault, for example, childhood sexual abuse, accident victims, experiences in the armed forces, sudden illness.

PTSD signs

These include:

- nightmares
- flashbacks (reliving the event)
- jumpiness (being easily startled)
- trying to avoid reminders of the traumatic event or situations (due to the extreme distress they cause).

The DSM-IV (APA, 2002) has a comprehensive listing of the symptoms of PTSD.

PTSD in practice

Some therapists use what they have seen work in clinical practice for problems such as PTSD. This does not necessarily mean that there is a substantial amount of research to back-up what is being practised by them. However, it is important for therapists to be able to provide a rationale for what they do, such as practice-based evidence supported by theory, as can be seen from the case vignette below.

PTSD CASE VIGNETTE

Six months before her initial visit to a therapist Elizabeth witnessed a traumatic event and she consequently suffered from PTSD. Her therapist used a little-known technique known as the Fast Phobia Cure (Griffin and Tyrrell, 2004), a process of ten steps he had used successfully many times with traumatised clients (although there was a paucity of research on it, theory being ahead of the research).

1 Initially, Elizabeth's therapist built good rapport and trust.
2 Next, Elizabeth was guided into a relaxed state, where she was invited to visualise herself sitting very comfortably in a place she felt safe and secure.
3 From this place, the therapist enabled Elizabeth to relax more fully.
4 When this happened, he invited her to imagine a cinema screen in front of her.
5 Once Elizabeth could do this, she was asked to imagine holding a remote control for a film she was about to watch.
6 After this, the therapist suggested that Elizabeth see herself floating to one corner of the room where she could watch herself sitting on the comfortable chair watching the blank cinema screen (thus being substantially emotionally distanced from any events on the screen which she would view).
7 Next, Elizabeth was asked to imagine seeing herself watching a film of the traumatic event, from the point of the event to a point at the end where she could see herself in a place feeling safe.
8 After this, she was asked to imagine pressing the rewind button on the remote control to see the film rewinding backwards from the safe place, through the trauma, to a safe place before the traumatic event.
9 Once Elizabeth did this, she was gently instructed by her therapist to fast-forward the film from safe place, through the trauma, to safe place.
10 This process of rewinding and fast-forwarding was done repeatedly at the speed dictated by Elizabeth, as many times as she deemed necessary, until there was no emotional arousal from her. When Elizabeth was feeling confident in her relaxed place, the therapist gradually talked her back into the here-and-now of the therapy room.

Elizabeth did not at any point have to explain the traumatic event. Due to the process used for the Fast Phobia Cure, instead of the memory traumatising her, it became stored in a place within her memory (the neo-cortex) that did not elicit trauma and allowed the memory to be put into perspective. Consequently, Elizabeth stopped having the flashbacks that had plagued her during the previous six months.

PTSD prevalence, research, theory, intervention and outcome

Reportedly, 7.8 per cent of the population in the USA suffer from PTSD; over 10 per cent of women and 5 per cent of men (APA, 2006). Brain function is affected if profound stress is experienced (van der Kolk, 2006). According to researcher van der Kolk, this leaves the traumatised person susceptible to responding in irrelevant and often dangerous ways because reminders of the traumatic events fire up the parts of the brain associated with intense emotions while dampening down the central nervous system. This results in an impaired ability to integrate information coming in from the senses with physical action, coupled with an incapacity to control physiological arousal and an inability to use words as a means of communicating experience. With failing memory and attention (due to PTSD) obstructing engagement with the here-and-now, PTSD sufferers are unable to 'find their way'. Due to such research findings, van der Kolk theorises that for a positive outcome, an intervention of choice must include learning to tolerate sensations and emotions, control arousal and take appropriate action after experiencing physical helplessness.

Another therapeutic approach for PTSD that seems to be gaining popularity is EMDR (2012); it may be that the number of therapists using this approach will increase further as more valid and reliable research accumulates, supporting its efficacy. In the UK, NICE guidelines however, and recent developments in the NHS such as IAPT (Improving Access to Psychological Therapies) and the HCPC (Heath and Care Professions Council), create an impact on the way that therapists working within the NHS have on clients, for example, which therapeutic approach is chosen and how many therapy sessions are allocated to a particular client/patient with a problem such as PTSD. As a result, the therapy model chosen for a particular mental health problem may not be the therapist's choice.

SEPARATION ANXIETY

In adults, this usually relates to parents when their sons and daughters leave home (Kins et al., 2011). Researchers Kins and team found a link between a controlling style of parenting and the parents experiencing separation anxiety while their offspring found it more difficult to settle into their individual adult lives without feeling that they had to conform to perceived parental control, irrespective of whether they lived with the parents or not (2011). This suggests that parenting style has an effect on parents and their offspring's mental wellness, even after daughters and or sons have moved out of the parental household. One reason for a controlling style of parenting may be due to parents having survived abuse as children and wanting to keep control of their offspring in the hope that they do not experience similar abuse.

Role-play

Before moving on in this chapter, I suggest a consolidation of what has been gleaned so far regarding the five anxiety disorders. Role-playing is one way of doing this. Therefore, I would encourage students to gather into groups of between three and five people, to do the activities below. One person in the group can role-play the client, a second can role-play the therapist and the others can observe. After a few minutes of role-playing, the observers can see if they can identify the anxiety disorder being role-played, then the 'therapist' can guess the role-played disorder, before the 'client' discloses it. Group discussion will subsequently occur where reasons for the interventions used can be deliberated on. Each person in the group can take turns in playing different roles for the various disorders. Only the person role-playing the client knows the disorder, which they must not name while in that role.

Role-playing activities (for the tutor to photocopy)

1 GAD role-play scenario

Zak is a recently retired sixty-five-year-old whose wife is fed up with his negative attitude and has given him the ultimatum: 'Get some therapy to change your attitude or I'll leave you!' He explains that although he has come for therapy, he does not believe that it can help. Zak's self-description is that he blows up problems out of all proportion and dwells on them. He appears stressed and says that he has been stressed for years. Any problem concerns him so much that he is continuously negative in his attitude. Due to this, other people keep away from him. Now he thinks he'll lose his wife, but wants to save the marriage.

This client has self-referred.

The therapist works independently in a rented room at a Wellness Centre.

2 Agoraphobia role-play scenario

Esme is a thirty-five-year-old single, childless Turkish woman who lives alone in England and works from home doing piece-work. The only time she sees her friends is if they visit her. Although she needs to go shopping, she fears that she cannot go without fainting. Therefore she has asked a voluntary agency for help. In every respect, Esme seems normal, except that if she goes into a shop she feels sick, her heart starts thumping and she breaks out into a sudden sweat; so she stays at home.

This client was referred by the voluntary agency (which does Esme's shopping for her).

The therapist works for the voluntary agency and visits Esme in her home.

3 OCD role-play scenario

Amanda is eighteen years old and will shortly be starting her university course. She seems well adjusted, but if she touches money she becomes very anxious and feels that she must wash her hands immediately. Believing that the money is dirty, she thinks that she will pass on the 'bad bacteria' (that is on her hands due to touching the money) to all her loved ones. They will then become very ill and consequently die. If she is unable to wash her hands immediately, washing them is all she can think about, she feels tremendously nervous and her heart beats too rapidly. Eventual hand-washing temporarily relieves her high anxiety.

This client was referred by her family doctor.

The therapist works in a room within a GP surgery under the umbrella of a local Health Centre.

4 Panic disorder role-play scenario

Caroline is an unemployed twenty-nine-year-old single mother living with her parents who is afraid to go out alone in case she has what she describes as a 'heart attack' in a public place with nobody to help her. She is a Christian and her mother gives her a lift to the counselling service attached to her local church. 'My heart beats like it's gonna jump out o' me chest, I feel like I'm chokin', that I'll puke up, my heart aches and I'm all trembly' is how she describes what happens to her, all of a

(Continued)

(Continued)

sudden, for no apparent reason. Caroline has had medical tests that did not show any sign of a heart attack or any other physical problems.

This client self-referred after receiving the results of her medical tests.

The therapist is a Christian who offers therapy at the Christian Therapy Centre.

5 PTSD role-play scenario

Senaisha, an actress, was taking a short cut across a park one weekday morning, when she was seven weeks pregnant, to go and audition for a children's TV programme. In the park, a man grabbed her from behind and held a knife against her throat with one hand and her left breast with the other, ordering her to do as he said, or he'd kill her. She believed that she was miscarrying – in fact she was not having a miscarriage, but was urinating due to the fear she felt. A passer-by was seen so the man with the knife fled and Senaisha stood frozen due to the terror she experienced. To the therapist, she complains of difficulty getting to sleep and of nightmares about the event, saying she repeatedly thinks of it, even though she tries not to. She will not walk in a park any more for fear of flashbacks and she is afraid that something dreadful will happen to her baby, whose birth is expected at full term, in six weeks time.

This client's GP referred her to an Adult Community Mental Health Team.

The therapist works within the Adult Community Mental Health Team.

ADULT SURVIVORS OF SEXUAL ABUSE

The word 'survivors' is used to describe living people who have experienced sexual abuse (SA). Often called 'molestation', SA is the unwanted sexual action of one person onto another. There are many forms of SA, including spousal, incest, non-consensual verbal sexual demands, exposing genitalia, sexual kissing, voyeurism, sexual assault, attempted rape, rape or any unwanted sexual activity. When the victim is under the age of consent, it is known as 'childhood sexual abuse' (see also Chapter 3). These are some of the affects survivors of sexual abuse can experience:

- flashbacks
- shame
- insomnia
- nightmares
- guilt
- fear of anything related to the abusive incident/s
- pain
- addiction
- somatic complaints
- depression
- stress
- anxiety.

Adult survivors of SA research, theory and prevalence

According to a research team headed by Bottoms, those who have survived childhood SA are six times more likely to attempt suicide than those who have not and eight times more likely to attempt suicide repeatedly than those who have not; however, it is abusers who are more likely to commit suicide (Bottoms et al., 2003). In the USA, approximately 20 per cent of women and 10 per cent of men report being survivors of childhood SA (Bottoms et al., 2003). Statistical figures from the NSPCC show that, alarmingly, one in nine young adults in the UK are survivors of SA (NSPCC, 2011). Most reported abuse is committed by men who are members of the family of the person they abuse (see also Chapter 3). Those who have been abused as children tend to be revictimised as adults, and many with developmental disorders are at risk of sexual abuse (Bottoms et. al., 2003). Popular theories, based on beliefs that SA is somehow the fault of the victim and that the perpetrator has also always been sexually abused, are myths (Murtagh, 2010)!

Nevertheless, adult survivors of adult or child SA can take on board such 'myths' and often partly attribute self-blame about the abuse. This results in further distress, even in survivors who have completed a therapy programme but continue self-blaming (Kingston and Raghaven, 2009). However, research shows that using what is known in the field of mental health about sexual offenders can help survivors of SA (Murtagh, 2010). What is crucial is that therapists address any self-blame (rather than perpetrator-blame) attributions. A relatively new intervention programme named the Appropriate Attribution Technique (ATT; Murtagh, 2010) is a cognitive psycho-educational technique, which helps survivors rid themselves of the distress stemming from the originally attributed self-blame via a critical reattribution process. This process moves through four parts and can be conducted in one therapy session of approximately sixty minutes, either in a group or on a one-to-one basis. It supports survivors in learning how to form healthy and appropriate attributions regarding the SA.

SURVIVOR OF SA CASE VIGNETTE

Anna was date raped and felt lost in her world so she found a therapist who did the following during group therapy:

1 Pre-ATT the therapist discussed the choice of highlighting SA and using ATT with the group, and suggested that the next session could focus on the reasons why SA happened. The therapist informed the group that the next session would be a psycho-educational one, although the discussion would involve all in the group.
2 The next session commenced with Part 1 of ATT, Stage 1: giving information regarding sexual offenders and the popular beliefs about them (that all who are sexually abused become sexual offenders).
3 Stage 2 followed: a discussion and challenging of the popular myth about offenders, which consequently diminished it.
4 Stage 3: research findings were used to shatter another myth (that SA is partly the victim's fault) by explaining that 76 per cent of sexual abusers were abusing so as children and that 30 per cent were sexually abused themselves (Hindman and Peters, 2001). This reduced the group's (including Anna's) self-blame.

(Continued)

(Continued)

5   Stage 4: the therapist facilitated emotional-charge for the group while enabling them to realise that they were not responsible for the abusive situation/s they experienced, hence helping to clear their sense of self-blame. It was while laughing in-session that Anna and her group perceived that not all who are abused end up abusing; and this fact was overtly explained. The therapist also explained that consuming alcohol and other drugs does not make a person abusive, rather, it lowers inhibitions. Another myth that was busted regarded the fact that some victims of SA may experience a degree of pleasure (the myth being, 'they wanted it') – the therapist explained that as humans, our bodies are made so that they will often respond to stimulation, irrespective of whether we want it or not (for example if shot, we will bleed, even though we do not want to). Anna and the other survivors fully realised that they were not responsible for the abusive situation/s they experienced, hence again, helping to clear their self-blame.

6   Once the myths about why sexual offenders offend were exploded, Anna and her group were educated about why offenders offend.

The therapist then continued with Part 2 of the ATT programme, which focused on the four preconditions for abusing sexually:

• First precondition: having the motivation to express anger or gain control via a sexual act.
• Second precondition: either the offender's own internal inhibition must be overcome or the inhibition which informs the offender that the act is not right does not exist.
• Third precondition: the offender overcomes external inhibition.
• Fourth precondition: the opportunity must be there.

Learning about the four preconditions further helped Anna's group reduce self-blame, aiding them in making the attribution of responsibility appropriately. In Part 3 of the process, the therapist also explained the seven-phased cycle of abuse of a sex-offender:

• Phase i: the sexually abusive act.
• Phase ii: re-enforcement.
• Phase iii: psychological pain and trying to reduce it.
• Phase iv: defence mechanism kicks-in.
• Phase v: masking that the abuse was their responsibility.
• Phase vi: increased stress with negative mood.
• Phase vii: pre-assault victim-grooming and offence-planning.

Finally, Part 4 culminated in reattribution, by increasing offender-blame and deleting self-blame. Ensuring the group could handle it, Anna's therapist increased tension (because group members originally self-blamed under tension), followed by release which came with reattribution. Stages before Part 4 (which aided in understanding the steps the group members' perpetrators took before committing abuse) prepared Anna and the others for the final part of ATT, where the information gleaned about their sexual offenders was applied to their individual cases; in this way, tension was increased so that the very powerful emotional processing of fully attributing responsibility of the abuse to the perpetrator, could be completed (see Murtagh, 2010). This freed Anna into finding her way in the world.

NOTE: As this vignette shows, ATT is a delicate process and should only be utilised by a therapist who is highly skilled in working with SA survivors.

Specific research shows that SA survivors who self-blame are not healed as time goes by, and that those who attribute blame to external factors tend to be better adjusted (Wilson, 2010). It has been found that women who have survived SA (either as children from, for example, a family member, or as adults from, for example, rape) and who self-blame can have problems with their sexual functioning and are more likely to commit suicide than even those who are depressed but are not survivors of SA. Shame or self-blame is the greatest risk factor for emotional distress in adults (Whiffen and Macintosh, 2005). ATT helps adult survivors of SA to perceive the abuse as being fully the perpetrator's responsibility. The first three parts of ATT bring into relief why some people offend sexually, rather than focusing on the client's personal experience. The final fourth part is the reattribution process in which the knowledge that the client has learnt during parts one to three is brought into the client's personal experience in an emotional way and it is when the change in attribution is made. In the hands of a skilled therapist, this is a very powerful technique for healing.

AGE, GENDER AND CULTURE

Anxieties can occur in people of all ethnicities and cultures but are locally specific: OCD sufferers, for example, for whom blasphemous thoughts are the problem, may belong to a religious institution. Anxiety disorders such as OCD are found in individuals of all ages but tend first to emerge in juveniles or during early adulthood. PTSD can emerge at any age since it is related to trauma, and panic disorder tends to emerge during the teenage years, twenties or thirties. Yet, when an anxiety disorder is spotted in an older adult, it is not uncommon for some to suspect that it is because the person has a physical illness or that it is due to consuming drugs. Research findings reveal that significantly more women report feeling profoundly anxious than men (Ahmed and Bader, 2004). However, one study also revealed that from a total of 372 adult undergraduate students, it was mainly men who smoked and were more alert in the evenings rather than the mornings and experienced poor sleep quality, who tended to suffer from minor anxiety problems (Schneider et al., 2011). Since most adults have experienced some anxiety, it is not surprising that it is one of the most investigated concepts within the field of psychology (Ahmed and Bader, 2004).

Globally, the constructs used for identifying anxiety are based on ideas from the western world (see also Chapter 2). 'It is our contention that there is a great need to develop and validate psychological tests in Arabic by Arab-speaking psychologists, with good translations into English to address the growing interest in cross-cultural comparisons, thereby bringing alternative cultural perspectives to scale construction' (Ahmed and Bader, 2004: 650) – and, indeed, in Asian and African languages too!

CONCERN

Although NICE (2012) provides therapists and other health professionals in Britain with guidelines for best practice within the NHS based on available evidence, this evidence may not be as good as it could be and tends to be incomplete (Rawlins and Culyer, 2004). The individuals whose job is to formulate the advice which NICE offers, judge which research is good-enough and which is not, thus making scientific value judgements; they must also make decisions about which interventions are good for society as a whole, thereby making social value judgements. However, according to authors Rawlins and Culyer, the main basis for NICE arriving at judgements is cost-effectiveness. The annual health budget is decided by government. Whether something should be purchased from the fund that the government makes available is a decision stipulated by NICE, but the government can state that a certain treatment cannot be afforded (even though NICE say that it is cost-effective) because too many want it. A further concern is that NICE apparently make a value judgement about the meaning of quality of life: the judgement being that an increase in life expectancy is paramount. Seemingly, what is not taken into account is the quality of life in those extra years. Rawlins and Culyer suggest therefore that NICE should offer priority to new treatments if nothing else has worked, irrespective of social stigma, for example, due to mental problems such as anxiety disorders.

Points to ponder

- The over-pathologising of feeling anxious in a social situation by perceiving this as a disorder of social phobia or a dysfunction can be harmful.
- Although onset of most anxiety disorders is in childhood, during the teen years or young adulthood, when identified in older adults, there is suspicion that medication or illness is to blame.
- Non-westerners are labelled as suffering from anxiety if their symptoms match western notions of anxiety.
- Is it valid or reliable for those who are from, for example, Asian or African countries, to be assessed as having an anxiety disorder if a western assessment tool is used?
- Why might more women than men report suffering from anxiety disorders?

Exercise

(Answers are embedded in this chapter.)

1 When is the onset of most anxiety disorders?
2 What is the difference between shyness, social phobia and social anxiety?
3 How can an anxiety disorder be identified?
4 Name signs of a panic attack and OCD, respectively.
5 Which type of intervention can help adult survivors of SA?

CHAPTER SUMMARY

There are many anxiety disorders and five of the most common are phobia, GAD, OCD, PTSD and panic.

GAD is characterised by pessimistic mood, perceiving problems unrealistically and worrying persistently.

A phobia can be about anything; one of the most common is agoraphobia.

OCD is about having obsessive thoughts and repeating actions compulsively.

Most people with panic attacks improve if they follow an appropriate intervention programme.

Not all who have been stressed or suffered a trauma experience PTSD.

The ATT programme is an extremely powerful intervention for adult survivors of SA and should only be used by a therapist who is very experienced in working with this client group.

LIST OF USEFUL RESOURCES

- Hoffman, S.G. and Smits, J.A. (2008) 'Cognitive behavioural therapy for adult anxiety disorders: a meta-analysis of randomized placebo-controlled trials', *Journal of Clinical Psychiatry*, 69, 4, pp. 621–32.
- Rudd, B. (2010) *Stress Control* (game) (Milton Keynes, Speechmark).
- Stein, M.B., Goin, M.K., Pollack, M.H., Roy-Byrne, P., Sareen, J. and Simon, N.M. (2009) *Practice Guideline for the Treatment of Patients with Panic Disorder* (Arlington Vancouver, American Psychiatric Association).
- Taylor, C.T., Pollack, M.H., LeBeau, R.T. and Simon, N.M. (2008) 'Anxiety disorders: panic, social anxiety and generalised anxiety', in Stern, T.A. Rosenbaum, J.F., Fava, M., Biederman, J. and Rauch, S.L. (eds) *Massachusetts General Hospital Comprehensive Clinical Psychiatry* (Philadelphia, Mosby Elsevier).

RELEVANT WEBSITES

www.anxietyuk.org.uk
www.hope4ocd.com/overview.php
www.nopanic.org.uk
www.stress.org/americas.htm

REFERENCES

Abramowitz, J.S., Moore, E.L., Braddock, A.E. and Harrington, D.L. (2009) 'Self-help cognitive-behavioral therapy with minimal therapist contact for social phobia: a controlled trial', *Journal of Behavior Therapy and Experimental Psychiatry*, 40, pp. 98–105.

Ahmed, M. A.-K. and Bader, M.A. (2004) 'Gender differences in anxiety among undergraduates from ten Arab countries', *Social Behavior and Personality*, 32, 7, pp. 649–56.

Alvarado, G.F., Storr, C.L. and Anthony, J.C. (2010) 'Suspected causal association between cocaine use and occurrence of panic', *Substance Use and Misuse*, 45, 7/8, pp. 1019–32.

Anestis, M. (2010) *Comparing Treatment for Generalized Anxiety Disorder (GAD)*, www.psyhotherapybrownbag.com/psychotherapy_baga/generalized_anxiety_disorder/, accessed 23 January 2012.

(Continued)

(Continued)

APA (2002) *DSM-IV-TR® Diagnostic and Statistical Manual of Mental Disorders* (Fourth Edition, revised) (Vancouver, American Psychiatric Association).

APA, (2006) *Facts about PTSD*, http://psychcentral.com/lib/2006/facts-about-ptsd/, accessed 23 January 2012.

Beck, A.T. and Emery, T. (1985) *Anxiety Disorders and Phobias* (New York, Basic Books).

Bernstein, B.E. (2011) *Social Phobia*, http://emedicine.medscape.com/article/290854-overview, accessed 23 January 2012.

Bling, B.E. (2005) *Obsessive Compulsive Disorder Research* (New York, Nova Science Publishers).

Bottoms, B.L., Nysse-Carris KL, Harris, T. and Tyda, K. (2003) 'Developmental and intellectual disabilities', *Law and Human Behavior*, 27, 2, pp. 205–27.

EMDR Network (2012) *A Brief Description of EMDR Therapy*, www.emdrnetwork.org/description.html, accessed 22 October 2012.

Fairfax, H. and Barfield, J. (2010) 'A group-based treatment for clients with Obsessive Compulsive Disorder (OCD) in a secondary care mental health setting: Integrating new development within cognitive behavioural interventions – an exploratory study', *Counselling and Psychotherapy Research*, 10, 3, pp. 214–21.

Fireman, B.M.S., Koran, L.M., Leventhal, J.L. and Jacobson, A. (2001) 'The prevalence of clinically recognized obsessive-compulsive disorder in a large health maintenance organization', *The American Journal of Psychiatry*, 158, 11, pp. 1904–10.

Friedman, H.S. and Silver, R.C. (eds) (2007) *Foundation of Health Psychology* (New York, Oxford University Press).

Gerhardt, S. (2004) *Why Love Matters: How Affection Shapes a Baby's Brain* (Hove, Brunner-Routledge).

Green, S.M., Antony, M.M., McCabe, R.E. and Watling, M.A. (2007) 'Frequency of fainting, vomiting and incontinence in panic disorder: a descriptive study', *Clinical Psychology and Psychotherapy,* 14, 3, pp. 189–92.

Griffin, J. and Tyrrel. I. (2004) *Human Givens, A New Approach to Emotional Health and Clear Thinking* (Chalvington, HG Publishing).

Gros, D.F., Antony, M.M., McCabe, R.E., Randi, E. and Lydiard, R.B. (2011) 'A preliminary investigation of the effects of cognitive behavioural therapy for panic disorder on gastrointestinal distress in patients with comorbid panic disorder and irritable bowel syndrome', *Depression and Anxiety*, 28, 11, pp. 1027–33.

Gundelfinger, E.D., Fischnecht, R., Choquet, D. and Heine, M. (2010) 'Converting juvenile into adult plasticity: a role for the brain's extracellular matrix', *European Journal of Neuroscience*, 31, 12, pp. 2156–65.

Hayano, F., Nakamura, M., Asami, T., Uehara, K., Yoshida, T., Roppongi, T., Otsuka, T., Inoue, T. and Hirayasu, Y. (2009) 'Smaller amygdala associated with anxiety in patients with panic disorder', *Psychiatry and Clinical Neurosciences*. 63, 3, pp. 266–76.

Hindman, J. and Peters, J. (2001) 'Polygraph testing leads to better understanding of adult and juvenile sex offenders', *Federal Probation*, 65, pp. 8–15.

Hinton, D.E., Hofmann, S.G., Pitman, R.K., Pollack, M.H. and Balowe, D.H. (2008) 'The panic attack-post traumatic stress disorder model: applicability to orthostatic panic among Cambodian refugees', *Cognitive Behaviour Therapy*, 37, 2, pp. 101–16.

Honeycutt, J.M., Choib, C.W. and DeBerry, J.R. (2009) 'Communication apprehension and imagined interactions', *Communication Research Reports*, 26, 3, pp. 228–36.

Keeley, M.L., Storch, E.A., Merlo, L.J., and Geffken, G.R. (2008) 'Clinical predictors of response to cognitive-behavioral therapy for obsessive-compulsive disorder', *Clinical Psychology Review*, 28, pp. 118–30.

Kingston, S. and Raghaven, C. (2009) 'The relationship of sexual abuse, early initiation of substance abuse, and adolescent trauma to PTSD', *Journal of Traumatic Stress*, 22, 1, pp. 65–8.

Kins, E., Soenens, B. and Beyers, W. (2011) '"Why do they have to grow up so fast?" Parental separation anxiety and emerging adults' pathology of separation-individuation', *Journal of Clinical Psychology*, 67, 7, pp. 647–64.

Kircanski, K., Craske, M.G., Epstein, A.M. and Wittchen, H.-U. (2009) 'Subtypes of panic attacks: a critical review of the empirical literature', *Depression and Anxiety*, 26, 10, pp. 878–87.

Leahy, R.L. and Holland, S.J. (2000) *Treatment Plans and Interventions for Depression and Anxiety Disorders* (New York, Guilford Press).

Life Extension (2012) *Obsessive-Compulsive Disorder*, www.lef.org/protocols/emotional_ health/obsessive_compulsive_disorder_01.htm, accessed 10 January 2012.

Maglione-Garves, C.A., Kravitz, L. and Schneider, S. (2005) 'Cortisol connection: tips on managing stress and weight', *ACSM's Health and Fitness Journal*, 9, 5, pp. 20–3.

Michelson, S.E., Lee, J.K., Orsillo, S.M. and Roemer, L. (2011) 'The role of values – consistent behavior in generalized anxiety disorder', *Depression and Anxiety*, 26, 5, pp. 358–66.

Mind (2012) *Panic Attacks*, www.mind.org.uk/help/diagnoses_and_conditions/panic_ attacks, accessed 10 January 2012.

Mineka, S. and Zinberg, R. (2006) 'A contemporary learning theory perspective on the etiology of anxiety disorders: it's not what you thought it was', *American Psychologist*, 61, 1, pp. 10–26.

Murtagh, M.P. (2010) 'The Appropriate Attribution Technique (ATT): a new treatment technique for adult survivors of sexual abuse', *North American Journal of Psychology*, 12, 2, pp. 313–34.

NICE (2012) *Clinical Guidelines Development Methods*, www.nice.org.uk, accessed 05 January 2012.

NSPCC (2011) *Statistics on Sexual Abuse*, www.nspcc.org.uk/Inform/resourcesforprofessionals/ sexual_abuse_statistics_wda8020 4.html, accessed 27 January 2012.

O'Kearney, R.T., Ansty, K., von Sanden, C. and Hunt, A. (2010) *Behavioural and Cognitive Therapy for Obsessive Compulsive Disorder in Children and Adolescents* (San Francisco, John Wiley and Sons).

Peterson, S. (2009) *Fears and Phobias – How Many People Suffer from Phobias?* www. completeMindCare.co.uk, accessed 23 January 2012.

Phobics-Awareness (2012) *What is Agoraphobia?*, www.phobics-awareness.org/agoraphobia. htm, accessed 09 January 2012.

(Continued)

(Continued)

Priyamvada, R., Kumari, S., Prakash, J. and Chaudhury, S. (2009) 'Cognitive behavioural therapy in the treatment of social phobia', *Industrial Psychiatry Journal*, 18, 1, pp. 60–3.

PsychCentral (2013) *What Causes General Anxiety Disorder?* http://psychcentral.com/lib/2006/what_causes_generalized_anxiety_disorder/, accessed 12 February 2013.

Rawlins, M.D. and Culyer, A.J. (2004) 'National Institute for Clinical Excellence and its value judgements', *British Medical Journal*, 3, 29, pp. 224–7.

Santana, L. and Fontenelle, L.F. (2011) 'A review of studies concerning treatment adherence of patients with anxiety disorders', *Patient Preference Adherence 2011*, 5, pp. 427–39.

Schaefer, C.E. (ed.) (1987) *Handbook of Parent Training: Parents as Co-Therapists for Children's Behaviour Problems* (New York, Oxford University Press).

Schneider, M.L.DeM., Vasconcellos, D.C., Dantas, G., Levandovski, R., Caumo, W., Allebrandt, K.V. Doring, M. and Hidalgo, M.P.L. (2011) 'Morningness-eveningness, use of stimulants and minor psychiatric disorders among undergraduate students', *International Journal of Psychology*, 46, 1, pp. 18–23.

Shackman, A. (2007) 'Physical abuse amplifies attention to threat and increases anxiety in children', *Emotion*, 7, pp. 838–52.

Sikazwe, H.C. (2009) *Behavioural Theories and the Impact on Human Interactions: A Compilation of Articles, Essays and Discourses Around the World* (Newcastle upon Tyne, APX Business Management Consultants Ltd).

Skapinakis, P., Lewis, G., Davies, S., Brugha, T., Prime, M. and Singleton, N. (2010) 'Panic disorder and subthreshold panic in the UK general population: epidemiology, co-morbidity and functional limitation', *European Psychiatry*, 6 Sept., 26, pp. 354–62.

Stein, M.B., Goin, M.K., Pollack, M.H., Roy-Byrne, P., Sareen, J. and Simon, M.N. (2009) *Practice Guidelines for the Treatment of Patients with Panic Disorder* (Vancouver, American Psychiatric Association).

van der Kolk, B.A. (2006) *Clinical Implications of Neuroscience Research in PTSD*, http://64.34.215.212/products/pdf_files/NYASF.pdf, accessed 17 January 2012.

Ulrich, R.S. (2000) 'Environmental research and critical care', in Hamilton, D.K. (ed.) *I C U 2010: Design for the Future* (Houston, Center for Innovation in Health Facilities), pp. 195–207.

University of Maryland Medical Center (2011) *Anxiety Disorders – Causes,* www.umm.edu/patiented/articles/what_causes_anxiety_disorders_000028_2.htm, accessed 12 February 2013.

Vassilopoulos, S. (2005) 'Social anxiety and the effects of engaging in mental imagery', *Cognitive Therapy and Research*, 29, 1, pp. 261–77.

Whiffen V.E., and Macintosh, H.B. (2005) 'Mediators of the link between childhood sexual abuse and emotional distress', *Trauma, Violence and Abuse*, 6, 1, pp. 24–39.

Wilson, D.R. (2010) 'Health consequences of childhood sexual abuse', *Perspectives in Psychiatric Care*, 46, 1, pp. 56–63.

Wilson, R. and Veale, D. (2005) *Overcoming Obsessive–Compulsive Disorder* (London, Constable and Robinson).

Wittchen, H., Gloster, A.T., Beesdo-Baum, K., Fava, G.A. and Craske, M.G. (2010) 'Agoraphobia: a review of the diagnostic classificatory position and criteria', *Depression and Anxiety*, 27, 2, pp. 113–33.

5

Cognitive Disorders

LEARNING OBJECTIVES FOR THIS CHAPTER

- Understand what is meant by cognitive disorders
- Recognise signs of Alzheimer's, vascular dementia and amnesia
- Know what a neurodevelopmental disorder is

In this chapter I spotlight direct cognitive disorders such as amnesia and dementia (rather than anxiety, mood and psychotic disorders, which are discussed elsewhere). Therapists are not trained to deal with these direct cognitive problems, which is reflected in the chapter's shortness. Cognitive disorders affect cognition and are mainly associated with forgetfulness, which in turn is associated with old age. In today's population, the number of aging individuals is growing. Considering cognitive disorders is important because clients suffering from such a disorder may seek a therapist for a problem they believe is unrelated to it. Indeed, many individuals suffer from cognitive disorders or are carers for those who suffer from dementia, therefore it is likely that most therapists in their career will have contact with clients who have signs of one of the dementias; it may therefore be wise to know what the symptoms are and perhaps one of the tests that can be used, such as the Mini Mental State (Alzheimer's Society, 2012). Unfortunately, there is stigma attached to perceived mental disorder and old age (at least in the UK). Perhaps due to this, there is not much knowledge and understanding of all the dementias.

What is known is that overall, if suffering from dementia, the brain fails to function mainly in areas relating to emotion, personality and cognition (Houston, Joiner and Trounce, 1982). Those with dementia are usually emotionally labile. Their personality changes with increasing loss of behavioural control. Cognitively, there is inability to remember and retain information recently acquired, worsening over time. There are over a hundred dementias. This chapter focuses on a few major ones.

DELIRIUM, AMNESIA, ALZHEIMER'S AND VASCULAR DEMENTIA

These are the main types of cognitive disorders that tend to be written about. Here are their meanings: 'Delirium' means going off-track. Therapists do not see clients who are delirious therefore I do not deliberate further about this. 'Amnesia' means memory loss. It can be short or long-term, permanent or temporary. Alzheimer's disease involves nerve degeneration and is a type of dementia ('dementia' is a term describing symptoms); its cause/aetiology is unknown. Another type of dementia is vascular dementia; 'vascular' means that there is a reduction of blood-flow to the brain.

Signs

Although not everyone who forgets suffers from a cognitive disorder, forgetfulness is associated with neurological decay due to deterioration of connectivity between brain cells. There is a belief that this decay is a normal part of aging. However, work at Massachusetts Institute of Technology (MIT) questions this belief because investigations reveal that at any age, having low magnesium accelerates brain-cell aging and memory loss, while magnesium-L-threonate (MgT) supplementation enhances memory and cognition (Alessio, M. 2012; Slutsky, Abumaria and Wu, 2010). I explain this further below. Other factors can contribute to dementia, including genetic predisposition to its development, especially Alzheimer's.

Major problems encountered by individuals suffering from dementia are increasing short-term memory loss and getting lost. For instance, they can get lost while trying to find their local shop – due to their diminishing memory they can forget where the shop is, or where they live and why they went out of their house in the first place. In the majority of dementias, short-term memory and the ability to learn new skills are lost, but long-term memory is the last to be lost. For example, an elderly person might lose the ability to recognise his or her grandchildren or forget their names in the beginning, but remember her or his children's and spouse's names.

One critical function of memory is to fill in missing information appropriately. For instance, when driving a car in snow, although some landmarks are hidden by it, others are still seen. With these partial cues, most people fill in the missing ones and are able to find their destination. However, if suffering from neurological decay, these partial cues may not be enough, which is why it is possible to get lost in the dark. Finding a familiar place on a routine trip does not cause a problem during daylight hours.

Recent research significantly links hearing loss in older adults with developing dementia over time (Frank et. al., 2011). Reasons for this have yet to be discovered; perhaps because not many have looked at how hearing loss affects brain function. Maybe the isolation which deafness brings with it, due to not being able to hear the conversation of others and therefore not being able to join in, might have something to do with the degeneration seen in dementia.

Intervention

A simple remedy regarding hearing loss can be to obtain a hearing aid. Such a step might delay or prevent dementia. However, it is important to bear in mind that the purported possible outcome of taking this step is speculative because of the lack of cross-talk between geriatricians and otologists. Yet, with a hearing aid, better hearing would result and the hearing-challenged individuals may not be as isolated once they can hear what others say; they can choose to attend therapy without fearing that they will not hear what the therapist says.

Amnesia

Amnesia is usually a temporary problem, in which only part of a person's experience is lost. There are several causes. Common ones are:

- brain damage because of poisoning (often due to alcohol intake)
- an acute event such as an accident (causing brain injury or concussion)

- stress and anxiety
- dementia.

What these causes have in common is that there is either a psychological factor present or the nerve tissue to the brain suffers physical damage.

Many symptoms are present with amnesia, for example: an altered state of awareness or consciousness, an impairment of judgement or problem solving, behaviour or emotions that are not normal for the person and problems with muscles or strength that were not there previously. If amnesia is due to concussion after an accident, episodes before the accident often cannot be remembered. Events of the previous days, weeks or months can be forgotten yet the person suffering from amnesia is still able to carry on with life (Mumenthaler,1983). Often, an episode of bad memory is caused by a disturbance of the blood supply to the brain.

Amnesia is not normally a problem that therapists deal with unless it is to support managing associated stress and anxiety (see also Chapter 4). If a therapist is faced with a client who displays symptoms of amnesia, it is imperative to obtain the services of a medical practitioner. Medical tests and investigations may need to be performed, for example, a brain scan, to check for any damage such as haemorrhage. Many who suffer from amnesia improve as time goes by or as a result of effective treatment. Others live their day-to-day lives with support from specialist help.

Alzheimer's

This is the most common dementia. Increasingly, aged individuals suffer from Alzheimer's (Alzheimer's Association, 2008). 'The horrific progression of Alzheimer's disease … afflicts between 24–30 million people worldwide' (Alessio, 2012: 3).

Unfortunately, no cure is currently available but new research offers hope (MIT, 2010), as correctable factors connected to the early onset of Alzheimer's have been identified as well as a novel nutritional intervention that may target them in an effective way. Researchers Slutsky and team (2010) have discovered a special, extremely absorbable, type of magnesium; MgT (mentioned earlier). They state that this rebuilds degenerated neuronal connections seen in forms of memory loss such as Alzheimer's, restoring ruptured synapses. Their experimental findings reveal 18 per cent improvement in short-term memory and 100 per cent in long-term (Slutsky, Abumaria and Wu, 2010).

Vascular dementia

Not as common as Alzheimer's, though not rare, is vascular dementia. Stroke is one type of vascular dementia. If there is a vascular dementia, the sufferer is arteriosclerotic. This means that the arteries are clogged up, therefore there is lack of oxygen to brain tissue, causing it to die. Although senior citizens see therapists for all sorts of issues; for example, loss and bereavement, if there is a vascular dementia problem, medical intervention is required. Sadly, not much medical intervention can be offered in the chronic, well-established stage, but there are medications that can reduce the risk factors (hypertension, diabetes, hypercholesterolaemia) thereby slowing down the disease's progression.

Amnesia, Alzheimer's and vascular dementias in practice

It is unusual to see clients in a therapist's consulting room who suffer from amnesia, Alzheimer's or any of the vascular dementias. They are usually treated medically. But, a therapist may see a client who has a relative or family member suffering from a dementia syndrome.

NEURODEVELOPMENTAL AGE-RELATED AND ACQUIRED INJURY COGNITIVE DISORDERS

If there is an abnormality or loss in the development and growth of the central nervous system or brain, then a neurodevelopmental disorder is likely to be present. When this happens during babyhood or childhood, consequences can include autism spectrum disorders (such as Asperger's syndrome), Down's and fragile-X syndromes, communication disorders and traumatic brain injury. A leading cause of neurodevelopmental disorders (as well as birth defects and mental retardation) is prenatal exposure to alcohol (Ozonoff and Jensen, 1999). For more on pre-adult problems, see Chapter 3.

An acquired brain injury is an injury to the brain acquired after birth. For support to sufferers of either acquired brain injury or neurodevelopmental age-related cognitive disorders, services should be sought from medical doctors, not therapists. However, for psychological problems related to, for example, head injuries, it is not unusual to see a therapist who works within a team of health professionals for support (which is usual within Community Adult Mental Health Services in England).

COGNITIVE DISORDER CASE VIGNETTE

Unemployed fifty-nine-year-old Ron was worried about his forgetfulness. Both his parents suffered from Alzheimer's before they died. He has three grown-up children and describes himself as happily married. His family, concerned about his increasing memory loss, urged him to seek help. Ron self-referred to a therapist who noticed that he seemed a little deaf. The therapist listened to his concerns and taught him stress-reducing techniques for managing his tendency to worry. Being up-to-date with her continuing professional development (CPD), the therapist had read about the link between hearing loss and dementia. Consequently, she referred him to a medic, which led to Ron taking tests related to dementia. The test results were positive. Ron's wife, Daisy, with his blessing, also saw the therapist due to her concern for him. The therapist empowered Daisy, who was then more able to support her husband with the dementia. Daisy was helped by the therapist to manage her worries aptly. The therapist also spotlighted the importance of offering kind-based care to Ron. Daisy managed to do this, with love for Ron, which enabled him to have more periods of lucidity than expected. Particularly empowering for Daisy was being given information by the therapist about errorless learning for Ron, and also about not making demands on him. Indeed, Daisy noticed that when demands were made on him, he went from lucidity to non-lucidity and when demands were not made of him (but he was listened to with warm, accepting positive regard) he went from non-lucidity to lucidity, particularly when walking outdoors while they conversed. Often, they prayed together. Daisy continues to see the therapist, which in turn enables her apt communication with Ron, such as walking with physical contact while conversing (their favourite physical contact on walks was holding hands, although sometimes they chose to be arm-in-arm).

The importance of religiosity, physical contact, errorless learning and loving care for individuals who suffer from dementia is clearly explained in de Vries' latest scholarly publication (2012).

AGE, GENDER AND CULTURE

Worldwide there are approximately thirty million individuals reported as suffering from dementia. In Europe, 98 per cent of them are over sixty-four years. Within this figure, there are a few more women than men with the problem. Az (2008) states that there is less dementia in the developing countries when compared with the developed, but why this difference exists is unknown. However, Az's statement has many confounders. First, the life expectancy in most developing countries is lower than developed countries; hence the number of individuals affected by dementia is fewer. Second, healthcare services can be variable and lacking in developing countries, so people with dementia may not be identified and therefore not treated. Third, there is lack of reliable and consistent data-collecting in these developing countries, making it difficult to keep track of developments.

CONCERN

I am concerned that there is a paucity of interactions between many primary health care practitioners, researchers and therapists. If more primary health care practitioners knew and understood cutting-edge research results, they could perhaps more effectively help an increasing number of patients. Similarly, if more therapists knew and understood up-to-date investigative findings, they could perhaps make more effective client referrals. To help, researchers could make their findings more widely known (see also Chapter 2). Unfortunately, most literature on psychopathology overlooks cognitive disorders. It is of vital importance to consider these disorders in our current society with its expanding aging population and consequent concerns about increases in cognitive problems.

Points to ponder

- Ageing does not equate with loss of mental agility.
- We have something to learn from the people of Abkhasia because they live long lives in good mental and physical health; indeed, they are not the only culture who represent the possibility of doing so (Robbins, 2006).
- How is it possible to live to a ripe old age with robustly good mental health?
- Perhaps certain cognitive disorders have something to do with the stigma that much of the western world attach to aging; whereas in some places such as Abkhasia, old age is something to look forward to (Robbins, 2006).
- A therapist may think that a client is forgetful due to bereavement, but the forgetfulness may be due to mild cognitive impairment.
- For Abkhasians 'The psychological climate of the old is so positive that rest homes which are available through government avenues are rarely utilized, as even in the smallest families there are many relatives who covet the honor of housing an elder' (Robbins, 2006: 16, ll.509).

Exercise

(Answers are embedded in this chapter.)

1   Name a few amnesia symptoms.
2   Is there a cure for Alzheimer's?
3   What does 'vascular dementia' mean?
4   Why is it important for therapists to know about cognitive disorders?

CHAPTER SUMMARY

Older clients who have mental health issues with concomitant undiagnosed early pathological deterioration may see a therapist, therefore it is important for the therapist to spot some of the signs so that a medical doctor can be alerted.

Stroke may lead to a vascular dementia.

Forgetfulness is a main feature of cognitive disorders such as Alzheimer's.

Problems related to cognition are generally linked to neurodegeneration.

LIST OF USEFUL RESOURCES

- Hughes, J.C. (2011) *Alzheimer's and other Dementias (The Facts)* (Oxford, Oxford University Press).
- James, I.A. (2011) *Understanding Behaviour in Dementia that Challenges: A Guide to Assessment and Treatment* (Bradford, Bradford Dementia Group Good Practice Guides).
- Marcantonio, E.R. (2008) 'Clinical management and prevention of delirium', *Psychiatry*, 7, 1, pp. 42–8.
- Rudd, B. (2010) *Awareness* (game) (Milton Keynes, Speechmark).

RELEVANT WEBSITES

- www.alzheimers.org.uk/site/scripts/documents_info.php?documentID=100
- www.esa.un.org/wpp/Sorting-Tables/tab-sorting_aging.htm
- www.medscape.com/viewarticle/706300_10
- www.nhs.uk/pathways/dementia

REFERENCES

Alessio, M. (2012) 'Novel magnesium compound reverses neurodegeneration', *Life Extension*, 18, 2, pp. 2–97.

Alzheimer's Association (2008) 'Alzheimer's disease facts and figures', *Alzheimer's and Dementia*, 4, 2, pp. 110–13.

Alzheimer's Society (2012) *The Mini Mental State Examination*, www.alzheimers.org.uk/site/scripts/documents_info.php?documentID=121, accessed 22 October 2012.

Az (2008) *Alzheimer's Disease International*, https://docs.google.com/viewer?a=v&q=cache:eFokzRKZBlYJ:www.alz.co.uk/adi/pdf/prevalence.pdf+dementia+age+gender+culture&hl=en&gl=uk&pid=bl&srcid=ADGEESgnKdlgRDqndSyCP9bcRthpXa754QQ42HPya8otrOMa0-nwWS5IQFbVbRnT1V5H0GYfatXownq9F-Ys5qXps05XND60CdAIBBzsUpBibNLPtr-QQzEVNrUMyksj7wFayLe1E9aN&sig=AHIEtbTqsIZ-Wp987LI89YJGpb-eMkTd3w, accessed 6 February 2012.

de Vries, K. (2012) 'Becoming a person in society: dementia', in Jarvis, P. and Watts, M. (eds) *The Routledge International Handbook of Learning* (Abingdon, Routledge), pp. 319–29.

Frank, R., Lin, E., Metter, J., O'Brien, R.J. and Resnick, S. (2011) 'Hearing loss and incident dementia', *Archives of Neurology*, 26, 2, pp. 214–20.

Houston, J.C., Joiner, C.L. and Trounce, J.R. (1982) *A Short Text Book of Medicine* (London, Hodder and Stoughton).

Mumenthaler, M. (1983) *Neurology* (New York, Thierne-Stratton).

MIT (2010) *Magnesium Supplement Helps Boost Brain Power*, www.mit.edu/press/2010/magnesium-supplement.html, accessed 2 February 2012.

Ozonoff, S. and Jensen, J. (1999) 'Brief report: specific executive function profiles in three neurodevelopmental disorders', *Journal of Autism and Neurodevelopmental Disorders,* 29, 2, pp. 171–7.

Robbins, J. (2006) *Healthy at 100* (New York, Random House).

Slutsky, I., Abumaria, N. and Wu, L.J. (2010) 'Enhancement of learning and memory by elevating brain magnesium', *Neuron*, 65, 2, pp. 165–77.

6

Mood Problems, Depression, Self-harm and Suicide

LEARNING OBJECTIVES FOR THIS CHAPTER

- Recognise mood disorders
- Understand self-harm
- Know about suicide
- Be aware of research and theory regarding self-harm and suicide
- Discuss theoretical and empirical perspectives on depression
- Have an insight into seasonal affective disorder
- Differentiate between type 1 bi-polar disorder and type 2

There are four types of mood disorders. These are

1 Depression
2 Cyclothymia
3 Seasonal affective disorder
4 Mania and hypomania.

Before deliberating on them (which can be cross-referenced with Chapter 3), I discuss suicide and self-harming behaviour.

SELF-HARM AND SUICIDE

Suicide is about killing one's self. It is the most extreme form of self-harm. The term 'self-harm', however, is not as easy to define as it might appear to be at first glance. This is because it covers a plethora of behaviours from, for example, pierced ears to self-poisoning and wrist-cutting. Self-harm can be divided into two categories: non-suicidal self-harm and self-harm with suicidal intent (Nock, 2009). Often, it is associated with borderline personality disorder (cross-reference with Chapter 11).

Self-harm theory and research

Deliberate self-harm (DSH) is about hurting oneself without suicide. Currently, the term 'DSH' is used throughout the mental health field; but this may change because as I write (23 February 2012), the fifth edition of DSM is being planned for publication in 2013, so the categorisation of self-harm may be different from that presented in the fourth version.

Despite the term 'DSH' being used extensively in literature (for example, Hawton and Harris, 2008; Haw and Hawton, 2011) the Royal College of Psychiatrists dislike its use (2010). They argue that it is misleading to use 'DSH' because some who abuse drugs (including nicotine cigarettes and alcohol) may not be self-harming deliberately, but might, for instance, be doing so from a sense of wanting to fit in with peers (see also Chapter 8). I therefore use the term 'self-harm', instead. Overall however, experts have yet to agree on its definition.

Much research links self-harm with eventual suicide (for example, Barr, Leitner and Thomas, 2004; Cooper et al., 2005). What can be deciphered from such a pool of research? These investigations were conducted within medical institutions, and although I value them, they do not offer an overview of purported links between self-harm and suicide, as the remainder of the population who self-harm are not taken into account. Without further research to back up a connection between self-harm and suicide within the population as a whole, a valid and reliable correlation between self-harm and suicide is impossible.

Looking deeper at this issue, certain statistics show that approximately a third of the UK individuals who killed themselves previously self-harmed (Royal College of Psychiatrists, 2012). Within the whole population though, the number of people that self-harm and eventually kill themselves does not appear as a statistically significant figure (Plante, 2007; Kern, 2010). With this in mind, perhaps most who self-harm do not want to kill themselves.

Although a sea of research focuses on connecting self-harm with suicide (for example, Owens and Horrocks, 2002; Netdoctor, 2012) a stream of other research is emerging which does not make a connection (such as Castille et al., 2007). While this contradiction exists, separating misconception from fact is difficult.

Why do individuals self-harm?

There appears to be a popular belief that those who self-harm are manipulative attention-seekers. They do not seem to bring out a sense of compassion from others. Yet many who self-harm do so secretly (for instance, self-cut on areas of the body where the injuries are hidden, such as the top of the arms).

Most people who self-harm do so to cope (Klonsky, 2007). Numerous works theorise that self-harming acts as a type of coping which has meaning to the person who self-harms, such as relief from what seems unbearable; for example, flashbacks, deeply painful emotions and dreadful thoughts (see Klonsky, 2007 and Gratz, 2007). Self-harming, therefore, is probably not attempting suicide, but rather a form of dealing with the unbearable. When self-harming brings relief, the behaviour is likely to be repeated.

Suicide theory and research

Unfortunately, there are basic methodological flaws in much research, but a good-enough investigation was conducted by researchers Ceccherini-Nellie and Priebe (2011) who found that a correlation exists between suicide rates and economic factors. Whether in the USA, Italy, France or the UK, rates of suicide rise when unemployment increases with consequent financial problems. Another theory is that those who want to kill themselves are less sensitive to pain. This is supported by researchers Smith et al. (2010). Their work shows that those who self-harm, attempt suicide and wish to die are more fearless and less sensitive to pain than those who do not.

Self-harm and suicide signs and intervention

The greatest risk factor for predicting suicide is deliberate self-harm. Related to this, the National Institute for Health and Clinical Excellence (NICE, 2012a) recommend interventions that include problem-solving, cognitive behaviour therapy or psychodynamic elements and suggest offering three to twelve sessions of a psychological intervention programme. In practice, a longer and more integrated case formulation is sometimes required (see the case vignette below). Identifying someone who self-harms can be difficult, so look out for apparently inexplicable signs: symptoms can include unexplained injuries, for instance, cuts, bruises or cigarette burns as well as change in weight or drug misuse. Since self-harming is probably a type of coping, a way of intervening is to introduce healthier coping strategies. When such an intervention is taken on board, self-harming can reduce.

Prevalence of self-harm and suicide

When compared with the general population, in the USA, research shows that it is those aged over sixty years who have the highest rate of suicide (Marty, Segal and Coolidge, 2010). Sadly, the research focusing on this age group relating to suicide prevention is meagre (Marty, Segal and Coolidge, 2010). Although self-harming behaviour varies between countries, alarmingly, a recent investigation conducted by Kokkevi et al. (2012) shows that suicide is a leading cause of death among teenagers throughout Europe. Within the UK however, Department of Health (2012) statistics show that suicide is most likely in men aged 35–49. Much research supports the popular perspective that mainly women self-harm (for example, Heath et al., 2008). Yet, this is likely to be because the majority of participants involved in such investigations are female, since findings from research using equal numbers of men and women do not show a significant difference between the number of males and females who self-harm (see Klonsky, Oltmans and Turkheimer, 2003).

Outcome of self-harm and suicide

Of course, death is the outcome of suicide. What about the outcome of those who self-harm with suicidal ideation? It is hopeful (Egan, Koff and Moreno, 2013). Very recent research reveals that training in 'experiential exercises emphasising awareness and empathic responding and practice of those skills' contributes towards stopping suicide and reducing self-harm (Pasco et al., 2012: 134). When there are reasons for living, problem-solving skills and good-enough ways of coping emotionally, then resilience to suicide is strong. When these ways of dealing with life are weak, resilience to suicide is also weak (Marty, Segal and Coolidge, 2010).

Self-harm and suicide in practice

During a therapist's career, sadly, it is not unusual for at least one client to kill themselves. Unsurprisingly, self-harm is very challenging for therapists to work with: fear of eventual suicide might be the reason, or it may be because of the stigma attached to self-harming behaviour. Therefore, many therapists refuse to accept clients who harm themselves. If the therapists who do see those who self-harm initially attempt to stop such behaviour, then without the relief that self-harming brings suicide may be a consequence. Imperative for therapists, therefore, is to ensure that clients who self-harm have healthier coping mechanisms in place, such as the skills of expressing their thoughts and emotions healthily (see Levenkron, 1998). Additionally, if therapists bear in mind the findings of researchers Marty, Segal and Coolidge (2010), revealing that adequate emotional literacy, a reason for being alive and problem-solving skills buffer against suicide, then helping to build these coping strategies in their clients, is apt. Tremendous feelings of guilt and shame, confusion and worry may be experienced by the person who self-harms, and therefore he or she needs to be approached very tenderly, with care and compassion. If those who self-harm do not wish to discuss their behaviour, they may like to ring a helpline or see their GP.

SELF-HARM AND SUICIDAL IDEATION CASE VIGNETTE

Alfredo was nineteen years old, with parents who were bothered about his negative mood and self-harming behaviour (bouts of heavy alcohol consumption). He worked in the family business, helping to run a tea-room. This young man was easily angered and became violent, shouting at customers he did not like and throwing tea cups against a wall. The tea-room business deteriorated and his family suffered. Alfredo then ignored his family, spending much time with his sixteen-year-old girlfriend. She was strongly disapproved of by Alfredo's family members, which isolated him from them even more. Eventually, his girlfriend left him. He felt devastated and said that he wanted to die. His family were extremely concerned and Alfredo agreed to see a therapist.

The therapist ascertained that he needed to be heard, as well as his brother, sister, mother and father. Alfredo declared that he disliked indoor work, disclosed discovering that he was adopted and felt betrayed that his parents never told him. He also revealed his suicidal ideation. This alerted the therapist and with Alfredo's permission he was admitted into hospital, where he continued with therapy. In hospital, Alfredo was passive in groups but spent time in one-to-one therapy blaming his family for all the negative aspects in his life, complaining bitterly without showing awareness of his part within the family situation.

The therapist liaised with a psychiatrist who prescribed anti-depressants. Alfredo complied with the medication but continued denying his role within the family problem. However, he stopped self-poisoning (binge-drinking). The therapist also saw the rest of the family (without Alfredo) who were highly motivated to heal the family rift. In sessions with Alfredo's parents and siblings, each was facilitated in becoming aware of his situation and given work to do between sessions, such as not calling Alfredo negative names and endeavouring to understand his feelings. With better family communications, Alfredo was less aggressive and more open to having dialogue with his family.

(Continued)

(Continued)

As usual, the therapist was having regular supervision. She and her supervisor agreed that Alfredo might be ready to face his family during dialogue-intervention sessions with the therapist, where every family member in turn could voice frustrations, disappointments and hopes. These intervention sessions took place. Concerns and hopes were heard (including the adoption issue). Gradually, during one-to-one therapy, Alfredo's thought processes changed. Also, he was observed as being increasingly involved in the community, such as group therapy – a welcome change from his previous isolated life. He became able to perceive some of his weaknesses and take responsibility for his behaviour. Initially, Alfredo's psychiatrist prescribed a mood-stabilising drug. Six months later, he gradually reduced it to a significantly lower dose (by then, Alfredo was no longer an in-patient). Its reduction continued and after a further twelve months the psychiatrist prescribed a very small amount.

Alfredo no longer wishes to die. He has left the family home and enjoys a new job as a gardener at an estate where he also has a residence as part-payment for work. He continues with 'follow-up' therapy sessions and voluntarily attends an art therapy group each week as well as mindfulness sessions.

There was a sea-change in Alfredo after the whole-family dialogue interventions. Since then, overall, he is blossoming: able to share his thoughts and emotions in a more insightful, open way and to behave appropriately. Specifically, what helped him was an integrative approach manifesting as a balance of interventions incorporating ongoing consultations with a psychiatrist, regular therapy, respite from his lifestyle during the hospital stay where he was enabled to stop his unhealthy intake of alcohol, family sessions and, particularly, family-dialogue interventions, as well as the regular structure of art therapy, mindfulness meetings and outdoor work with plants.

DEPRESSION

Impacting on mind and body, depression is more than feeling sad and may be linked to suicide.

Depression theory and research

There are four main theories on depression:

1 Genetic
2 Psychological
3 Environmental
4 Biological.

According to the genetic theory, depression is passed on genetically; there may, therefore, be a family history of the illness. If we follow this theory, we are at the mercy of our genes. A counter-argument to the gene theory is that being depressed can be learnt, particularly if there is a role model for depression in the family.

The psychological theory is concerned with being emotionally vulnerable enough to become depressed. For example, a lack of problem-solving skills may result in a person having low emotional literacy or lacking self-esteem. By following this theory, we can use psychological techniques to move in a therapeutic direction. A counter-argument to this is that many who do not seem to be emotionally literate enough are not depressed.

Environmental theory has to do with life events. For example, if we live our lives in a country where there is not enough light, we may experience depression (see SAD, further down), or other stressors may trigger the illness, such as a major loss. If we go with this theory, by changing lifestyle we can do something about depression. A counter-argument to this is that most who live in countries that go through a gloomy winter, or have experienced a major loss, do not suffer from depression.

Biological theory is concerned with physiological change, such as infection or childbirth. With physiological change, there is a change in, for example, the balance of hormones. If we believe this theory, then we are likely to believe that medication can lift depression. A counter-argument to the biological theory is that many suffer from depression who have not experienced such physiological change.

There are research findings that support all the above theories. Research results indicating that depression is a disorder of the brain supports the genetic and biological theories (for example, Hunter and NIMH, 2012). Other research, showing that psychological factors such as trauma can trigger depression, offers support to the psychological and environmental theories (for example, Porcelli and Sonino, 2007).

Clearly, exact reasons for depression are inconclusive and may be multifactorial. Irrespective of which research findings are favoured to back up a theoretical model which might be used to support a depressed client, there is agreement regarding how to identify a person who can be classified as suffering from depression.

Depression signs

These include being lethargic, feeling dejected, inadequate and without self-esteem. Other symptoms encompass fatigue, very low mood, lack of enjoyment in previously enjoyed activities, inability to concentrate, no sex drive, difficulty in making decisions, feeling guilty, restless, experiencing sleep problems and thinking of suicide. Such a depressive state paints a negative worldview, opening the gates to believing that the future is hopeless.

Depression prevalence

According to the World Health Organization (WHO, 2012), approximately two-thirds of the adult population experience depression severe enough to affect their daily lives. WHO also states that one in four women and one in ten men are so depressed that they need professional intervention. Sadly, in the UK, depression is the most commonly reported mental health problem and the most common reason for consulting a mental health practitioner (WHO, 2012). Also in the UK, a fifth of primary care patients who have been diagnosed with unipolar depression may have an undiagnosed bi-polar disorder, and almost all who suffer from mania will experience a depressive state (Rull, 2012).

Depression intervention

Various interventions that are available, such as medication and therapy, seem to help most individuals who suffer from depression. NICE guidelines (2012b), suggest between six and nine sessions of CBT for mild to moderate depression, with medication if more severe (2012b).

Depression expected outcome

Treatment outcome for depression, when appropriate intervention is used, shows significant improvement (see Ruskin et al., 2004).

Depression in practice

When seeing a client, watch out for risk factors relating to depression, such as interpersonal loss (whether perceived or factual), co-morbidity and drug use (Martin-Merino et al., 2012). Other risk factors are sociocultural, for instance, work stress, sexual abuse, family responsibilities such as child-care and financial problems. Risk factors can also be hormonal, such as puberty, child-birth, menstruation, pregnancy or menopause. Others are a family history of depression, isolation, health problems, being divorced or widowed, chronic pain, sleep difficulties, isolation or a neurological problem such as stroke (Simon, 2012). Many therapists use the Beck Depression Inventory as standard practice when first seeing a client, even if depression is not suspected (to rule it out) because it is so quick and easy to utilise (Beck, Steer and Brown, 1996). (See also Chapter 2.)

DEPRESSION CASE VIGNETTE

Paul has worked as an accountant for fifteen years. Despite being intelligent, he feels low self-worth and experiences ongoing tiredness due to sleep problems he has suffered for what he describes as, 'a very long time'. He finds concentrating difficult and believes that he could have done better with his career if he had not procrastinated so much about important decisions.

Eventually, Paul plucked-up enough courage and confided to a friend at work who had heard about CBT and encouraged him to see a therapist. He found one who specialised in CBT and had nine weekly sessions. Paul has much more energy now, which he attributes to running again (something he used to enjoy and has come back to, as suggested by his therapist). His increased use of energy also helps him sleep better. During Paul's final therapy session, the therapist suggested a self-help book. He can use it if he feels he needs a boost. To his surprise, he now experiences a certain amount of joy in life.

SEASONAL AFFECTIVE DISORDER

SAD is sometimes known as the 'winter blues' because, apart from wanting to eat and sleep more, it is like depression that only emerges in winter when there is a lack of sunshine.

SAD theory and research

The main theory is that SAD is caused by inadequate light (Dalgleish, Rosen and Marks, 1996). Certain research shows that with lack of light, the amount of serotonin in the brain decreases (for example, Lambert and Reid, 2002), which backs up this prevailing theory. With this in mind, light therapy, as suggested decades ago, makes sense (Jacobsen, Wehr and Sack, 1986).

SAD signs

Not enough sunlight can affect appetite (over-eating), sex drive (absent), mood (depressed) and energy level (low). If these signs are seasonal, they are symptoms of SAD. If suffering, the winter period results in feeling gloomy, stressed, unhappy, tired and lethargic. Other signs include gaining weight, sleeping more and not wanting to be active. With low mood there can be a loss of interest in what was previously found interesting (NHS, 2012).

SAD prevalence

About seven out of every hundred people and approximately twice as many women as men are purported as suffering from SAD in the UK (NHS, 2012).

SAD intervention

Several interventions exist for SAD. They include light therapy, CBT, and medication for depression (NHS, 2012). NICE do not currently offer clinical guidelines for SAD, but are in the process of developing them (2012c).

SAD expected outcome

Theoretical and empirical models of mental health treatment for SAD are incomplete. Treatment outcome is therefore anecdotal: apparently, sufferers experience improvement if on a winter sunshine holiday! As discussed, it is thought that signs of SAD appear in the winter due to lack of sunshine; not getting enough sun can make us feel sleepier and eat more whereas sunshine makes us feel better, alleviating the symptoms of SAD (NHS, 2013).

SAD in practice

One way of dealing with clients in order to de-escalate their SAD, which I have found useful in practice, is to have different coloured spotlights on when they are in my consulting room. Additionally, I may walk outdoors with clients (on the sunny side of the road, if possible), which is beneficial for them.

> ## SAD CASE VIGNETTE
>
> Savas suffered his first period of SAD in his early twenties when he moved from Cyprus to UK for the purpose of studying law at university. It happened when he experienced his first winter in England. He seemed to perk up when it snowed and there was a crispy sunny winter period, but as soon as the snow melted and skies were grey again, his SAD was triggered. He became lethargic, stopped seeing friends, stopped telephoning home. He seemed to become 'invisible' apart from using his computer to do his homework and send it electronically to his tutor. Savas would just sleep, morning, afternoon and night, waking up to eat substantially. He found himself becoming excited about visiting his homeland in the summer, where he could feel and see the sunlight. This became an annual pattern. Savas seemed to only want to eat and 'hibernate' in the winter yet felt energised and alive during the sunny summer time. His university tutor informed Savas that his work was deteriorating and if he felt sad, he should see a therapist. The therapist kept up to date with her CPD so she was knowledgeable about the link between needing bright light in order to rapidly suppress levels of melatonin (which are sleep-inducing). During therapy, Savas felt better; this was because he sat where natural light streamed into the room. The wallpaper was also light-coloured and there was bright artificial light in the therapy room. This was explained to him, as was the option of obtaining a light-therapy box. When he went to his accommodation, he moved his furniture so that natural light streamed into his room. He decorated the dark walls with a light colour and replaced low voltage lights with bright, full spectrum bulbs. Therapy helped him realise that to feel alive, England, with its mainly grey sky, was not the place he would spend his life living in. He no longer needs therapy, finishes his law degree soon and will be returning to his homeland.

BI-POLAR DISORDER

Bi-polar disorder is characterised by extreme ups and downs. In the worst instances, sufferers may even kill themselves. But, for the most part, the problem is manageable.

Individuals suffering from what the DSM–IV–TR (APA, 2002) describes as type 1 bi-polar, experience mania and may have psychotic episodes (2002). It is the severest form of manic depression. Type 2 bi-polar embraces cyclothymia and hypomania. It is sometimes called type 2 affective disorder.

MANIA AND HYPOMANIA

Mania is an abnormally high mood, although individuals experiencing elevated mood along the mania continuum can also experience periods of normality and depressive states.

Hypomania is a milder form of expressed mania. Hypermania relates to an inner felt excessive enthusiasm without outward manifestation (which would mean it was either hypomania or mania, depending on the degree of expression). It is generally overlooked because it is not spotted.

Mania signs

If people experience being manic (type 1 bi-polar), they are a danger to themselves or others, their relationships are jeopardised as well as their employment, and a psychotic episode can result in being admitted to hospital. Sometimes, mania is difficult to differentiate from schizophrenia. Onset of mania can be sudden and last for weeks – one week is the minimum it can last. If manic, individuals experience increased self-worth, expanding sociability, burgeoning drive and heightened alertness. Feeling euphoric is experienced with unrealistic optimism. Although mood is elevated, emotions are volatile, so sufferers can suddenly become intensively irritated. If grandiose delusions develop, overspending and socially inappropriate behaviour can occur, distressing loved ones as well as the sufferer of mania.

Mania prevalence

One per cent of the population purportedly suffer from mania. Approximately two-thirds of sufferers reportedly experience psychosis. This is why mania might be confused with schizophrenia.

Mania intervention

Overall, interventions are offered under the umbrella of a hospital. The sufferer is usually cared for by a team of professionals. Medication is often prescribed, but if stopped there is a risk of mania rebound.

Mania outcome

For movement in a positive direction, therapy is considered imperative, coupled with medication (Scott, Colom and Vieta, 2007). Most remit within a few months. Full recovery takes longer, especially if there is co-morbidity.

Hypomania signs

This is similar to mania but symptoms are less severe therefore not as easy to spot. With hypomania (type 2 bi-polar) there is less sleep, more talk, and fast-flying thoughts (when compared with the general population) which, unlike type 1 bi-polar, does not lead to hospitalisation. Other symptoms of hypomania are being fidgety, easily distracted and excessively immersed in perceived pleasurable behaviour that can have unfortunate consequences. Mood is noticeable over a specific time period: hypomania lasts for at least four days.

Hypomania prevalence

Even though there have been a considerable number of investigations into hypomania, knowledge of its incidence is incomplete. However, it is purported that approximately one person in every two hundred are sufferers. Onset is mainly during the teen years or early adulthood.

Hypomania intervention

A community adult mental health services team, which includes a therapist, tends to deal with those suffering from hypomania. A sufferer should be evaluated on an ongoing basis, frequently monitored to ensure that the disorder has not progressed to mania, and a support network should be available. Therapy can be beneficial in enabling the client to expand insight and manage mood swings. Indeed, therapy appears to be an essential adjunct to any other intervention, including medication (Scott, Colom and Vieta, 2007).

Hypomania outcome

Many do not comply with a therapeutic programme and the condition may worsen. For those who do, the risk of relapse can be low. Overall outcome therefore, if an appropriate therapeutic programme is adhered to, is positive.

Research and theory on mania and hypomania

Causes are largely unknown, but there are several speculative theories. One is that suffering from bi-polar type 1 or 2 is because of generally eating non-nutritionally (Fogiolini et al., 2005). Another is that it is due to stress (Andreazza et al., 2008). There is a theory however, researched almost continuously for over the last thirty years, that suffering from one of the bi-polar disorders is a result of taking drugs, specifically cannabis or marijuana (for example, see Richardson, 2012 and Strakowski et al., 1998). However, this does not mean that everyone who has tried these drugs will suffer from a bi-polar disorder. Neither does it mean that if cannabis has never been used, a bi-polar disorder will not be suffered. More research is needed focusing on mania and hypomania, where findings can be put into effective clinical practice.

Mania and hypomania in practice

Mania is extreme, that is why it is not difficult to identify in practice. Where one client experiencing hypomania buys, for example, six jackets, the one with mania buys sixty jackets. Hypomania is not as excessive and therefore, although identifiable, not as easily spotted. Within IAPT services under the umbrella of the NHS, dynamic interpersonal therapy can be offered (for up to sixteen sessions) to treat mood disorders – this is a brief psychodynamic psychotherapy that has been developed specifically for this purpose.

CYCLOTHYMIA

An uncommon form of type 2 bi-polar disorder that many people have not heard of and which might be mistaken for borderline personality disorder is cyclothymic disorder (see also Chapter 11).

HYPOMANIA CASE VIGNETTE

When Tina, a woman in middle-age, visited her therapist, he listened while she described times in her life when she had felt that she would always have the best ongoing luck ever. Tina disclosed that now her feelings of excessive elation may be at the cost of the relationship with her life partner. The therapist asked Tina to clarify what she meant.

Tina replied, 'I remortgaged my house and used all the money investing in high-risk shares, positive that my prospects were outstandingly successful, with nothing going wrong and having a wonderful life'.

The therapist responded, 'Sounds as if you took a major risk, thinking you couldn't fail due to feeling lucky and invulnerable in that luck. What were the consequences?' In such a way, the therapist was able to facilitate Tina in becoming aware of the links between her thoughts, emotions and how they affected her behaviour, leading to certain consequences.

Tina answered, 'I lost every invested penny and the house was repossessed, just because of my impulsiveness when I felt, oh-so-high. Then my partner [Linda] and I went to live with my old mum. Linda's really fed up with my high moods. Don't know what I'll do if she goes.'

The therapist communicated his understanding to Tina. He also continued to ensure that she became aware of the connections between her thoughts, feelings and actions, by his use of open (Socratic) questions.

In addition, the therapist also used psycho-education by explaining that one way of achieving her aim of managing herself better was to spot thoughts such as 'my life will be perfect' and to interfere with them before the sense of being manic intensified. He said, 'Think of a time you were completely optimistic about the future'.

'Last winter! Although a ski beginner, I took a chance, and went off-piste,' declared Tina.

'What were the consequences?' asked the therapist.

'I broke my arm.'

The therapist responded, 'Although you were a ski beginner: You went off-piste, resulting in a broken arm.'

'Exactly!' Tina exclaimed.

'Your emotions at the time?'

'Oh,' replied Tina, 'I felt on top of the world! That I could fly! Like I was on the best drug ever! I thought nothing could go wrong.'

In order to re-enforce for Tina the links between her thoughts, emotions, actions and their consequences during her 'high' times, he stated, 'This led to taking a risk you would not take under normal circumstances.'

'Precisely!' Tina exclaimed while nodding.

Then, to consolidate Tina's learning experience within the session, the therapist explained, 'In future, challenge totally positive thoughts; deliberate on possible alternatives in order for your sense

(Continued)

(Continued)

of impulsiveness to be interfered with. When feeling what you describe as "high" [which can also be termed as a 'hypomania' stage] put off dealing with major issues such as important money matters, avoid taking drugs during that stage; because the positive feelings might lead you to believe that you can do anything. Instead, chat to a friend you can trust. How do you think you can avoid future problems?'

Tina thought for a moment then said, 'I can discuss matters with Linda. She'd like that very much. I know she has my best interests at heart. I can use the relaxation techniques you taught me. I can remember the other times I felt invulnerable and what that led to.'

As a result of the therapy, Tina had a heart-to-heart talk with Linda, who now supports her wisely through the 'high' times. Tina accepts that support. She also attends relaxation classes, which she finds very useful for managing her mood.

Cyclothymia theory and research

Surprisingly, despite many investigations, the causes of cyclothymia are unknown. There are several theories. One is that it is triggered by a virus. Another is that it is brought on by stress. A further theory is that it is hereditary. The favourite theory is that it is a disorder of the brain due to a chemical imbalance. None of these theories, however, are supported by research.

Cyclothymia signs

Symptoms of cyclothymic disorder involve long-term (chronic) fluctuating disturbance of mood incorporating several hypomanic episodes and depressive periods (APA, 2002). In other words, the sufferer's mood moves through periods of highs and lows with periods of normality, but they are not free of the high or low moods for more than eight consecutive weeks. The high episodes do not include hallucinations or other psychotic features, and when feeling low it is not so low that the person is incapacitated or suicidal. Mood swings persist for more than twenty-four months and are rapid. They can occur every few weeks, days, or even hours.

Cyclothymia prevalence

Approximately 1 per cent of the population is considered to be suffering from cyclothymia (4therapy, 2011).

Intervention for cyclothymia

Focusing on interpersonal therapy as well as self-image is the favoured therapeutic approach. Other options are treatment with antidepressants, or for severe cases, lithium (prescribed by a medical doctor who is likely to be a psychiatrist).

Cyclothymia expected outcome

If cyclothymia is not treated the outcome can be mania, leading to hospitalisation. This is because without intervention the cyclothimic condition might change for the worse. When the cyclothymic disorder is mild, therapy alone is usually sufficient. The outcome can be significantly beneficial if an interpersonal model embracing self-image is used. For more severe cases, taking prescribed drugs often reduces mood swings.

Cyclothymia in practice

When faced with a client who reveals feeling on top of the world one day and hopeless the next, cyclothymic disorder may be the problem and needs attending to otherwise it can develop into full-blown mania. If the therapist is inexperienced, it may be best if the client is referred to one who is a specialist in mood problems (see also Chapter 2).

CYCLOTHYMIA CASE VIGNETTE

At the mercy of her moods, is how Eve could be described. She was in her thirties with two toddlers and had experienced sudden mood swings since her teens. A neighbour suggested that she sought help after seeing Eve smack her twin toddlers while shouting. She visited her GP, who referred her to a therapist.

During therapy, Eve disclosed that when feeling high she could be really loud and rude. She revealed that once, when a friend called at an inconvenient time, she slammed the telephone down so hard that it broke. When feeling low, she said, 'I'm just depressive'. The therapist recognised cyclothymia and was concerned about the children, so offered Eve and her life partner parenting sessions, which they experienced as supportive. Eve also learnt relaxation techniques (useful for balancing her 'up' and 'down' swings) and appropriate communication skills so that she could interact with others in a civil way.

Eve still however was unable to have full control over her moods. She bought each twin, and herself, seven pairs of shoes during an up mood. It was extremely costly! She had an ugly argument with her partner and stopped trusting her emotions. Eve's GP prescribed a drug which made her put on weight and seemed to dull all her emotions. During therapy, she was too 'zonked-out on medication' to talk. She stopped taking it and asked her GP for a second opinion. He referred her to a psychiatrist who liaised with the therapist and prescribed a low dosage of a drug that was very effective regarding Eve's depressed moods and mildly effective with her 'highs'. This, with the support of her therapist, enabled her to start trusting her emotions again. Eve also became skilled in using the psychological techniques she had learnt regarding communicating well, parenting appropriately and using relaxation skills to balance mood. She and her partner communicated better and agreed to discuss financial matters before any major spending, so they could come to a mutual agreement. Via therapy Eve was enabled to gain insight into herself, learn to be rational and deal with her moods. She is no longer in therapy.

AGE, GENDER AND CULTURE

A problem with mood tends to rear its ugly head during the teen years, occurring in both sexes, and in any culture. Self-harming behaviour too can manifest regardless of culture and gender, and emerge at any age. Similarly, depression can occur in individuals from any race and socio-economic status. Mounting evidence shows a direct link between the use of cannabis and depression, especially if cannabis was taken before the age of fifteen years; girls are particularly vulnerable (Pattern, 2004). Indeed, in the UK, the majority of people who are depressed appear to be women (Martin-Merino et al., 2010). Purportedly, twice as many women as men suffer from SAD.

CONCERN

Importantly, trainee therapists should have some idea of what to look for when clients may suffer from mood problems or self-harming behaviour. It is a question of recognising what is beyond normal variation. Any individuals, can be, for instance, extremely happy for a specific reason – this does not mean that they suffer from a mood disorder. What is of concern is that some trainees on placements may not have adequate training in dealing with clients who are depressed, self-harm or suffer from a mood disorder, and are consequently unprepared for facing the demands that these clients present. Can this be legal? Expertise in dealing with such clients can be found, for example, within multiprofessional care.

Points to ponder

- If the majority of those who self-harm are 'invisible', what may help them?
- When faced with a suicidal client, is it ethical to break client-therapist confidentiality?
- At a time of international economic difficulty (bearing in mind the evidential link between economic decline and burgeoning suicide rates) should governments cut back on mental health spending or should they increase it so that suicide prevention strategies are set up?
- 'To prevent SAD, perhaps those of us living in northern latitudes would be better taking a winter-sunshine holiday, rather than a summer-sunshine holiday' (Rudd, 2012).
- Mood problems, suicide and self-harm cut across age, gender and cultural boundaries.
- Over years of clinical work, therapists can become vicariously traumatised (profoundly impacted in the way they perceive the world) due to their care for clients. This can lead to feeling overwhelmed and even helpless, resulting in burnout (see for example, Brady et al., 1999).
- More recent thinking on vicarious growth has changed from being negative, to perceiving it as not all bad, and that the tears therapists 'shed on behalf of their clients represent an extraordinary opportunity for personal growth' (Arnold et al., 2005: 260).

Exercise

(Answers are embedded in this chapter.)

1 State four types of mood disorders.
2 Why may the term 'deliberate self-harm' be misleading?
3 Is self-harming likely to be an attempt at suicide?
4 Can CBT be an appropriate intervention for mild depression?
5 Are marijuana and depression linked?
6 What has been shown to improve SAD?
7 Which can lead to hospitalisation: mania or hypomania?
8 Name a drug that might trigger a bi-polar disorder.
9 Identify a mood disorder where research lags behind theory.

CHAPTER SUMMARY

Self-harming tends to be a way of coping.

NICE recommend CBT as a clinical intervention for mild to medium depression (2012b).

SAD differs from depression mainly because it is cyclical.

Reasons for suffering cyclothymic disorder are inconclusive.

Mania can lead to hospitalisation and is categorised under type 1 bi-polar disorder (APA, 2002).

Hypomania does not lead to hospitalisation and is categorised under type 2 bi-polar disorder (APA, 2002).

If cyclothymia or hypomania are untreated, full mania may develop.

It seems that at some time in a therapist's career, a client will die by suicide.

LIST OF USEFUL RESOURCES

- FMG (2011) *Mood Disorders and Suicide* (film) (New York, Films Media Group).
- Freeman, J. (2010) *Understanding Self-Harm* (Dublin, Veritas).
- Joiner, T. (2005) *Why People Die by Suicide* (Massachusetts, Harvard University Press).
- Lukas, C. and Seiden, H.M. (2007) *Living in the Wake of Suicide* (London, Jessica Kingsley Publishers).
- O'Connor, R. (2010) *Undoing Depression: What Therapy Doesn't Teach You and Medication Can't Give You* (New York, Little Brown and Company).

(Continued)

(Continued)

- Power, M. (2005) *Mood Disorders: A Handbook of Science and Practice* (Chichester, John Wiley and Sons).
- Rudd, B. (2009) EQ (card game) (Milton Keynes, Speechmark).
- Rudd, B. (2010) Handling Emotion (game) (Milton Keynes, Speechmark).

RELEVANT WEBSITES

http://selfharm.net/

www.angelfire.com/ne/cre8vityunltd/sumania.html

www.mooddisorders.net/

www.mind.org.uk/help/diagnoses_and_conditions/suicidal_feelings

www.nhs.uk/Conditions/Depression/Pages/Introduction.aspx

www.webmd.com/bipolar-disorder/guide/cyclothymia-cyclothymic-disorder

REFERENCES

Andreazza, A.C., Kauer-Sant'Anna, K., Frey, B.N., Bond, D.J., Kapczinski, F., Young, L.T. and Yatham, L.N. (2008) 'Oxidative stress markers in bipolar disorder: a meta-analysis', *Journal of Affective Disorders*, 111, 2, pp.135–44.

APA (2002) *DSM-IV-TR® Diagnostic and Statistical Manual of Mental Disorders* (Fourth Edition, revised) (Vancouver, American Psychiatric Association).

Arnold, D., Calhoun, L., Tedeschi, R. and Cann, A. (2005) 'Vicarious traumatic growth in psychotherapy', *Journal of Humanistic Psychology,* 45, 2, pp. 239–63.

Barr, W., Leitner, M. and Thomas, J. (2004) 'Short shrift for the sane? The hospital management of self-harm patients with and without mental illness', *Journal of Psychiatric and Mental Health Nursing,* 11, 4, pp. 401–06.

Beck, A.T., Steer, R.A. and Brown, G.K. (1996) *Manual for the Beck Depression Inventory* (San Antonio Texas, Psychological Corporation).

Brady, J. L., Guy, J. D., Poelstra, P.L., and Brokaw, B. F. (1999) 'Vicarious traumatization, spirituality, and the treatment of sexual abuse survivors: a national survey of women psychotherapists', *Professional Psychology: Research and Practice,* 30, 4, pp. 386–93.

Cooper, J., Kapur, N., Webb, R., Lawlor, M., Guthrie, E., Kevin Mackway-Jones, K. and Appleby, L. (2005) 'Suicide after deliberate self-harm: a 4-year cohort study', *American Journal of Psychiatry*, 162, 2, pp. 297–303.

Castille, K., Prout, M., Geoffrey, M., Schmidheiser, M., Yoder, S. and Howlett, B. (2007) 'The early maladaptive schemas of self-mutilators: implications for therapy', *Journal of Cognitive Psychotherapy*, 21, 1, pp. 58–71.

Ceccherini-Nellie, A. and Priebe, S. (2011) 'Economic factors and suicide rates: associations over time in four countries', *Social Psychiatry and Psychiatric Epidemiology,* 46, 10, pp. 975–82.

Dalgleish, T., Rosen, K. and Marks, M. (1996) 'Rhythm and blues: the theory and treatment of seasonal affective disorder', *British Journal of Clinical Psychology*, 35, 2, pp. 163–82.

Department of Health (2012) *Update on Suicide* www.dh.gov.uk/health/files/2012/09 Statistical-update-on-suicide.pdf, accessed 29 January 2013.

Egan, K.G., Koff, R.N. and Moreno, M.A. (2013) 'College students' responses to mental health status updates on facebook', *Mental Health Nursing*, 43, 1, pp. 46–51.

Gratz, K.L. (2007) 'Targeting emotional dysregulation in the treatment of self-injury', *Journal of Clinical Psychology*, 63, 11, pp. 1,092–103.

Fogiolini, A., Frank, E., Scott, J.A.,Turkin, S. and Kupfer, D. (2005) 'Metabolic syndrome in bipolar disorder: findings from the bipolar center for Pennsylvanians', *Bipolar Disorders*, 7, 5, pp. 424–39.

4therapy (2011) *Cyclothymia*, www.4therapy.com/conditions/bipolar-disorder/cyclothymia/what-cyclothymia-2173, accessed 07 March 2011.

Harwood, R.H. (2012) 'Dementia for hospital physicians', *Clinical Medicine Journal of the Royal College of Physicians*, 12, 1, pp. 35–9.

Haw, C. and Hawton, K. (2011) 'Problem drug use, drug misuse and deliberate self-harm trends and patient characteristics, with a focus on young people, Oxford 1993–2006', *Social Psychiatry and Psychiatric Epidemiology*, 46, 2, pp. 85–93.

Hawton, K. and Harris, L. (2008) 'The gender ratio in occurrence of deliberate self-harm across the life-span cycle', *Crisis*, 29, pp. 4–10.

Heath, N.L., Toste, J.R., Nedecheva, T. and Charlebois, A. (2008) 'An examination of nonsuicidal self-injury among college students', *Journal of Mental Health Counseling*, 30, 2, pp. 137–56.

Hunter, J. and NIMH (2012) *Research and Depression*, http://psychcentral.com/disorders/depressionresearch.htm, accessed 6 March 2012.

Jacobsen, F.M., Wehr, T.A. and Sack, D.A. (1986) 'Seasonal affective disorder, a review of the syndrome and its public health implications', *American Journal of Psychiatry*, 143, 3, pp. 356–8.

Kern, J. (2010) *Scars That Wound: Scars That Heal* (Cincinnati, Standard).

Klonsky, E.D., Oltmans, T.F. and Turkheimer, E. (2003) 'Deliberate self-harm in a non-clinical population: prevalence and psychological correlates', *American Journal of Psychiatry*, 160, 81, pp. 1501–08.

Klonsky, E.D. (2007) 'The functions of deliberate self-injury: a review of the evidence', *Clinical Psychology Review*, 27, 2, pp. 226–39.

Kokkevi, A., Rotsika, V. Arapaki, A. and Richardson, C. (2012) 'Adolescents' self-reported suicide attempts, self-harm thoughts and their correlates across 17 European countries', *Journal of Child Psychology and Psychiatry*, 53, 4, pp. 381–9.

Lambert, G. and Reid, C. (2002) 'Effect of sunlight and season on serotonin turnover in the brain', *The Lancet*, 360, 9348, pp. 1840–2.

Levenkron, S. (1998) *Cutting: Understanding and Overcoming Self-mutilation* (New York, Norton).

Martin-Merino, Ruigomez, A., Johansson, S., Wallander, M. and Garcia-Rodriguez, L.A. (2012) 'Study of a cohort of patients newly diagnosed with depression in general

(Continued)

(Continued)

practice: prevalence, incidence, comorbidity, and treatment patterns', *Medical Care*, 50, 1, pp. 1–108.

Marty, M.A., Segal, D.L. and Coolidge, F.L. (2010) 'Relationships among dispositional coping strategies, suicidal ideation and protective factors against suicide in older adults', *Aging and Mental Health*, 14, 8, pp. 1015–23.

Netdoctor (2012) *Self-harm*, www.netdoctor.co.uk/diseases/depression/suicideanddeliberate selfharm_000 600.htm, accessed 24 February 2012.

NHS (2012) *Seasonal Affective Disorder*, www.nhs.uk/conditions/Seasonal-affective- disorder/ Pages/Introduction.aspx, accessed 26 February 2012.

NHS (2013) *Seasonal Affective Disorder*, www.nhs.uk/conditions/Seasonal-affective- disorder/Pages/Introduction.aspx, accessed 12 February 2013

NICE (2012a) *Intervention for Self-harm*, http://pathways.nice.org.uk/pathways/ self-harm#path=view%3A/pathways/self-harm/longer-term-management-of-self-harm- assessment-and-treatment.xml&content=view-node%3Anodes-interventions-for-self-harm, accessed 6 March 2012.

NICE (2012b) *Clinical Guideline 90 – Depression*, www.nice.org.uk, accessed 6 March 2012.

NICE (2012c) *Using Evidence to Inform the Best Quality and Social Care*, www.nice.org. uk/, accessed 8 March 2012.

Nock, M.K. (2009) 'Why do people hurt themselves?', *Current Directions in Psychological Science*, 18, 2, pp. 78–83.

Owens, D. and Horrocks, A. (2002) 'Fatal and non-fatal repetition of self-harm: a systemic review', *British Journal of Psychiatry*, 181, 3, pp. 193–9.

Pasco, S., Wallack, C., Sartin, R.M. and Dayton, R. (2012) 'The impact of experiential exercises on communication and relational skills in a suicide prevention gate-keeper training program for college resident advisors', *Journal of American College Health*, 60, 2, pp. 134–40.

Pattern, S.B. (2004) 'Drug-induced depression: a systematic review to inform clinical practice', *Psychotherapy and Psychosomatics*, 73, 4, pp. 207–15.

Plante, L.G. (2007) *Bleeding to Ease the Pain: Cutting, Self-injury, and the Adolescent Search for Self* (Westport, Praeger).

Porcelli, P. and Sonino, N. (2007) *Psychological Factors Affecting Medical Conditions* (New York, Karger).

Richardson, T.H. (2012) *A Review of the Relationship Between Cannabis Use and Affective Disorders*, www.kon.org/urc/v8/bath.htm, accessed 09 March 2012.

Royal College of Psychiatrists (2010) *Self-harm, Suicide and Risk: Helping People who Self-harm*, https://docs.google.com/viewer?a=v&q=cache:4SgG2Oto_XUJ:www.rcpsych. ac.uk/files/pdfversion/CR158.pdf+better+services+for+people+who+self-harm+royal+coll ege+of+psychiatrists&hl=en&gl=uk&pid=bl&srcid=ADGEEShmr-RsOPZEE_ Qs03BkuZIf12ECHfpbq9brkQNWxBa4on-nFSaGJms8sADXw_rCnpOE4vmod5Bd3k4V- AnAfp6n26c56M2hS8LnTvPmclCHtuVPkI2EfSmW1zNdWxpkoWE78Q8n&sig=AHIEtbQ cjhe-FiWWXq9YngKjuErWbBwR3A&pli=1, accessed 23 February 2012.

Royal College of Psychiatrists (2012) *Self Harm*, www.rcpsych.ac.uk/mentalhealthinfoforall/problems/depression/self-harm.aspx, accessed 24 February 2012.

Rudd, S. (2012) Personal conversation, 06 March 2012, 6.30 pm, Ashdown Chiropractic and Natural Health Centre, Uckfield.

Rull, G. (2012) *Mania and Hypomania*, www.patient.co.uk/doctor/Mania-and-Hypomania.htm, accessed 26 February 2012.

Ruskin, P.E., Silver-Aylalan, M., Kling, M.A., Reed, S.A., Bradham, D.D., Hebel, J.R., Barrett, D., Knowles, F. III and Houser, P. (2004) 'Treatment outcomes in depression: comparison of remote treatment through telepsychiatry to in-person treatment', *American Journal of Psychiatry*, 161, 8, pp.1,471–6.

Scott, J., Colom, F. and Vieta, E. (2007) 'A meta-analysis of relapse rates with adjunctive psychological therapies compared to usual psychiatric treatment for bipolar disorders', *The International Journal of Neuropsychopharmacology*, 10, 1, pp. 123–9.

Simon, H. (2012) *Depression – Risk Factors*, www.umm.edu/patiented/articles/what_risk_factors_depression_000008_3.htm, accessed 07 March 2012.

Smith, P.N., Cukrowioz, K.C., Poindexter, E.K., Hobson, V. and Cohen, L.M. (2010) 'The acquired capacity for suicide: a comparison of suicide attempters, suicide ideators, and non-suicide controls', *Depression and Anxiety*, 27, 9, pp. 871–7.

Stratkowski, S.M., Sax, K.W., McElroy, S.L., Keck, P.E., Hawkins, J.M. and West, S.A. (1998) 'Course of psychiatric and substance abuse syndromes co-occurring with bipolar disorder after a first psychiatric hospitalization', *Journal of Clinical Psychiatry*, 59, pp. 465–71.

WHO (2012) *Depression – Background Information*, www.cks.nhs.uk/depression/background_information/prevalence#-402794, accessed 6 March 2012.

7

Eating and Sleeping Disorders

LEARNING OBJECTIVES FOR THIS CHAPTER

- Understand bulimia and anorexia nervosas
- Recognise insomnia and hypersomnia
- Know that environmental factors can maintain eating or sleeping disorders
- Realise that internal factors of affect, cognition and biology impact on disorders

---

Before focusing on sleep problems I spotlight eating disorders, of which there are two major forms: anorexia nervosa and bulimia nervosa.

BULIMIA AND ANOREXIA NERVOSAS

Three main categories of theory are used to understand the nervosas:

1 Biological: this postulates that the nervosas are passed down from parent to offspring via the genes. In this way they become part of the person's biological make-up.
2 Environmental: something in the environment impacts, triggering an eating disorder. For example, if parents are over-controlling or unduly concerned about eating matters or weight, then this can have such an impact on their children that either anorexia nervosa or bulimia results.
3 Psychological: mind matters can underpin an eating problem. For instance, when an individual does not experience being in control of any areas of life, eating/not eating and weight are at least areas in which they can assert control.

Clearly, definitive reasons for suffering an eating disorder are inconclusive.

Anorexia nervosa

Anorexia nervosa is a serious disorder with high mortality rates.

Anorexia nervosa research

Unfortunately, controlled studies of therapy focusing on anorexia nervosa are chronically lacking, although recent research does indicate that no more than half of those who suffer from this problem recover (Lockwood, Serpell and Waller, 2012). Anorexia strikes mostly women – the number of male sufferers is very small and for this reason, I presume, men have hardly ever been used in research investigations. A recent US study however, shows that anorexia nervosa is increasing in men (N.A.M.E.D., 2011). Certain investigative findings indicate that anorexia runs in families (Pinheiro, Root and Bulik, 2009), but this does not explain why it is females, rather than males, who are more likely to suffer from the disease. Other researchers speculate that 'an important contributing factor to the disorder is the social pressure young women experience when extreme body shapes and images are rewarded ... Even a cursory inspection of supermodels in the hottest fashion magazines reveal an emphasis on unhealthy and unnatural thinness ... it's not hard to imagine impressionable young teenagers taking too seriously the value of losing weight and being thin' (Nathan, Gorman and Salkind, 1999: 27). An imbalance of a chemical in the brain may cause anorexia, but within my search, I have not found research supporting this perspective. Intriguingly, therapists Long, Fitzgerald and Hollin offer hope. They looked at individuals 'who fulfilled Diagnostic and Statistical Manual of Mental Disorders, Fourth Edition diagnostic criteria for anorexia nervosa' (2012: 1). Their findings revealed that clients over the age of eighteen with chronic anorexia nervosa had favourable results, even after a four-year follow-up, when eclectic interventions were used. These interventions embraced dealing with emotional distress, psychological problems, perception of body image and coping skills, along with resolving the symptoms of anorexia nervosa. By contrast, research findings appear unfavourable when CBT is an intervention (Lockwood, Serpell and Waller, 2012).

Anorexia nervosa signs

The main features of this disorder are being very afraid of putting on weight, a distorted self-body image and a refusal to maintain a healthy body weight. Other characteristics are:

- not acknowledging the sensation of hunger
- reducing food intake
- feeling fat, regardless of appearance
- experiencing a sense of low self-worth
- using laxatives, diuretics and or exercising to excess, due to a fear of putting on weight
- if a female of menstruating age, missing at least three consecutive periods, although not pregnant
- being a minimum of 15 per cent below the normal range of body weight that is expected, if no physical illness is causing the weight loss (Swenne et al., 2005; Nordo et al., 2006; Merwin et al., 2011).

(This list takes into account the DSM-IV-TR's criteria for anorexia nervosa, but it is important to bear in mind that these listed symptoms, used as guidelines for psychiatrists to diagnose the problem, may differ in the forthcoming DSM-V.)

Anorexia nervosa prevalence

Approximately one in every 500 women are reported to suffer from anorexia at some time during their lives; and one in every 10,000 men (Rutigliano, 2012).

Anorexia nervosa treatment

Intervention for those suffering from anorexia is aimed at changing the way sufferers think about themselves and enabling them to achieve a healthy body weight. In cases of severe malnourishment hospitalisation can be a necessary part of treatment. Overall, when the person is under the age of eighteen years, intervention that focuses on family therapy has been found to be more effective than one-to-one therapy and can have a good prognosis if sufferers have had the disorder for less then thirty-six months (Nathan, Gorman and Salkind, 1999; Eisler et al., 2007).

For those who are eighteen years old and over or have had the disorder for longer than thirty-six months, an eclectic approach (see case vignette) offers promise (Long, Fitzgerald and Hollin, 2012).

Anorexia nervosa outcome

The most serious outcome of anorexia, due to starvation, is death. Before this, a consequence is an imbalance of electrolytes within the body, such as sodium and potassium: these are needed by the nervous system for the adequate functioning of muscles and nerves. Low blood pressure, coupled with low heart rate, are also often associated with this disorder, and a further issue is that while sufferers lose weight, they store water and swell up. Edema is the way that the body responds to the loss of water, by attempting to retain it. Researcher Steinhauser looked at 119 studies, published in English and German, incorporating 5,590 patients suffering from anorexia (2002). The findings revealed that 20 per cent of sufferers remained chronically unwell with anorexia nervosa and that just under 50 per cent recovered (if 'recovered' means 'symptom-free'). Unfortunately, there was a lack of definition within the studies regarding the meaning of 'outcome measures'. Due to a paucity of data relating to the studies, the exact calculation of the outcome of anorexia nervosa is inconclusive. This is because follow-up of patients after treatment ranged from between one and twenty-nine years. There are insufficient randomised trials taking into account interventions as well as outcome. Consequently, this does not allow for rigorous evaluation of outcome.

ANOREXIA NERVOSA CASE VIGNETTE

Anne was eighteen years old and had suffered with anorexia nervosa for two years. One day, when walking to a local shop to buy a fashion magazine, she collapsed. A passer-by called an ambulance. In hospital, medics initially treated her for impending kidney failure resulting from anorexia nervosa. The mode of intervention then assigned for Anne was a team approach incorporating medical care, a therapist and nutritionist.

Initially, Anne found it difficult talking to the therapist because she did not trust her or perceive herself as having a food problem, even though she weighed herself daily, was on an extreme diet of very restricted calories, and obsessed about appearing thin rather than fat. She felt ashamed of secretly taking laxatives, diuretics and exercising excessively.

The therapist was a good listener and it did not take long for Anne to confide in him. Medics treated her kidney problem. From the nutritionist, Anne learnt what a normal healthy diet meant. During therapy she decided to keep away from looking at fashion and fitness magazines as well as websites to do with weight. When not in impeding physical danger, and having put on approximately 1kg per week while in hospital, she was discharged from being an in-patient but continued therapy as an out-patient.

Working within the NHS, Anne's therapist adhered to interventions suggested by the NICE guidelines (2004). Of the therapies NICE suggest, the therapist chose to use family interventions because she knew that Anne lived with her parents. Therapy included spotlighting Anne's attitude to her shape, weight and eating behaviour, as well as broader psychosocial issues. Throughout, Anne was carefully monitored and the therapist liaised closely with an experienced physician.

Over one year, Anne gained an average of 0.5kg per week, her energy increased and she took the daily nutrients necessary for her health. After a year of weekly sessions, the therapist, Anne and her parents deemed the therapy successful. Although Anne's daily urge to relapse is still with her, she seems to have recovered because she no longer has symptoms of anorexia nervosa.

Bulimia nervosa

Many of us have looked to food for comfort when lonely or tired. Bulimia nervosa is different however – it is more of a compulsion, rather than an occasional chocolate bar. Overeating followed by extreme attempts to lose weight characterise this disorder. Although the planned DSM-V may offer a new definition of bulimia, currently it is defined by self-purging: bulimia sufferers use laxatives and diuretics or, more commonly, self-induced vomiting. Enemas are used too, but they are not as popular as the other methods (Mehler, 2011).

Bulimia nervosa research

Investigations conducted by researcher Mehler (2011) show that there can be detrimental outcomes regarding vomiting, the use of laxatives, diuretics and enemas. For example, self-induced regurgitation (irrespective of whether a finger or something else is used), can eventually lead to vomiting as a reflex action. If a laxative is used to stimulate colonic activity, it results in a large amount of watery diarrhea. When diuretics are used, dehydration can occur. Other difficulties associated with bulimia, are heartburn, a sore throat, problems with teeth, gums, esophagus, ulcers and more serious medical conditions.

Bulimia nervosa signs

Spotting who suffers from bulimia is difficult because sufferers may appear healthy and of normal weight (Newton et al.,1993). Binging (consuming large quantities of food quickly, usually of high calorific value) then frantically trying to lose weight (for example, by exercising excessively) are its hallmarks.

Bulimia nervosa prevalence

It is estimated that 1 per cent of the population suffers from bulimia (Hoek and Hoeken, 2003).

Bulimia nervosa intervention

Therapeutic approaches encompass not only psychosocial interventions, but also nutritional rehabilitation, counselling and treatments from professionals other than therapists, such as medication. The remedies relevant to therapists who have clients suffering from bulimia are psychosocial. These embrace interventions such as group psychotherapy, support groups, family and marital therapy (US Department of Health and Human Services, 2012).

Bulimia nervosa outcome

On average, onset of bulimia is at eighteen years of age. Most sufferers lead an active life. After following an appropriate intervention programme, approximately 60 per cent appear recovered

(Best Practice, 2012), although this rate may be misleading because while some may seem to recover after adhering to treatment, specific findings show that after a five-year follow-up, only 5 per cent have fully recovered (Keski-Rahkonen et al., 2009).

BULIMIA NERVOSA CASE VIGNETTE

Amy was again making herself a liquid diet drink, but she craved food. Her willpower collapsed: she opened a new tin of biscuits and ate them in minutes. After looking around for anything else to eat, she found cheese, chocolates, ice cream and plenty of bread and butter. Amy ate the lot. After nearly an hour of binging, and afraid of gaining weight from the approximate 4,000 calories consumed, she dashed to the toilet and vomited before weighing herself; making an inner promise that she would change her eating behaviour tomorrow. The next day, she found a therapist.

'You've taken a big step towards healing by admitting that you have an issue with food and that you want to gain control over what is happening with cravings and the binge–purge cycle. By collaborating together, I can help you break that cycle and achieve the health you want,' summarised the therapist after listening to Amy, offering hope. The therapeutic approach chosen was eighteen sessions of CBT over a period of four and a half months, as suggested within the NICE guidelines (2004).

The first thing Amy learnt was that she needed to stop her liquid diet. By doing this and eating normally, her cravings ceased.

Initially, Amy seemed angry and defensive during therapy but talking to the therapist about things that were hard to disclose, about her feelings of shame, fear, and being judged, helped her enormously.

Low self-esteem was at the heart of Amy's problem. Her therapist's support and compassion helped. Amy adopted stress-busting techniques that her therapist showed her. She developed a healthier attitude towards food, resulting in normal eating and a healthier body. She also stopped buying fashion magazines that were full of skinny models.

It was Amy's own decision to move in a therapeutic direction that boosted her the most. She developed a support network with individuals who listened non-judgementally and did not try to 'fix' her. Overall, the core aspects that helped Amy were threefold: first, breaking her cycle of binge–purge by dealing with stress appropriately and eating normally and regularly; second, using skills she learnt during therapy to identify and change the beliefs that were dysfunctional about her self-worth, body, diet and weight; third, learning to problem-solve the emotional issues that initially underpinned her eating problem.

Eating disorders in practice

Facing clients with eating disorders is challenging for therapists, particularly if there is a problem with anorexia nervosa. If working with clients suffering from bulimia, binge–purge is not always what manifests; instead, clients may try to compensate for ingesting food by fasting, dieting or taking excessive exercise (Smith and Segal, 2012).

Mindfulness can be used in working with people with eating disorders, particularly in attending to the eating process. For example, here is how one therapist explains his intervention: 'I'll have a client watch their tongue as they eat … it is an amazing experience to see what the tongue does all by itself and helpful if one trains the tongue to not push down the gullet but to push food to where it can be chewed' (Shepard, 2012). Recent research by Ertelt et al. (2011) suggests that bulimia sufferers prefer on-line therapy to face-to-face work. This is not a difficult way of delivering therapy and the research showed that the outcome seemed favourable if CBT was used. Within clinical practice, clients attending with apparent eating problems generally suffer with unprocessed emotional issues that need resolving yet which seem too painful to face. The consequence is that they use food unhealthily as a coping mechanism, and tend to continue doing so until equipped with a different, healthier way of dealing with emotions.

Interestingly, as we move on to the next section, sleep deprivation and increased eating are linked (WebMD, 2012).

SLEEPING DISORDERS

Insomnia and excessive, ongoing oversleeping (hypersomnia) are sleeping disorders. Most of us spend a third of our lives asleep, though some do not need to sleep as much – although many subscribe to the idea that eight hours sleep are necessary, there are individuals who require either less or more. Sleeping is essential for our growth and brain development. Without enough sleep, we are grumpy, forgetful and cannot concentrate properly. Sleep deprivation impacts on emotional wellbeing, physical health and cognitive functioning.

Insomnia

If falling asleep, staying asleep and not getting restful sleep is experienced long-term, then the problem is insomnia.

Insomnia theory
There are three categories of theory.

1 Biological: this relates to the body. For instance, Garde et al. (2012) suggest that the excretion of a stress hormone (cortisol) causes insomnia.
2 Psychological: mind matters, for example, thoughts keeping people awake, are said to be the culprit (Belanger et al., 2005).
3 Environmental: a change in the environment, such as following the birth of a baby, causes insomnia (Barclay et al., 2012).

There is no bank of research that can back-up or dispute these theories validly and reliably.

Insomnia research
Investigative findings from Harvard Medical School (2011) show that when a combination of the following techniques is used, insomnia can be overcome:

- lifestyle changes (for example, having a bedtime ritual)
- reconditioning (for example, only using bed for sex or sleep)

- psychotherapy (for example, CBT)
- medication (for example, melatonin)
- sleep restriction (for example, only being in bed for the amount of time that is slept)
- relaxation exercises.

Further research conducted by staff at the Mayo Clinic (2011) shows that a structured CBT programme supports insomnia sufferers in overcoming the causes that underlie their sleeping problems and promotes better sleep: by identifying and replacing negative thoughts and behaviour, emotions change. For example, if worrying is causing sleep problems, then changing that worry to calmness thereby allows unproblematic sleep to occur.

Insomnia signs
These include:

- sleeping poorly at night
- waking up several times during the night
- not being able to fall asleep for a long time after going to bed
- irritability
- finding concentration difficult, unable to function properly during the day
- inability to sleep after waking up very early
- tiredness
- unrefreshing sleep.

Insomnia prevalence
Approximately 50 per cent of the population suffer from insomnia at some time during their lives (Cooperberg, 2012).

Insomnia intervention
Some sufferers self-medicate with alcohol, but this can cause fragmented sleep with more awakenings during the night, as well as other problems. If one alcoholic drink was needed on Monday night, for example, five may be needed on Sunday, because alcoholic tolerance happens quickly and therefore more is needed to achieve the same effect.

Rather than self-medicating, a therapist specialising in sleep disorders can help with better sleep hygiene. There is also a computer device for delivering behavioural intervention for insomnia (Riley et al., 2010). For hospital in-patients, researchers Davidson et al. (2007) recommend a quiet, calm-inducing room, neither too big nor too small, too hot or too cold, and going to bed having dealt with concerns which might otherwise keep the mind active.

Insomnia expected outcome
Insomnia can cause depression, though if caught early, depression can be stopped from manifesting (National Sleep Foundation, 2012). Ongoing insomnia can also cause relapse of a previous dependence on alcohol. Researchers Fong and Wing (2007) conducted a longitudinal study, the findings of which reveal a relationship between insomnia and possible subsequent psychiatric disorder. There is hope, however, as the case below exemplifies.

Insomnia in practice
Educating clients to link bed with only sleep and sex is useful. For example, here is what one therapist has found works when working with a client suffering from a sleep problem: 'working

on worry thoughts … rumination … mindfulness … relaxation and making changes in life … routines to accommodate sleep work well … not to stay in bed trying to sleep … link sleep with bed' (Vardi, 2012).

INSOMNIA CASE VIGNETTE

Forty-three-year-old Chang awoke daily at 3 a.m., tossing and turning, going over the next day's activities in his mind, unable to get back to sleep. He was concerned about his inability to stay awake at work, because of difficulty coping with only three hours nightly sleep. His GP offered him the choice of attending a sleep clinic or seeing a therapist. Chang chose therapy.

The therapist asked questions about his symptoms. Chang explained that for the last few years he had found sleeping difficult and had had restless nights.

'Insomnia,' the therapist said.

'Yes,' responded Chang.

She offered an integrative CBT programme, formulating therapy with seven factors:

1 Educating Chang about the different sleep cycles in order to give him knowledge about sleep basics.
2 Cognitive control: Chang learnt how his inner beliefs and actions, as well as external factors, affected his sleep. The therapist supported Chang in controlling his thoughts and eliminating both negative ways of thinking and the feeling of worry that kept him awake. This included discarding beliefs about sleep which were untrue, such as, 'Not falling asleep for a night will make me ill'.
3 Restricting sleep: bed was only for sleeping in.
4 Being awake passively: the therapist explained that it was not useful for Chang to spend eight hours in bed each night if he only slept for less than half that time. She suggested that he restrict the amount of time in bed to no more than four hours, but to still get up at the same time each morning.
5 Using stimulus control: this meant that Chang went to bed at 3 a.m., resulting in being sleepier when he went to bed and therefore more likely to fall asleep and stay that way until the morning. When Chang reported sleeping for four hours he and his therapist worked out a programme where he gradually increased the amount of time he spent in bed by twenty minutes whenever he was able to stay asleep for over three-quarters of the time that he spent in bed. Time spent in bed was adjusted on an ongoing basis, relating to his sleeping time, so that the amount of time Chang spent in bed was the time that he slept. His sleeping time became longer, and he went to bed earlier and earlier. He associated the action of going to bed with falling asleep, and controlled when he went to bed so that he did not experience the restless tossing and turning that had previously plagued him.
6 Training in relaxation: weekly bedtime adjustments were coupled with learning and using relaxation techniques such as progressive muscle relaxation, which helped in stopping Chang's unruly thoughts and was conducive to relaxing, helping him sleep.
7 Keeping a sleep diary to ascertain how much he slept.

Being passively awake was something else Chang learnt. By not trying to fall asleep, his therapist explained, paradoxically it helps sleep to happen. To Chang's surprise, he found that not worrying about sleeplessness helped him to relax, enabling sleep. Chang continues to have better sleep and no longer needs therapy.

Oversleeping

Some individuals oversleep often and regularly (NINDS 2012). This is not the same as feeling tired due to not getting enough sleep. Those who suffer from oversleeping can fall asleep at inappropriate times, such as at work or even behind a driver's wheel. Hypersomnia stops people enjoying daily life.

Oversleeping theory and research

Three main categories of theory are biological, psychological and environmental (Tolle, 2012). However, there is a paucity of valid and reliable research about these.

Oversleeping signs

Either prolonged daytime sleep or excessive night-time sleep (lasting ten or more hours nightly for at least two weeks) characterise hypersomnia (NINDS, 2012). Sufferers tend to be excessively sleepy. They feel that they must take naps during the day, but these do not alleviate their sleepiness.

Oversleeping prevalence

Approximately 7 per cent of the population suffer from hypersomnia (Right Diagnosis, 2012).

Oversleeping intervention

Treatment is usually symptomatic. Depending on the reason for the disorder, medication may be prescribed (Gibson, 2012). CBT can also be an intervention but further research is required to ascertain robust-enough reliability and validity of its effectiveness.

Oversleeping expected outcome

Prognosis of a sleep disorder is dependent on cause. For example, if clients suffer from hypersomnia mainly due to inhaling nicotine and consuming caffeine, and their lifestyle practices remain the same, then hypersomnia can persist, as found by researchers in China (Zhang et al., 2011). Unfortunately, this study only took children as participants, therefore transposing results onto an adult population is speculative. A very recent outcome study though shows that when seven adults took flumazemil, their sleep problem improved (Rye et al., 2012). This small number of participants does not make it possible to generalise; more good outcome studies related to oversleeping are required.

Oversleeping in practice

If no physical problems such as asthma or heart disease (which can be referred to a medical doctor) cause hypersomnia, then stress may be the culprit, so suggesting lifestyle changes to clients can help. For instance, if stressful issues in life may be contributing to hypersomnia therapists can teach lifestyle changes such as incorporating daily stress-management time to help with a sleep problem (Helpguide, 2013).

OVERSLEEPING CASE VIGNETTE

This is not the first time and probably not the last that Tom oversleeps, feels guilty about being late for work and sleepy all day. He sleeps over ten continuous hours and has done each night for at least a fortnight. He sees his primary health practitioner. After a check-up from which the doctor finds nothing physically wrong, he recommends Tom accesses a sleep clinic. As Tom is not happy staying nights there, he sees a therapist instead. She and Tom endeavour to find the cause of his hypersomnia. His lifestyle is looked at, any drugs he may be taking, and his emotional state. What emerges is that Tom feels anxious about asking for help relating to problems at work, and has done ever since his new boss took over a month ago. Tom likes having a doughnut, a cigarette and a coffee with brandy while watching a DVD at night. He falls asleep on the sofa, wakes up a few hours later and drags himself to bed, where he curls up under two duvets. Knowing this useful information, the therapist explains a few self-help strategies:

- eat nutritiously and if hungry at night, have an apple
- no cigarettes, alcohol or caffeine at bedtime; hot milky cocoa instead
- watch a DVD earlier
- go to bed when sleepy
- have less bed covers, so that it is not too hot in bed.

Determined to stop his hypersomnia problem, Tom makes these lifestyle changes.

During therapy, Tom has the insight that he can go to personnel at his workplace and discuss how he feels about work-related anxieties. He does so, which makes him feel less anxious. Quickly, he notices improvement. Tom sleeps less with an improved quality of sleep and gets to work on time. He takes a short refreshing power-nap at lunchtime which enables him to stay alert for the rest of the day.

AGE, GENDER AND CULTURE

Although anthropologists have rarely studied diverse sleep habits in various cultures, different coun-tries do not necessarily have the same sleeping habits. In Spain and Greece, for instance, siestas are the norm, but not in Germany. In the UK, although some individuals oversleep, most people do not sleep enough (PsychNet-UK, 2012). Overall, women are believed to need more sleep than men, teenagers more than adults, children more than teens and babies more than children.

Regarding eating disorders, men and women manifest with the same symptoms but far more females than males suffer from bulimia (Mehler, 2011). As for anorexia nervosa, its onset is almost exclusively during the teenage years and sufferers are mainly female (Rutigliano, 2012). A belief exists that it is women in the western world who are susceptible to suffering from an eating disorder, however, research does not entirely support this: Wildes, Robert and Simons (2001) found that non-white women in the western world, irrespective of age, experience much less disturbance with their eating and less body dissatisfaction than their white counter-parts. Future research is needed for debunking myths related to eating disorders and highlighting the reasons behind not only cultural, but also ethnic differences.

Points to ponder

- If most in the UK undersleep, might it make sense to introduce siestas?
- It behoves researchers to not only look at reduction of symptoms in a client when dealing with hypersomnia, but also quality of life.
- If a private client complains of oversleeping, and the therapist knows about research relating this with a potential heart problem and other physical ailments, might it be best to ensure that the client has a physical check-up or should the therapist offer the intervention they think may work in enabling their client to sleep less?
- Culture within the western world bombards us with images of so-called 'ideal' female models who are too thin, thereby pressurising women, especially girls who are young and vulnerable, to copy an unhealthy body image.
- Although we do not know for sure why there is a massive discrepancy between the numbers of women and men who suffer from anorexia nervosa, it may be because the media images of the ideal male within the western world are muscular; such images can be very powerful for easily-influenced young men.
- What may be the reasons that in western cultures, being fat is popularly perceived as unattractive while in other cultures such as the Pacific islanders and the sub-Saharan Africans, fatness is deemed attractive?

Exercise

(Answers are embedded in this chapter.)

1 Identify two eating disorders.
2 Name the psychological approach that the NICE (2004) guidelines recommend for bulimia nervosa.
3 Is it mostly men or women who suffer from anorexia?
4 What is a sleeping disorder?
5 What does 'hypersomnia' mean?
6 Which techniques can be used to help alleviate insomnia?

CHAPTER SUMMARY

Anorexia nervosa and bulimia nervosa are eating disorders.

Three major theories about them are: biological, environmental and psychological.

NICE guidelines recommend CBT for bulimia nervosa (2004).

Most people in the UK do not sleep enough but are not insomnia suffers.

Approximately 50 per cent of people, at some time in their lives, suffer from insomnia (Tamara, 2012).

Some people sleep more than is healthy for them.

LIST OF USEFUL RESOURCES

- Jacobs, G.D. (2009) *Say Goodnight to Insomnia: A Drug-Free Programme Developed at Harvard Medical School* (London, Pan MacMillan).
- Thorpy, M.J. and Billard, M. (2011) *Sleepiness: Causes, Consequences and Treatment* (Cambridge Medicine) (Cambridge, Cambridge University Press).
- Robinson, P. (2009) *Severe and Enduring Eating Disorder (SEED): Management of Complex Presentations of Anorexia and Bulimia Nervosa* (Chichester, Wiley-Blackwell).
- Rudd, B. (2010) *Compassion* (game) (Milton Keynes, Speechmark).
- Rudd, B. (2010) *Self-image* (game) (Milton Keynes, Speechmark).

RELEVANT WEBSITES

www.behavenet.com/anorexia-nervosa

http://eating-disorders-help.co.uk/Eating-Disorders/Bulimia-Nervosa.html

www.sleepdisordersguide.com/

REFERENCES

Barclay, N., Eley, T., Buysse, d. Maughan, B. and Gregory, A. (2012) 'Nonshared environmental influences on sleep quality: a study of monozygotic twin differences', *Behavior Genetics*, 42, 2, pp. 234–44.

Belanger, L., Morin, C.M., Gendron, L. and Blais, F.C. (2005) 'Presleep cognitive activity and thought control strategies in insomnia', *Journal of Cognitive Psychotherapy*, 19, 1, pp. 19–28.

Best Practice (2012) *Bulimia Nervosa*, http://bestpractice.bmj.com/best-practice/monograph/441/follow-up/prognosis.html, accessed 30 March 2012.

Cooperberg, J. (2012) *The Causes of Insomnia*, www.med.upenn.edu/psyhotherapy/user_documents/CausesfInsomnia2.html, accessed 30 March 2012.

Davidson, J.R., Feldman-Stewart, D., Brennenstuhl, S. and Ram, S. (2007) 'How to provide insomnia interventions to people with cancer: insights from patients', *Psycho-Oncology*, 16, 11, pp.1028–38.

Eisler, I., Simic, M., Russell, G.F.M. and Dare, C. (2007) 'A randomised controlled treatment trial of two forms of family therapy in adolescent anorexia nervosa: a five-year follow-up', *Journal of Child Psychology and Psychiatry*, 46, 6, pp. 552–60.

Ertelt, T.W., Crosby, R.D., Marino, J.M., Mitchell, J.E., Lancaster, L. and Crow, S. (2011) 'Therapeutic factors affecting the cognitive behavioral treatment of bulimia nervosa via telemedicine versus face-to-face delivery', *International Journal of Eating Disorders*, 44, 6, pp. 687–91.

Fong, Y. and Wing, S.Y.K. (2007) 'Longitudinal follow up of primary insomnia patients in a psychiatric hospital', *Australia and New Zealand Journal of Psychiatry*, 41, 7, pp. 611–17.

Garde, A.H., Albertsen, K., Persson, R., Hansen, A.M. and Rugulies, R. (2012) 'Directional associations between psychological arousal, cortisol, and sleep', *Sleep Medicine*, 10, 1, pp. 28–40.

(Continued)

(Continued)

Gibson, M.C. (2012) *Hypersomnia*, www.wikidoc.org/index.php/Hypersomnia, accessed 31 March 2012.

Harvard Medical School (2011) 'Overcoming insomnia: options include lifestyle changes, psychotherapy and medication', *Harvard Mental Health Letter*, 27, 8, pp. 3–5.

Helpguide (2013) *Can't Sleep?* www.helpguide.org/life/insomnia_treatment.htm, accessed 11 February 2013.

Hoek, H. and Hoeken, D. (2003) 'Review of the prevalence and incidence of eating disorders', *International Journal of Eating Disorders*, 34, 4, pp. 383–96.

Keski-Rahkonen, H., Hoek, H.W., Linna, M.S., Raevuori, A., Sihvla, E. and Bulik, C.M. (2009) 'Incidence and outcomes of bulimia nervosa: a nationwide population-based study', *Psychology of Medicine*, 39, 5, pp. 823–31.

Lockwood, R., Serpell, L. and Waller, G. (2012) 'Moderators of weight gain in the early stages of outpatient cognitive behavioral therapy for adults with anorexia nervosa', *International Journal of Eating Disorders*, 45, 1, pp. 51–6.

Long, C.G., Fitzgerald, K.A. and Hollin, C.R. (2012) 'Treatment of chronic anorexia nervosa', *Clinical Psychology and Psychotherapy*, 19, 1, pp. 1–13.

Long, C.G., Fitzgerald, K.A. and Hollin, C.R. (2012) 'Treatment of chronic anorexia nervosa', *Clinical Psychology and Psychotherapy*, 19, 1, p. 1.

Mehler, P.S. (2011) 'Medical complications of bulimia nervosa and their treatments', *International Journal of Eating Disorders*, 44, 2, pp. 95–104.

Mayo Clinic Staff (2011) *Insomnia Treatment: Cognitive Behavioral Therapy Instead of Sleeping Pills*, www.MayoClinic.com, accessed 12 March 2012.

Merwin, R. M., Timko, C.A., Moskovich, A.A., Ingle, K.K. Bulik, C.M. and Zucker, N.L. (2011) 'Psychological inflexibility and symptom expression in anorexia nervosa', *Eating Disorders*, 19, 1, p. 62–82.

N.A.M.E.D. (2011) *Males and Eating Disorders*, www.namedinc.org/statistics.asp, accessed 30 January 2013.

Nathan, P.E., Gorman, J.M. and Salkind, N.J. (1999) *Treating Mental Disorders: A Guide that Works* (Oxford, Oxford University Press).

National Sleep Foundation (2012) *Depression and Sleep*, www.sleepfoundation.org/article/sleep-topics/depression-and-sleep, accessed 1 April 2012

Newton, J.R., Freeman, C.P., Hannan, W.J. and Cowen, S. (1993) 'Osteoporosis and normal weight bulimia nervosa – which patients are at risk?', *Journal of Psychosomatic Research*, 37, 3, pp. 239–47.

NICE (2004) *Eating Disorders*, www.nice.org.uk/CG009quickreferenceguide, accessed 29 March 2012.

NINDS (2012) *Hypersomnia Information Page*, National Institute of Neurological Disorders and Stroke, www.ninds.nih.gov/disorders/hypersomnia.htm, accessed 30 March 2012.

Nordo, R.H.S., Ragnfrid, H.S., Espeset, E.M.S., Gulliksen, K.S., Skarderud, F. and Holte, A. (2006) 'The meaning of self-starvation: qualitative study of patients' perception of anorexia nervosa', *International Journal of Eating Disorders*, 39, 7, pp. 556–64.

Pinheiro, A.P., Root, T. and Bulik, C.M. (2009) 'The genetics of anorexia nervosa: current findings and future perspectives', *International Journal of Child and Adolescent Health*, 2, 2, pp. 153–64.

PsychNet-UK (2012) *Hypersomnia*, www.psychnet-uk.com/x_new_site/DSM_IV/hypersomnia.html, accessed 1 April 2012.

Right Diagnosis (2012) *Sleep Disorder*, www.rightdiagnosis.com/h/hypersomnia/stats.htm, accessed 31 March 2012.

Riley, W.T., Mihm, P. Behar, A. and Morin, C.M. (2010) 'A computer device to deliver behavioral interventions for insomnia', *Behavioral Sleep Medicine*, 8, 1, pp. 2–15.

Rye, D.B., Bilwise, D.L., Parker, K., Trotti, L.M., Saini, P., Fairley, J., Freeman, A., Garcia, P.S., Owens, M.J., Ritchie, J. and Jenkins, A. (2012) 'Sleep-modulation of vigilance in the primary hypersomnias by endogenous enhancement of GABA receptors', *Science Traditional Medicine*, 4, 161, pp. 151–61.

Rutigliano, A. (2012) *Anorexia Nervosa, an Issue of Control*, http://serendip.brynmawr.edu/bb/neuro03/web2/arutigliano.html, accessed 20 March 2012.

Shepard, G. (2012) Personal communication, 23 March 2012.

Smith, M. and Segal, J. (2012) *Bulimia Nervosa*, www.helpguide.org/mental/bulimia_signs_symptoms_causes_treatment.htm, accessed 22 March 2012.

Steinhauser, H. (2002) 'The outcome of anorexia nervosa in the 20th century', *The American Journal of Psychiatry*, 159, 8, pp. 1284–93.

Swenne, I., Belfrage, E. Thurfjell, B. and Egstrom, I. (2005) 'Accuracy of reported weight and menstrual status in teenage girls with eating disorders', *International Journal of Eating Disorders*, 38, 4, pp. 375–9.

Tamara, S. (2012) *Insomnia Statistics*, http://sleepcottage.com/insomnia-statistics/ accessed 1 April 2012.

Tolle, D. (2012) *Causes of Oversleeping*, www.ehow.com/about_5076826_causes-oversleeping.html, accessed 1 April 2012

US Department of Health and Human Services (2012) *Specific Guidelines for Bulimia Nervosa*, www.guideline.gov/content.aspx?id=9318, accessed 30 March 2012.

Vardi, B. (2012) Personal communication, 23 March 2012.

WebMD (2012) *Sleep Less Eat More*, www.webmd.com/sleep-disorders/news/20120314/sleep-less-eat-more, accessed 30 March 2012.

Wildes, J.E., Robert, E.E. and Simons, A.D. (2001) 'The roles of ethnicity and culture in the development of eating disturbance and body dissatisfaction: a meta-analytic review', *Clinical Psychology Review*, 21, 4, pp. 521–51.

Zhang, J., Lam, S.P., Li, S.X., Lai, K.W. and Wing, Y.K. (2011) 'Longitudinal course and outcome of chronic insomnia in Hong Kong children: a 5-year study of a community cohort', *Sleep*, 34, 10, pp.1395–402.

8

Substance Dependence

LEARNING OBJECTIVES FOR THIS CHAPTER

- Identify behavioural addictions
- Gain insight into theoretical perspectives on substance and behavioural dependence
- Know about the three categories of illegal drugs
- Learn that specific theories are supported empirically
- Discuss the key concepts of substance dependence

The British Medical Association (BMA) (2009) state that individuals are addicted if they crave and depend on a drug such as alcohol, heroin, cocaine or morphine, and that if the intake of drug is reduced or stopped the consequence is a psychological and or physiological sign of distress such as feeling anxious and or trembling. The BMA further declare that extensive use of a substance can elicit a psychological feeling of being warmly at peace and unconcerned about any situation as well as a physiological tolerance of its use, resulting in a need for an increase in the amount of the substance used in order to produce the same effect.

CURRENT PERSPECTIVES ON PROBLEMATIC AND DEPENDENT USE OF SUBSTANCES

Up to the end of the twentieth century, the term 'drug addict' was used within the field of therapy when referring to a person who was physically or psychologically dependent on a substance. However, the current perspective is that such an individual has a 'substance dependency'. 'Substance' refers to toxins (such as inhalants) as well as drugs.

During the late part of the twentieth century, a substance disorder was perceived as present when the user manifested with one or more of these four characteristics:

1 Interpersonal problems, such as marital issues, parenting concerns or social problems linked to substance use.
2 Illegal activity linked to using substances, for example, drug dealing or underage drinking.
3 The substance being used in a place that may be hazardous to the user, for example, drinking and driving.
4 Problems related to the substance user's school or work, such as non-attendance, being suspended or not finishing tasks on time (Nathan, Gorman and Salkind, 1999).

Currently, the view is that although a substance user may not be dependent, there is still a problem if any of the characteristics numbered above are present. There is therefore a possibility of having a problem with taking substances without being dependent on them; for example, some people may feel obliged to drink alcohol and become intoxicated in order to fit in to a social group.

Substances can be divided into two main categories: legal and illegal. There is currently a huge issue with 'legal highs' which many therapists working with young people are dealing with (US Food and Drug Administration, 2012).

LEGAL SUBSTANCES

Legal substances include tobacco, alcohol and caffeine. It is possible to have dependency problems with legal substances, and/or feel social pressure to take them. Medicinal drugs are also legal, under certain circumstances.

Prescription drugs

If drugs are accessed with a prescription, they are not illegal as long as they are used in the way that is prescribed, and used by the person the prescription is for. Often, it is the case that drugs should not be mixed. otherwise, drug interaction occurs.

Drug interactions

If two drugs are taken simultaneously, and one of the drugs has an effect on the other, drug interaction is occuring (this is why, for example, many prescribed and over-the-counter drugs should not be taken with alcohol). This can either decrease the drug effect (be antagonistic) or increase it (be synergistic), or there can be a different effect that cannot be produced by taking one of the drugs alone. Drug-food interactions also exist: for example, if taking anti-depressants containing monoamine oxidase and a food containing tyramine (such as smoked meats, chocolate or fermented foods), then hypertension may occur (US Food and Drug Administration, 2012). Drug interaction can also happen between a drug and herbs, for example, aspirin is affected by ginseng, warfarin by St John's wort (hypericumperforatum) and anticoagulants by ginger (US Drug and Food Administration, 2012). It is important that a therapist has some psychopharmacological knowledge, because if a client, whether wittingly or unwittingly, takes two drugs (or more) their interaction may produce a heightened risk of side effects, or one drug may increase the effect of the other and cause an overdose. Conversely, if a drug's effect is decreased, therapeutic effect may not be of any use due to underdose.

Caffeine

Some daily household substances, not normally thought of as drugs, can be addictive, such as sugar (Conason, 2012), but there is one substance that is worldwide by far the most popular legal drug (Magithia, 2012): caffeine. This mind-altering drug is found in many plants and is ingested widely in various substances such as tea, cola nut, guarana, cocao pod and coffee. It is said that 100 grams of caffeine can lead to dependence and withdrawal symptoms upon abstinence, yet an average of

280 milligrams daily are taken in the United States per adult (Griffiths, Juliano and Chausmer, 2003). Caffeine can be linked to numerous psychological issues such as dependence, sleep problems, withdrawal, anxiety and intoxification. Low doses (less than 200 milligrams) can produce feelings of well-being in those not accustomed to it, while large doses (more than 200 milligrams) can produce feelings of negativity, though individual differences vary considerably (Griffiths, Juliano and Chausmer, 2003).

Caffeine theory and research

Caffeine is one of the most researched drugs with a consequent enormous amount of literature on it. However, most investigations either focus on an extremely limited area or are conducted by people with little background in scientific research (Spiller et al., 2006). Therefore, theories such as 'it takes a week to stop being dependent on caffeine' tend not to be backed up by valid and reliable findings (Democratic, 2010).

Caffeine dependence symptoms, prevalence, intervention and expected outcome

Signs of being dependent on caffeine include feeling dizzy, tired, having poor concentration, being sleepy in the day and suffering from headaches and moodiness unless caffeine is consumed. Prevalence is unknown, although a vast number feel the need for it to feel alert.

Caffeine increases dopamine levels in the brain just as some other drugs do, including heroin, amphetamines and cocaine. Repeated use can lead to greater amounts of caffeine being ingested daily. Outcomes of taking too much caffeine can include high blood pressure, difficulty with fine motor skills, shaking and increased respiration rate. A gradual decrease in taking this drug is an appropriate intervention. There are many caffeine-free drinks available that can be taken instead.

Caffeine in practice

Within clinical practice, it is not uncommon to come across clients who consume a large quantity of caffeine and feel anxious or suffer from panic attacks. It may be wise, therefore, for them to either reduce intake of this drug or avoid it altogether. If totally avoided, clients can experience signs of withdrawal such as feeling tired and irritable, having a headache and symptoms of influenza, and being sleepy with decreased motivation. Withdrawal may take seven days. However, approximately 900 milligrams of the drug, spread out throughout the day, can produce tolerance of it (Griffiths, Juliano and Chausmer, 2003). With the above information in mind, it may be best not to offer tea or coffee (with biscuits or anything sugary) to clients.

Alcohol

Consuming alcohol to 'wind down' (and coffee to 'perk up'), is not rare. This drug can be very pleasurable. Indeed, most adults in the western world celebrate important occasions such a new year or weddings with alcohol. It is socially acceptable, legally available and can grease communication mechanisms at social gatherings. Yet alcohol can be dangerous due to its addictive and depressant qualities. Individuals can easily cross the line of having a pleasant drink to drinking at a level that causes damage. Although it is possible to drink too much while not being addicted, if a client is dependent on the drug, their dependency must be addressed. Drinking excessively is dangerous. If dependent on alcohol, it feels as if alcoholic consumption is a necessary part of life. Withdrawal can be fatal, therefore it is crucial that any withdrawal is undertaken under medical supervision. Psychological dependence can also cause severe problems: broken marriages, severed friendships, lost jobs, depression and health problems. In my search, I have not found evidence to show that any amount of alcohol is safe: one drink can cause a car crash; binging once can result in dangerous bleeding from the stomach (Butler and Hope, 1999). Unmistakenly, staying below the recommended limit for alcohol consumption is important, as is the importance of learning to say 'no' clearly and convincingly.

ALCOHOL MISUSE CASE VIGNETTE

Enya and Hans seemed the perfect couple. They had one daughter, one son, a house with a garden and a pedigree cat. They had graduated from different universities and first met one another in their early twenties at their local amateur dramatic society. Both had followed their chosen careers. Hans knew that Enya liked to drink alcohol but did not realise that there was a problem. Only years later, when she was dismissed from work due to not doing her job properly, and when she started shouting at their children, hitting the pet and was verbally abusive to Hans, did he spot that she had a drink problem. Hans noticed that the time Enya required to recover from her drinking bouts was becoming longer and the marital problems that her drinking behaviour caused seemed insurmountable, dwarfing all other problems between them. Consequently, he divorced her and obtained custody of their children, as well as keeping the house and cat. Enya lost everything – her family, career and home.

Feeling isolated and afraid of her situation deteriorating from bad to worse, Enya sought support from her GP who referred her to a substance abuse clinic where she voluntarily became an in-patient and complied with a detoxification programme, adhering to taking medication that reduced her craving while helping her to avoid a relapse. Having gone through this process, she became an out-patient. She now attends local Alcoholics Anonymous meetings and sees a therapist who works for an agency on a voluntary basis. Enya shares her deepest thoughts with the therapist who uses CBT, because this is what he understands to be of value with clients who have a substance issue, due to evidence based on his clinical experience.

What Enya finds particularly helpful from her therapist is social skills training which focuses on developing her assertiveness and communications techniques. Also importantly, Enya's nutrition is improved because she follows the advice of a nutritionist whom her therapist referred her to for added support. She continues attending the AA meetings where she has made a few friends with whom she can disclose her emotions – at the meetings, it is the community reinforcement that she experiences as most helpful. Though she takes each day as it comes, and nothing for granted, due to support gleaned, Enya is able to deal with the ups and downs of daily life in an appropriately effective way, rather than use alcohol.

ILLEGAL DRUGS

Illegal drugs are divided into classes A, B and C:

- Class A drugs include ecstasy, LSD, heroin, morphine, cocaine and methadone; they are considered the most addictive or dangerous.
- Class B drugs include amphetamine, cannabis and dihydrocodeine; they are considered addictive but not as much so as Class A drugs.
- Class C drugs include GHB, temazepam, valium and temgesic; they are considered addictive but not as much so as Class B drugs (SDEA, 2012).

Drug-dependency consequences

Almost all legal or illegal drugs resulting in dependence increase levels of dopamine in the brain, producing pleasurable feelings. Since drug taking produces more dopamine, the brain adapts over time to produce less dopamine, resulting in less pleasure being experienced. Therefore, the dependent person takes more and more of their drug of choice, attempting to buffer the unpleasant experience of withdrawal and experience the same level of pleasurable feeling they previously achieved. Unfortunately, this dependence can over-ride the area of the brain dealing with decision making (the pre-frontal cortex) and which is related to the ability to delay short-term gratification for a long-term goal. Sadly, such dependence (whether to legal or illegal substances) can lead to brain damage (MedHelp, 2012).

Cannabis

Only cannabis is discussed here because although many therapists work with people who use other substances, according to the United Nations, cannabis is the most favoured of the illegal drugs, worldwide (2011). It is known by various names, such as weed, skunk, pot, grass, marihuana, hash or hashish and, when smoked, a joint. In most countries, cannabis is illegal, however it is legal in Canada, Austria, Spain and the Netherlands if used medicinally.

Cannabis theory and research

A popular misconception is that cannabis is harmless. However, delta-9-tetrahydrocannabinol (THC), the main active chemical in it (Narconon, 2012), quickly travels from the lungs to the bloodstream and so is taken to the brain and other organs all over the body. When there is withdrawal from this chemical, stress increases. Investigations indicate that the risk of suffering a heart attack increases fourfold during the first hour after smoking cannabis (Mittleman, Lewis and Maclure, 2001; Buddy, 2012), and another research investigation, studying 450 people who often smoked cannabis (without tobacco), found them to have more health problems and sick leave (due to respiratory illnesses) than non-smokers (Polen, Sidney and Tekawa, 1993). Certain research also shows that smoking cannabis may be more dangerous than smoking tobacco (for example, Sridhar, Raub and Weatherby, 1994; Grimes, 2012). Mounting investigations link cannabis use with problems such as schizophrenia (see for example, Harrison, 2012) and other long-term detrimental effects when taken by young people (see NIH, 2012).

Cannabis dependence signs, prevalence, intervention and expected outcome

Symptoms of cannabis intake are a rise in heart rate and drop in blood pressure (Riedel and Davies, 2005). Other signs include impaired short-term working memory, such as forgetting the reason for going upstairs; changes in mood, for instance violent mood-swings; and changes in perception, for example hallucinating (Science Direct, 2008). Long-term effects are inconclusive (Science Direct, 2009). I have not found any valid and reliable information on cannabis dependence, although what has emerged is that in the USA, the number of people dependent on cannabis is less than one per cent (Stinson et al., 2006). More recent research shows that one in ten who buy the drug become dependent on it (ADAI, 2012). Interventions for cannabis dependence recommended by NICE, are psychosocial (2007). Regarding cannabis intake outcome, death is rare and mostly due to hashish oil injected straight into a vein. I have not discovered evidence to suggest that smoking a joint can be fatal. Valid and reliable research on all forms of cannabis use is limited so researchers continue debating whether its use causes dependence: the medical journal the *Lancet*, for example, has ranked it as one of the least harmful drugs (Nutt et al., 2007); yet other research (Hickman et al., 2007) revealed a causal relationship between cannabis and schizophrenia.

DRUG ABUSE CASE VIGNETTE

Victor works as a therapist in a clinic for drug dependency. He is on a late shift and knows there is only one available bed for an in-patient.

Pamela, in her early thirties and addicted to heroin, shows signs of withdrawal. She has muscle spasms, stomach cramps, cold tremors and a pounding heart. She asks to see a medical doctor for some drugs to see her through until the morning. When Victor refuses, she becomes angry and threatens that she will steal and may even harm someone, shouting that she is likely to kill herself unless she is given what she wants. Eventually, Pamela practically begs to be given the drug of her choice and a bed for the night.

However, Lynne, a woman in her late fifties, also arrives at the hospital, with a neighbour. She looks unkempt and is sweating and trembling. The neighbour says that he found her trying to open her garage door, saying that she had to enter for her shop work, but the neighbour knew that she stopped working in a shop when she was fifty. She has a big belly, her hands shake and there are red thread veins on her face. There is a smell of alcohol on her breath; she sweetly says that she does not have a problem with alcohol, although she did have some to drink earlier but cannot remember how much. Lynne also politely says that it is not necessary for her to have a bed at the clinic.

Victor knows that the heroin addict is manipulative, saying anything that may get her drugs in order to get relief from her withdrawal symptoms. He also knows that Pamela is not in severe danger and so he refers her to an out-patient drug recovery programme for detoxification and therapy.

From Victor's understanding, Lynne is in more danger due to her withdrawal symptoms from alcohol. He witnesses her signs of delirium tremors that can lead to death. Victor sees to it that she is given the remaining bed and immediate medical attention. After her detoxification process, Victor supports her through a social-model residential programme, which Lynne complies with. Over a period of time, she is well enough to become an out-patient. Therapy is a very important part of her healing process. She remains 'dry' after eighteen months, is able to sit with others who consume alcohol, and say 'no' to drink.

SUBSTANCE AND BEHAVIOURAL DEPENDENCE

Just as a person who is dependent on a substance feels compelled to take it, so an individual who feels compelled to perform a certain behaviour can be described as being addicted to that behaviour. Behavioural addiction can include gambling, internet, exercise, sex and shopping.

Unsurprisingly, the notion that addictive behaviour is learnt is considered seriously. A relatively new way of looking at how behaviour is acquired and maintained is known as Mower's (Klein, 2012). Mower considers a two-pronged approach for explaining any type of behaviour: acquisition and maintenance. The acquisition stage explains how a specific behaviour is gleaned. For instance, an association is built between a substance and relaxation, or gambling and excitement, or there is also the possibility that seeing others enjoying a substance or, for example, seeing lottery winners in the media, initiates the same actions in certain individuals. This type of learning is known as social learning. During the maintenance stage, seeing others experience a sense of pleasure from a substance, or a buzz from gambling, acts as reinforcement; for example, a person then chooses to take a drug of choice in search of that positive after-effect. The initial positive feeling from taking a chemical substance or from, for example, winning at gambling, acts as a further re-enforcer, and so makes the behaviour more likely to occur again in the future. In order to maintain behaviour, an irregular re-enforcer is necessary. Throughout amusement arcades, bingo halls and casinos, for example, reinforcement is not regular – if the gambling behaviour is not stopped, dependence continues on the promise of the eventual irregular 'reward'.

This type of conditioning (reinforcement), is very powerful in explaining dependence, whether to a substance or behaviour; although the explanation can be criticised as being reductionist. They do not explain the fact that most of us are exposed to similar opportunities and pressures from our society yet few of us have a problem with dependency, or take into account issues such as differences between individual thinking processes.

DEPENDENCE, THEORY AND RESEARCH

Why, precisely, do some become dependent when others, do not? There are two main theories: biological and psychological. The biological theory of dependence on a drug or behaviour is that the dependence results from something physical, such as brain chemistry, which is hereditary, passed down by a particular gene (McLellan, Lewis and O'Brien, 2009). This biological model provides a reductionist view of complex behaviour regarding dependence, and does not account for the complexities of a person's disposition, situation, cultural background and social environment.

The psychological theory is that dependence can be learnt either by conditioning (where a response becomes more frequent due to reinforcement or reward) or social learning (due to having learnt such dependence from someone else, either by having that person as a model for their actions, observing or imitating them), as explained above. There are two sides to the psychological theory. The first is the cognitive theoretical perspective, that dependence on a substance or behaviour is a result of dysfunctional thoughts; that is, faulty thinking. The other is the social theory view, that dependence is a result of a weak character coupled with situational variables. Importantly, specific research backs up the theory that environment and social factors, rather than heredity, are crucial for dependence (NIDA, 2008).

However, the American Academy of Child and Adolescent Psychiatry found that children whose parents abused alcohol were four times more likely to experience drink problems (AACAP, 2011). Although this information alone does not exclude the notion that a shared environment can be a contributing factor, this tendency towards alcoholic problems remained in children who were adopted by parents who did not have alcohol issues. Therefore, at first sight, this information seems to link with the medical theory that specific genes are related to substance abuse, particularly alcohol (Agrawal and Lynskey, 2008). But it is not easy finding a bank of valid and reliable research that can support this model. However, quite a lot of recent investigations show that the effects of in-utero alcohol exposure can be extremely detrimental to health, not only of the foetus but also after birth throughout the youngster's developmental years and eventually as an adult (see for example,

Government of Western Australia, 2013). Yet, one contributing factor relating to dependence may be that particular genes might predispose a person to exhibitionism (Goldman and Fishbein, 2000). However, the work of Tabery (2007) disputes the gene theory. Nevertheless research links attention-seeking to both gambling (Aasved, 2003) and alcohol problems (Blaney and Millon, 2008).

DEPENDENCY IN PRACTICE

There is much literature on dependence but full-time therapists usually have little time to read the latest relevant information; although it is important for them to keep up with the recent literature. It seems to me that within daily clinical practice, it is important to work with clients while bearing in mind clinical outcomes. When, for instance, faced with a client disclosing an issue such as substance dependence, instead of trying to talk the client into pre-existing treatments, using practice-based-evidence to tailor a programme for the individual client may be wiser. Psychologist Miller and his team (2005: 52) explain, 'imagine a treatment system in which clients are full and complete partners in their care, where their voice is used to structure and direct treatment … Notes and documentation will report events in treatment that have a direct bearing on outcome … Better to know what is working or not in the here and now, than … failure down the road'.

DISCUSSION

Research offering a simple explanation in support of a theory is seductive, but we need to remember to consider it with a broad view. A way to resist such seduction is by gaining a fuller perspective of what is being focused on while bearing in mind that the brain works in multiple ways. For example, one chemical can produce apparently incongruent results: nicotine, for instance, seems to decrease stress while increasing arousal – this seems an impossible state to be in! When we focus on gene theory, we see that it has implications for addictions but it does not offer an explanation regarding why there are many who are not dependent on a drug or behaviour, yet who do have that particular variant of gene. The gene DRD2, for example, which has been linked to those who feel that they must gamble, drink alcohol and smoke nicotine (Lowinson and Ruiz, 2011), can be found in a quarter of the population. Assuming that most of this population does not have a dependency issue, why they do not, when some do, is a mystery. Further, this gene is not found in many who do have a dependency problem. Nevertheless, the DRD2 gene has a role relating to dopamine pathways so it may seem an obvious candidate for playing a part in the process of addiction. Those with this gene have fewer dopamine receptors, so keeping in mind the basic role that dopamine plays in dependency issues, in order to obtain the presumed amount of pleasure that the majority of the population have, it may be deemed necessary for them to take part in perceived pleasurable activities such as drinking (more) alcohol.

This may also help to explain why those who are impoverished, either due to an unstimulating environment or poverty, and therefore might not experience themselves as having pleasurable lives, may seek compensation by taking 'pleasurable' substances (for example drugs) or by certain behaviours (for instance gambling); in a more stimulating, wealthy and pleasurable environment, it may not be perceived as necessary to engage in such actions. Although this example is more complicated than a simpler medical one, because there seems to be an overlap with the biological and psychological models, gene theory might explain the reason why, out of a number of individuals experiencing the same situational stimulus, some do not develop dependency problems while others do.

AGE, GENDER AND CULTURE

Although it is considered taboo to link senior citizens with dependency problems, approximately a third of those described as alcoholics do not develop dependency until after retirement. In post-retirement women, sleeping tablet and tranquillizer abuse are not uncommon. For many in their sixth decade and beyond, retirement is coupled with decreased contact with their surrounding culture and social interaction. This can leave people feeling empty, thinking that life is pointless; they may be at a loss regarding how to structure their days, and so can become vulnerable to misusing substances such as alcohol.

With regard to younger people, a drug such as tobacco is what many children become dependent on. They may think that smoking is 'cool', and therefore persevere beyond the nasty experience of a first cigarette; perhaps thinking that smoking is a 'grown-up' activity and not realising that they can become dependent on nicotine, very quickly. Alarmingly, approximately one-quarter of teenagers in the USA are at risk of nicotine-dependence (Hu, Davies and Kandel, 2006).

In the UK, teenage alcohol abuse is a problem, yet apparently perceived by many young people as acceptable. Disturbingly, if teenagers drink before they are fifteen they are seven times more likely to be in a car crash, and eleven times more likely to be unintentionally injured after drinking, when compared to other teens (Alcohol Education Trust, 2012). Binge drinking (not uncommon when young people go out together (Chainey, 2011)) is harmful and when alcohol is consumed by pre-teens or teens, it is very harmful indeed, risking, as time goes by, particular cancers, especially liver and oral, as well as high blood pressure and heart disease.

CONCERN

Teenage drinking has a detrimental effect on society (it behoves government to address this). Although many people visit their GP when there is a problem, being dependent on a substance or behaviour does not fit in with the medical model of psychopathology. One reason is that in certain social settings drinking is seen as acceptable (see above), as is taking cannabis in some societies. Unravelling a dependence problem is not straightforward because in many cases, substance dependence signals an underlying problem. For instance, alcohol can numb the emotions; an individual may therefore turn to drink when a loved one dies in order to numb the overwhelming feeling of grief. These underlying issues may explain the high relapse rate (approximately 75 per cent) following a purported cure (Soberplace, 2009).

Points to ponder

- Intriguingly, the Yi, a Chinese indigenous people, like to consume alcohol. When in their rural environment this consumption does not significantly impact on their health; however, when they move to a city and feel disconnected from social support there is a sharp increase in problems associated with alcohol consumption, such as a rise in blood pressure attributed to alcohol use, rather than to any other factor (Page, Damon and Moellering, 1974; McTaggart, 2011).
- If an individual is dependent on a behaviour then he or she feels compelled to perform it, increasingly even at the expense of friends and family. How can such dependence be differentiated from enthusiasm for a project? Perhaps for the enthusiast, the behaviour adds quality to life, whereas

for the one who is dependent, as with substance dependency, withdrawing from the behaviour causes trembling and irritability. Might these signs also occur though, if we are stopped from doing what enthuses us?

- If caffeine dependence is widespread, why do some therapists have tea and coffee available for clients?
- Alarmingly, if alcohol and tobacco were to be classified within the current A, B and C system, then they would be categorised as Class A and B drugs, respectively (Science and Nature, 2012).
- Why is it that only a minority of people exposed to drugs become dependent on them?
- There is a fine line between being a work addict and working long hours due to external pressure.

Exercise

(Answers are embedded within this chapter.)

1   Which drug withdrawal symptoms can be more dangerous, alcohol or heroin?
2   Why might it not be a good idea to offer a client tea or coffee?
3   Is there an amount of alcohol intake that is not dangerous?
4   Which class of drugs are considered to be the most addictive and harmful, A, B or C?
5   Can behavioural addiction be learned?

CHAPTER SUMMARY

Substance dependence is commonly known as drug addiction.

Compulsive use of a substance means that a person is dependent on it.

A person can use a substance without being dependent on it.

Individuals can feel addicted to certain behaviours, such as gambling.

Relapse rate after attending a recovery programme is high.

Illegal drugs are categorised into classes: A (most addictive and dangerous), B, and C (least addictive).

Dependence on a behaviour or substance tends to mask an underlying problem.

LIST OF USEFUL RESOURCES

- Coltart, C.E.M. and Gilmore, I. (2012) 'The need for a global alcohol strategy: upscaling the issue in a downstreaming environment', *Clinical Medicine*, 12, 1, pp. 29–34.
- Fortney, J., Tripathi, S., Walon, M., Cunnignham, R. and Booth, B. (2011) 'Patterns of substance abuse treatment seeking following cocaine-related emergency department visits', *Journal of Behavioral Health Services and Research*, 38, 2, pp. 221–33.

(Continued)

(Continued)

- Jongsma, A.E. Jr. and Bruce, T.J. (2012) *Evidence-based Treatment Planning for Substance Abuse DVD Workbook* (Evidence-based Psychotherapy Treatment Planning Video Series) (Chichester, Wiley John and Sons).
- Larson, J.M. (1997) *Seven Weeks to Sobriety* (New York, Fawcett Books).
- Murray, R., Leonardie-Bee, Marsh, J.L. and Britton, J. (2012) 'Smoking status ascertainment and interventions in acute medical patients', *Clinical Medicine*, 12, 1, pp. 59–62.
- Rudd, B. (2009) *EQ* (card game) (Milton Keynes, Speechmark).
- Rudd, B. (2010) *Problem Solving* (game) (Milton Keynes, Speechmark).
- Scott, T., Rotgers, W. and Rotgers, F. (eds) (2012) *Treating Substance Abuse: Theory and Technique*, Fourth Edition (New York, The Guilford Press).

RELEVANT WEBSITES

www.cmhc.com/guide/substance.htm

www.drugnet.net/behavioral-addictions

www.drugs.indiana.edu/

www.health.org/aboutn.htm

www.herbs2000.com/disorders/addictions.htm

REFERENCES

AACAP (2011) *Children of Alcoholics*, www.aacap.org/cs/root/facts_for_families/children_of_alcoholics, accessed 7 May 2012.

Aasved, M.J. (2003) *The Biology of Gambling* (Illinois, Charles C. Thomas).

ADAI (2012) *Dependence on Marijuana*, http://adai.uw.edu/marijuana/factsheets/dependence.htm, accessed 29 January 2013.

Agrawal, A. and Lynskey, M.A. (2008) 'Are there genetic influences on addiction: evidence from family, adoption and twin study', *Addiction*, 103, 7, pp. 1069–81.

Alcohol Education Trust (2012) *Facts and figures – Overview* www.dmdhwebspace.co.uk/AIM/Pages/factfig.html, acessed 11 February 2013.

APA (2002) *DSM-IV-TR® Diagnostic and Statistical Manual of Mental Disorders* (Fourth Edition, revised) (Vancouver, American Psychiatric Association).

Blaney, P.H. and Millon, T. (eds) (2008) *Oxford Textbook of Psychopathology*, Second Edition (Oxford, Oxford University Press).

British Medical Association (2009) *Addiction*, www.bma.org.uk, accessed 25 April 2012.

Buddy, T. (2012) *The Health Effects of Marijuana* http://alcoholism.about.com/od/pot/a/effects.-Lya.htm, accessed 14 February 2013.

Butler, G. and Hope, T. (1999) *Manage Your Mind* (Oxford, Oxford University Press).

Chainey, T.A. (2011) *'Let's get wasted!' A Discourse Analysis of Teenagers' Talk about Binge Drinking* (Manawatu New Zealand, Massey University).

Conason, A. (2012) *Is Abstinence the Best Treatment for Sugar Addiction?*, www.psychology-today.com/blog/eating-mindfully/201204/sugar-addiction, accessed 26 April 2012.

Democratic (2010) *How Long Does it Take to Kick a Caffeine Addiction?*, www.democratic underground.com, accessed 1 May 2012.

Goldman, D. and Fishbein, D.H. (2000) 'Genetic bases for impulsive and antisocial behaviors – can their course be altered?', in D.H. Fishbein (Ed.), *The Science, Treatment, and Prevention of Antisocial Behaviors: Application to the Criminal Justice System* pp. 914–19 (Kingston, Civic Research Institute).

Government of Western Australia (2013) *Foetal Alcohol Spectrum Syndrome (FASD)* www.communities.wa.gov.au/parents/parentingresources/Documents/Foetal_Alcohol_Spectrum_Disorder_FASD_Booklet.pdf, accessed 11 February 2013.

Grimes, S. (2012) *Marijuana Health Dangers Underestimated Study Shows* www.ksl.com/?nid=1012&sid=20737065, accessed 14 February 2013.

Harrison, P. (2012) *More Evidence Cannabis Use Linked to Schizophrenia* www.medscapecom/viewarticle/774128, accessed 14 February 2013.

Griffiths, R.R., Juliano, L.M., and Chausmer, A.L. (2003) 'Caffeine pharmacology and clinical effects', in Graham, A.W., Schwaltz, T.K., Mayo-Smith, M.F., Ries, R.K. and Wilford, B.B. (eds) *Principles of Addiction Medicine*, Third Edition (New York, American Society of Addiction) pp. 193–224.

Hickman, M., Vickerman, P., Macleod, J., Kirkbride, J., and Jones, P.B. (2007) 'Cannabis and schizophrenia model projections of the impact of the rise in cannabis use on historical and future trends in schizophrenia in England and Wales', *Addiction*, 102, 4, pp. 579–606.

Hu, M., Davies, M. and Kandel, D. (2006) 'Epidemiology and correlates of daily smoking and nicotene dependence among young adults in the United States', *American Journal of Public Health*, 96, 2, pp. 299–308.

Klein, S. (2012) *Learning* (London, Sage).

Lowinson, E. and Ruiz, P. (eds) (2011) *Substance Abuse: A Comprehensive Textbook*, Fifth Edition (Philadelphia, Lippincott Williams and Wikins).

Magithia, N. (2012) *Caffeine: Understanding the World's Most Popular Psychoactive Drug*, www.jyl.org/features, accessed 26 April 2012,

McLellan, T.A., Lewis, D.C., and O'Brien, P.O. (2009) 'Drug dependence, a chronic medical illness: implications for treatment, insurance and outcome evaluation', *Journal of the American Medical Association*, 284, 13, pp. 1689–95.

McTaggart, L. (2011) *The Bond* (London, Hay House).

MedHelp (2012) *Do Opiates Cause Brain Damage?*, www.medhelp.org/posts/Addiction-Substance-Abuse/Do-opiates-cause-brain-damage/show/971944, accessed 8 May 2012.

Miller, S., Mee-Lee, D., Plum, B. and Hubble, M. (2005) 'Making treatment count: client-directed, outcome-informed clinical work with problem drinkers', *Psychotherapy in Australia*, 11, 4, pp. 42–56.

Mittleman, M.A., Lewis, R.A. and Maclure, M. (2001) 'Triggering myocardial infarction by marijuana', *Circulation*, 103, 23, pp. 2805–09.

Narconon (2012) FAQ *About Marijuana*, www.drugrehab.co.uk/marijuana_explained.htm, accessed 1 April 2012.

(Continued)

(Continued)

Nathan, P.E., Gorman, J.M. and Salkind, N.J. (1999) *Treating Mental Disorders – A Guide to What Works* (New York and Oxford, Oxford University Press).

NICE (2007) *Drug Misuse: Psychosocial Interventions*, http://publications.nice.org.uk/drug-misuse-cg51, accessed 30 April 2012.

NIDA (2008) *Drugs of Abuse*, http://m.drugabuse.gov/publications/topics-in-brief/tobacco-nicotine-research, accessed 7 May 2012.

NIH (2012) *Drug Facts: Marijuana* www.drugabuse.gov/publications.drugfacts/marijuana, accessed 11 February, 2013.

Nutt, D., King, L.A., Saulsbury, W. and Blakemore, C. (2007) 'Development of a rational scale to assess the harm of drugs of potential misuse', *The Lancet*, 369, 9566, pp. 1045–53.

Page, L.B., Damon, A. and Moellering, R.C. Jr. (1974) 'Antecedents of cardiovascular disease in six Solomon Island societies', *Circulation*, 49, 6, pp. 1132–46).

Polen, M.R., Sidney, S. and Tekawa, I.S. (1993) 'Healthcare use by frequent marijuana smokers who do not smoke tobacco', *Western Journal of Medicine*, 158, 6, pp. 596–601.

Riedel, N. and Davies, S.N. (2005) 'Cannabinoid function in learning, memory and plasticity', *Handbook of Experimental Pharmacology*, 168, 168, pp. 445–77.

Schneider, M. (2008) 'Puberty as a highly vulnerable developmental period for the consequences of cannabis exposure', *Addiction Biology*, 13, 2, pp. 253–63.

Science Direct (2008) *Long Term Effects of Exposure to Cannabis*, www.sciencedirect.com/science/article/pii/S1471489204001973, accessed 30 April 2012.

Science and Nature (2012) *Is Alcohol Worse Than Ecstasy?*, www.bbc.co.uk/sn/, accessed 07 May 2012.

SDEA (2012) *Drug Classes and Penalties*, www.sdea.police.uk/drugsinfo.htm, accessed 30 April 2012.

Soberplace (2009) *Common Relapse Rates in Drug Recovery*, http://soberplace.com/common-relapse-rates-in-drug-recovery/, accessed 7 May 2012.

Spiller, G.A., Smith, B.D., Gupta, U.L.M.S. and Gupta, B.S. (2006) *Caffeine* (Varanasi, CBC Press)

Sridhar, K.S., Raub, W.A. and Weatherby, N.L. Jr. (1994) 'Possible role of marijuana smoking as a carcinogen in the development of lung cancer at a young age', *Journal of Psychoactive Drugs*, 26, 3, pp. 285–8.

Stinson, F.S., Ruan, W.J., Pickering, R. and Grant, B.F. (2006) 'Cannabis use disorders in the USA: prevalence, correlates and co-morbidity', *Psychological Medicine*, 36, 10, pp. 1447–69.

Tabery, J.G. (2007) *From a Genetic Predisposition to an Interactive Predisposition: Rethinking the Ethical Implications of Research on Gene-Environment Interaction* http://d-scholarship.pitt.edu9465/1/Tabery-From.GenPre.to.IntPre.pdf, accessed 11 February 2013.

United Nations (2011) *The Cannabis Market*, www.unodc.org/documents/data-and-analysis/WDR2011/The_cannabis_market.pdf, accessed 29 January 2013.

US Food and Drug Administration (2012) *Drug Interaction Study Design, Data Analysis, Implications for Dosing, and Labeling Recommendations*, www.fdon.gov/downloads/Drugs/GuidanceComplianceRegulatoryInformation/Guidances/ucm292362.pdf, accessed 29 January 2013.

9

Psychotic Disorders

LEARNING OBJECTIVES FOR THIS CHAPTER

- Identify diagnostic criteria for psychotic problems
- Discuss theoretical perspectives relating to psychoses
- Understand relevant research on psychoses
- Realise that age, gender and culture can impact on psychotic disorders

---

'Psychosis' literally means a state of mind or soul that is not normal. It stems from the Greek 'psyche', meaning 'soul', and 'osis', meaning 'not normal'. This meaning has changed over time. The contemporary perspective is that there is more than one psychosis, relating to mental state (rather than soul). Psychoses are understood under the umbrella of psychotic disorders. These include:

- schizophrenia (if a sufferer has hallucinated or experienced delusions lasting at least one month)
- brief psychotic disorder (this lasts for more than twenty-four hours but disappears after four weeks)
- psychotic disorder due to a medical condition (for example, suffering from psychosis as a result of lime disease due to a tick bite)
- puerperal psychosis (this can appear within twenty-eight days of giving birth).

Psychotic disorders nest under the overall term of psychopathology, as are all the disorders discussed in this book. Importantly, the term 'psychotic' should not be confused with 'psychopathy'.

PSYCHOPATHY

Those suffering from psychopathy reportedly constitute approximately 1 per cent of the population (Hercz, 2012). They appear charming but will, without conscience, be uncouth; for example, fabricate part of their CV in order to obtain a post with high authority (Babiak and Hare, 2006). A child suffering from psychopathy might torture and kill animals, set buildings alight and be automatically defiant. Adults suffering from psychopathy may be highly intelligent and seem nice, yet they can murder; or they may appear full of confidence while having unrealistic life goals and behaving irresponsibly (for example, they drive while drunk and kill someone, yet are remorseless when sober and know about the death). This short section on psychopathy is included here not as a way of diagnosing, but to show that it is different from psychosis.

PSYCHOSIS

This is not a specific disorder, although those who suffer from any one particular psychosis, such as schizophrenia, can be described as suffering from one of the psychoses. This difference between the generic term 'psychosis' and a more specific one such as 'schizophrenia' is sometimes confused.

Various risk factors can produce signs of a psychosis, such as trauma, negative emotional processing and social adversity. Many of us have experienced signs of a psychosis along the continuum from normality to displaying subclinical signs to having a clinical disorder.

Psychosis symptoms

Signs of psychosis include hallucinations, delusions, catatonia and thought disturbance (Gelder, 2005).

Hallucinations

These can include hearing voices, seeing others, smelling aromas (either sweet or unsavoury), seeing lights and having a sensation of being touched, which others cannot detect. Especially distressing, yet not uncommon, is to hallucinate voices saying negative comments.

Delusions

These can be paranoid (primary delusions) and can also be related to the sufferer's culture (secondary delusions).

Primary delusions: the world or parts of it are rendered by sufferers in a radically different way. For example, believing that they are at war (when it is in fact peace time).

Secondary delusions: these are understandable, bearing in mind the delusional person's experience. For example, suffering from an extremely low mood and subsequently believing that they are responsible for a horrific act (not committed by them).

Catatonia

There are two types of catatonia: classic and agitated. If agitated, sufferers are so extremely agitated that contact with the outside world is lost. For example, they might walk rapidly and repeatedly in tight circles or perform other seemingly purposeless behaviours coupled with a preoccupation with thoughts. Agitated catatonia should not be confused with bi-polar mania. (Chapter 6 can be cross-referenced with this.)

Classic catatonia involves being 'frozen' in a position, yet another person can move it. For example, if a sufferer sits with a frozen posture, an onlooker can move the sufferer's arm straight up, and the sufferer will stay frozen in that new position. These behaviours are typical if they occur after the onset of psychosis and if sufferers do not react to whatever happens in their environment.

Thought disturbance

Due to an underlying disturbance, conscious thought is disordered, manifesting as disconnected writing and speaking ('word salad').

Psychosis causes

The causes of psychosis are stress related (see the section on stress, further down). They can be drug induced or due to environmental reasons. For example, stress is cumulative (unless appropriately dealt with), so a current stress may be 'the straw which breaks the camel's back' and may trigger a psychotic episode (brief reactive psychosis). Brief reactive psychosis often recovers spontaneously within two weeks. However, psychosis can also last for years.

Hallucinations can also occur without suffering psychosis; for example, immediately before falling asleep or immediately upon waking. Additionally, legal and illegal drugs (such as caffeine and heroin) might induce psychosis (Cardinal and Bulmore, 2011). Further, if severely deprived of sleep, or experiencing sensory deprivation, signs of primary psychosis may emerge.

Secondary psychosis can be a result of of medical problems, for example neurodegenerative disorders such as Alzheimer's (Lesser and Hughes, 2006) as well as some sleep disorders, for instance, when wakefulness overlaps with REM sleep-state. It can also be a result of poisoning from drugs, or autoimmune and related disorders such as Hashimoto's encephalopathy (Wilcox et. al., 2008), or nutritional deficiency (Bull, 2008).

Psychosis prevalence

Reportedly, approximately 2 per cent of the US (Versola-Russo, 2006) and UK (Kender et al., 2012) populations suffer from a psychosis. Sufferers of the psychosis known as schizophrenia are about 1 per cent of the population (International Mental Health Research Organization, 2012). Out of 1,000 women, twelve are hospitalised with puerperal psychosis, which can be described as extreme post-natal depression. The cause is unknown and there is very little research on this, although a link has been found between puerperal psychosis and factors outside hormonal imbalances, such as low birth weight of the infant and caffeine use (Hay, 2009). Certain literature states that cannabis users are twice as likely to develop psychosis than non-cannabis users (Leweke and Koethe, 2008).

Psychosis expected outcome

Although there is a popular belief that outcome is poor for those diagnosed with a psychosis such as schizophrenia, long-term outcome studies show that the majority improve greatly, leading normal lives (Kua and Wong 2003; Thara, 2004). Studies also suggest that outcome is good if psychosocial intervention is combined with minimal medication (for example, see Bola and Mosher, 2003).

Psychosis research

Particular research shows that there is significantly less grey matter in the brains of individuals suffering from psychosis when compared with non-sufferers (Pantelis et al., 2003). What is unclear is whether the problem of psychosis causes this apparent damage. Our brains depend on stimulus from the outside world. When we are deprived of this, we develop psychotic symptoms. Some elderly people, for example, who are isolated as a result of failing eyesight, hearing and mobility, may consequently become unrealistically suspicious (Howard, 2005).

According to evolutionary theory, with the reduced reproduction of those suffering from schizophrenia symptoms, the number of individuals who are diagnosed as having schizophrenia should be reduced (CARTA, 2012). Yet this is not the case; those suffering within the general population remain at approximately 1 per cent (Avila, Thaker and Adami, 2001). Why is this? Even as recently as the earliest years of the twenty-first century the perspective that environmental factors were contributing causes to schizophrenia was 'regarded as implausible. However, recent epidemiological findings have strongly challenged this view. A number of environmental factors are now accepted as influencing the development of schizophrenia. These include urban birth and rearing, cannabis use and birth complications' (Garety et al., 2007: 138).

Psychosis theory

One theory links dysfunctional dopamine processing with psychosis (Cooper, Mizrahi and Li, 2005): this suggests that it is caused by dopamine shots gone awry in the brain. 'The dopamine hypothesis of schizophrenia proposes that the psychotic symptoms of the disorder result from hyper-activity of the mesolimbic dopaminergic system, which fires and releases dopamine independent of cue and context, creating experiences of aberrant novelty and salience' (Garety et al., 2007: 1379). Confusingly, this contradicts research on alcohol-induced psychosis, which does not show dopamine-processing dysfunction, implying that psychosis emerges irrespective of dopamine activity (Seeman, Scharz and Chen, 2006). Another theory is that a genetic component influences susceptibility to acquiring a type of psychosis such as schizophrenia (Craddock, Donovan and Owen, 2006). Overall, experts in this field disagree with each other.

However, they do agree that being unable to discern between inner and outer reality is a crucial aspect of psychosis (Renn, 2007). For example, many hear voices knowing that others do not and therefore realise that the voices are not 'real'; consequently, they are not described as or considered to be psychotic. If, however, hallucinatory experiences affect the consensual perception of reality, then the person is considered to be psychotic. Psychosis is complex and our knowledge of it only scratches the surface!

Stress

While some theorise that the problem of psychosis is passed via genes (for example, Crow, 2008), others theorise that it is due to adverse experiences (see Pitfield and Openheim, 2006). Mounting evidence shows that the lynchpin for tipping a person from apparently normal to psychotic behaviour is overwhelming stress (Startup, Freeman and Garety, 2006; Wiles et al., 2006). Many contemporary investigators comment on the evidential link between persistent trauma during childhood and psychosis (for example, Segal et al., 2006). Doubtlessly, stress affects the brain; for this reason, suffering from one of the psychoses may be as a result of environmental stress.

Psychosis in practice

When faced with a case of a type of psychosis such as schizophrenia, CBT (Birchwood and Trower, 2006) coupled with FI (family interventions) has been found to support the client therapeutically (Garety, 2003). Indeed, specific research shows that CBT can not only delay the onset of psychosis but also prevent it (Paul and Morrison, 2004).

Sufferers of a psychosis are assumed to lack insight into their inner experiences and how they relate to the outer world. Background and culture are influential factors. Hence, if a therapist does not share or understand these factors when relating with clients, the therapist may label clients as psychotic. Additionally, clients may perceive their therapist as lacking insight!

SCHIZOPHRENIA

Stresses in life and the result of these, such as difficulties in processing negative experiences, can result in schizophrenia.

Schizophrenia signs

According to the DSM-IV-TR (APA, 2002) these incorporate:

- hallucinations
- negative signs (such as 'flattened' emotion)
- delusions
- very disorganised or catatonic behaviour
- disorganised speech.

(Symptoms may be different in the forthcoming DSM-V.)

SCHIZOPHRENIA CASE VIGNETTE

Distressing life experiences which Agnes had difficulty processing, low self-esteem, and social isolation caused her to feel anxious and depressed and resulted in her hearing voices that others did not. At fifty-five years old Agnes lived with her mother Helen, who often called her 'mad'. They both felt hopeless about Agnes's condition and were not keen on medication; previously, medicine had seemed to bury her emotions and making her lethargic, sitting silently slumped each day. The GP referred Agnes to a therapist who offered regular weekly therapy and used skilled supervision wisely.

It took the therapist three sessions to create enough rapport for Agnes to trust him. In the fourth session, she learnt about keeping a voices diary. Using Chadwick and Birchwood's (1994) cognitive model, the therapist viewed the voices as an event or antecedent/A.

During session five, Agnes started realising that a pattern was emerging: the voices occurred when she did a certain activity. For example, when walking over a bridge, she heard voices saying 'Jump'. Agnes also recognised that the voices intensified when she felt distressed, for instance when believing that strangers stared at her (so she cursed them), and less intense when she felt calm, for example when listening to her favourite music.

(Continued)

(Continued)

In the weeks that followed, her therapist supported Agnes in identifying coping strategies that reduced the voices' intensity. By the tenth session she realised that to some extent she controlled the voices.

What also emerged from her voices diary was that Agnes became distressed when hearing a voice making sexual innuendos, such as, 'Do something wild and juicy with the next handsome man passing you on the pavement'. This was viewed in the therapy session as a triggering event with the underlying thought of 'I must not think about sex; if I think it, then I am promiscuous, will catch an incurable disease and kill myself because I am wicked; I should not have such a thought'. This thought was identified as an automatic thought/AT. It also identified belief/B: 'I am promiscuous ... wicked'; and consequence/C: 'I ... will catch an incurable disease and kill myself' (Chadwick, Lees and Birchwood, 2000).

During the next four sessions, Agnes's distress about unusual fantasies were normalised through education and positive reframing (as in Chadwick, 2011); for example, by the therapist explaining that fantasising can enrich the creative part of us. In addition, Agnes made a prediction log to discover the likelihood of putting her fantasy of having sex with strangers into action and of being wicked.

During the following two sessions Agnes started to accept her thoughts as her imagination and became able to create alternative, logical rationales to replace her dysfunctional, irrational ones and to gain the insight that it was highly unlikely that she would put her fantasies into reality.

Agnes uncovered a sense of fear of not being in control that led to strict day-to-day scheduling. The therapist assisted her in a cost-benefit analysis (the costs and benefits of a strict schedule). Agnes's 'should' statements were also addressed, enabling her to realise that she need not be so rigid. Her adherence to the therapy plan was facilitated by activities scheduling. This was achieved by planning in detail in such a way that long-term goals could be done in small steps.

Meanwhile, the FI part of the programme enabled Agnes's mother to relate to her honestly and positively. On an ongoing basis, Agnes's adaptive coping strategies, such as reading aloud, were fortified, while her maladaptive ones such as shouting curses publicly, were discouraged. Consequently, her distress reduced significantly and her progress was steady. Although she still hears voices after finishing therapy, they do not distress her.

Problems related to categorising schizophrenia

It is possible to see schizophrenia signs in other disorders. These include:

- mood (affective) disorders – for example, if a person experiences a psychotic episode while depressed, they may have persecutory beliefs, self-blaming delusions or hallucinations
- some personality disorders – for example, borderline personality disorder or during particularly stressful periods
- obsessive compulsive disorder – for example, during thought processes when suffering from OCD.

Sadly, labelling individuals as having schizophrenia can be harmful and lead to stigma. Indeed, the issue of whether there is any scientific basis for such a diagnosis, is contentious (CASL, 2010). There is no valid and reliable research to back up such a diagnosis, due to conflicting findings of investigators.

Currently, the APA suggests that there will be no schizophrenia subtypes categorised within their forthcoming DSM-V. No agreement has been reached among psychiatrists about the main signs of schizophrenia (for example, see Boyle, 2002 and Bentall, 2003). Although agreement with the diagnosis was imposed with the DSM-IV-TR's checklist of symptoms, this spotlights the validity issue about the concept of schizophrenia. I am not alone in thinking that perhaps the notion of attributing schizophrenia to a client is unhelpful because of not having pinpointed a biological marker across every purported sufferer (Anckarsater, 2010).

Over two decades ago, research conducted by Lefly (1990) revealed that those with signs of schizophrenia fared better if living in the Third World and in a rural society that had strong kinship networks. The researchers suggested that this may have been a result of there seeming to be buffering mechanisms against major stressors in developing countries, opportunities for low-stress and non-competitive roles within the local community, and high tolerance for individual difference.

BRIEF PSYCHOTIC DISORDER

There is a paucity of research on this uncommon disorder that can guide evidence-based treatment. Signs of this condition (hallucinations and delusions) usually appear suddenly and do not last longer than four weeks. Definite causes are unknown, although the majority suffer after an extremely disturbing event. The remedy typically incorporates therapy, sometimes including medication (MedicineNet, 2012).

PSYCHOTIC DISORDER DUE TO A MEDICAL CONDITION

When there is evidence indicating that as a result of a general medical illness, a physiological condition has developed manifesting as hallucinations or delusions, then this mental disorder can be diagnosed (BehaveNet, 2012). Since such a problem stems from a physical illness, a therapist does not usually work with individuals suffering from it; rather, a medical team deals with their care.

PUERPERAL PSYCHOSIS

This manifests after childbirth as hearing or seeing things that others do not, or having beliefs not shared by others. These disturbing experiences can be described as dreaming while awake. They are profoundly disruptive to daily life, such as mother-to-baby communications, work and relationships. The sufferer believes that what is going on is real.

(What seems to be sorely lacking in the literature are studies regarding the role that the partner plays in the staving off (or otherwise) of puerperal psychosis.)

CURRENT PSYCHOLOGICAL DEBATES

Contemporary debates on the various types of psychoses embrace the argument that life events such as parental childhood deprivation contribute to a person developing a schema (a 'template' from which the world is viewed) that attributes control and power not to the self but to others. This skews cognitive processes that perceive life events and creates vulnerability towards mental problems such as depression and anxiety.

Although hallucinations and delusions at some time in life are not uncommon, these experiences can lead to one of the purported psychoses and we can be diagnosed, for instance, as

PUERPERAL PSYCHOSIS CASE VIGNETTE

Irene had been born by caesarean section. She was raised in a deprived inner-city area. When in her early teens a friend introduced her to cannabis. Her father, of African-American origin, left her mother and filed for divorce while she was in hospital having another baby. Consequently, Irene was left with her grandparents who looked after her until her mother was out of hospital.

As a single parent with a demanding infant, Irene's mother was unable to give Irene the attention she needed, and Irene did not want to bother her about the ongoing bullying and sexual abuse she experienced at school. She felt powerless and isolated, truanted from school as much as she could and spent most of her time day-dreaming. Feeling miserable and worthless, Irene believed that nobody wanted to befriend her. Her mother called her 'good-for-nothing' and Irene believed she was in her mother's way unless she stayed in her room.

Once she left school Irene married and became pregnant. She stopped taking cannabis while pregnant, but drank several cups of coffee daily 'to keep going'. Nine months after the wedding, she was in hospital having the baby. Her husband told her to 'shut-up' if she made sounds during labour. He was so badly behaved that the midwife insisted that he left the delivery room. Despite complications, Irene gave birth to a normal but rather under-weight baby. One week later, she was home.

Two weeks after delivery, Irene visited her doctor informing him that she was seeing dead people saying 'fall under a bus with baby'. On top of this, she believed that her parenting skills were not good enough, that she might harm the baby and that her husband was unsupportive. The doctor instigated a community-based psycho-support system. Her husband was educated by a visiting therapist on how to communicate positively with Irene, and be involved in looking after their infant. In this way, Irene felt supported by him. The couple were also taught parenting skills by a social worker, and the midwife made daily visits, honestly informing Irene that she was doing 'a good job' in taking care of her baby.

Weekly, her husband 'babysat' while Irene went for therapy that dealt with her developmental issues, current concerns, where she talked about her deepest, most difficult-to-reveal emotions, and rehearsed new skills on being assertive. She was also empowered in seeing to her needs healthily. Her post-natal depression disappeared and her experiences of seeing dead people talking to her stopped.

suffering from schizophrenia. Assuming that it is normal for stressful life events to distress us, how can therapists label such distress as a 'mental health disorder' (Bentall, 2012; Boyle, 2012; Campbell, 2012; Cromby, Harper and Reavey, 2012; Harper et al., 2012; May, 2012; Moncrieff, 2012)? If we look at current relevant debates, they lead to the understanding that suitably skilled therapists can offer drug-free help (see for example, Bentall, 2012; Boyle, 2012; May, 2012).

On the one hand, I am not against medication. Drugs saved my life. Medicine has a rightful place. On the other hand, as therapists, it is important not to be swept off our feet by the prevailing tide of the biomedical model which has flooded the diagnosis and treatment with drugs of all the psychoses, but to hear the clients' stories, understand what they mean to them, their families and to us as their therapists, to empower them, to make space for the voice of clients to be heard within the therapeutic relationship, and to offer realistic hope rather than to block insight with drugs.

AGE, GENDER AND CULTURE

Although theories are contradictory and findings inconclusive, we know from investigations that psychosis such as schizophrenia strikes across all ethnic groups and cultures, inflicting women and men equally (Kaplan and Sadock, 2008). Irrespective of age and gender, in some parts of the world the signs of a psychosis are perceived and dealt with differently than in the west. They may, for example, be interpreted as spirits of ancestors or related to past lives, and individuals may be helped through such experiences by rituals or ceremonies.

Whereas in the western world experiences that can be described as psychotic are generally viewed as a mental illness needing medical attention, researchers McCabe and Priebe (2004) found that many non-whites, such as Africans, seek support from their traditional cultural healer. The Lao (living at the borders of Thailand and Cambodia) and the Khmer (a minority group in Vietnam) might seek Buddhist monks; while the Vietnamese may use Taoist teachers. Within the western world, when faced with a client from a minority group, it may be useful for a therapist to liaise with the client's folk-healer and/or family and to collaborate in relation to assessment and delivering healthcare in the best interests of the client (this can be cross-referenced with Chapter 2). Indeed, a folk-healer may have been the client's first port of call due to having known the family for many years and speaking the same native language.

Therapists must be sensitive to and respectful of a client's culture in order to minimise potential miscommunication. This is a cross-cultural issue. For instance, in western Europe it is polite to make eye contact when speaking to someone, and to accept support when offered by a professional. However, in some cultures, it is polite to look downwards when being spoken to, and to decline a professional's offer of support. In this way, varying beliefs of different cultures may lead a therapist to a misconstrued notion regarding a client's problem, with the result that a therapist-devised wellness programme may not be complied with. Individuals are unique and complex; it is not a case of 'one size fits all'.

Regarding schizophrenia, peak onset for men is between the ages of fifteen and twenty-five years. For women it is between twenty-five and thirty-five, although inception can be earlier or later (Kaplan and Sadock, 2008). One theory about this is that the female hormone estrogen acts as protection for the developing brain, delaying the onset in women (Versola-Russo, 2006). However, a study investigating a link relating to this hormone being a protective factor against schizophrenia onset did not find a causal relationship (Hochman and Lewine, 2004).

CONCERN

Although some individuals willingly accept a schizophrenia diagnosis, most find it unhelpful (Thornicroft et al., 2007). If I had major mental distress, rather than be judged 'mentally ill', I would want a few basic aspects in place, such as to be comforted, respected and non-judgementally listened to. I would want to be genuinely acknowledged, empathically facilitated towards moving in a therapeutic direction and included in fun. It would concern me deeply if symptom-control due to medication, was viewed as therapeutic movement. Although these issues are basic, some might be missing from a trainee's repertoire and it may be up to the trainee to see to it that they are embraced and that those who suffer from a psychotic problem are not excluded from basic attending-to. Many diagnosed with purported schizophrenia, if listened to respectfully, explain that they suffered trauma and abuse as children and or adults. Unless therapists endeavour to understand the origin and path of their clients' distressing experiences, then their problematic behaviour, which has the potential for being understood, can be mystifying (Dillon, 2006).

Also concerning is that pharmaceutical companies can be criticised for oversimplifying the theoretical biological basis of 'mental illness' in order to push the purported primacy of their drugs as treatments while factors relating to the environment and an individual's development, which are important influencers regarding psychosis, are ignored (Read, 2008). There is no agreement among researchers that sufferers have a biological imbalance, yet drugs tend to be prescribed for reversing such a purported imbalance. However, they are seen to work, due to their overall suppressant effects – suppressant to anyone in the population, not only those diagnosed with schizophrenia!

According to researcher Moncrief, these drugs buffer against recovery (2009). On the whole, we speak about recovery from surgery or a sore throat. But recovering from mental distress is different: we may want to tell our stories, have our voices heard and glean meaning from our experience (Faulkner and Lazell, 2000; May, 2000).

Points to ponder

- Therapists have a duty to strive towards improving quality of care for clients, so how can they take ownership of this and offer a programme of care to those suffering with psychotic symptoms, which may not be the care programme that most therapists use due to pressure from the prevailing culture?
- As a trainee, learning is not difficult, but once qualified, how can learning occur throughout a therapist's career so that they maintain an up-to-date understanding of mental health issues, including the psychoses?
- If there is no scientific basis for diagnosing a client with schizophrenia, and if that diagnosis is harmful, how can there be justification for it?
- Since we are all born with different genes, it follows that how we interact with our environment differs from person to person. Might this explain, for example, why some who take cannabis manifest signs of schizophrenia while others do not, and might it also explain contradicting findings in genetic studies?

Exercise

(Answers are embedded in this chapter.)

1 Is psychopathy one of the psychoses?
2 What does 'puerperal psychosis' mean?
3 Can a psychosis be induced by taking drugs?
4 How might the use of CBT help a client with a diagnosis of schizophrenia?
5 What are the difficulties in relation to diagnosing schizophrenia?

CHAPTER SUMMARY

Psychopathy is not categorised as one of the psychoses.

Psychosis can be induced by drug-taking.

Delusions, catatonia and thought disturbance are included in the signs of psychosis.

After giving birth, puerperal psychosis can be experienced.

The diagnosis of schizophrenia is contentious.

LIST OF USEFUL RESOURCES

- Basset, T., Cooke, A., Read, J. and Hathaway, J. (2007) *Psychosis Revisited* (Hove, Pavilion).
- Love, J. (2009) *Psychosis in the Family* (London, Karnac).
- Marneros, A. (2004) *Acute and Transient Psychoses* (Cambridge, Cambridge University Press).
- Rudd, B. (2010) *Communication* (game) (Milton Keynes, Speechmark).

RELEVANT WEBSITES

www.cassiopaea.com/cassiopaea/psychopath.htm

www.hearing-voices.org

www.mind.org.uk/help/diagnosis_and conditions/psychotic_experience

www.psychosis-bipolar.com

REFERENCES

Anckarsater, H. (2010) 'Beyond categorical diagnostics in psychiatry: scientific and medicolegal implications', *International Journal of Law and Psychiatry*, 33, 2, pp. 59–65.

APA (2002) *DSM-IV-TR® Diagnostic and Statistical Manual of Mental Disorders* (Fourth Edition, revised) (Vancouver, American Psychiatric Association).

APA (2012) *DSM-5: The Future of Psychiatric Diagnosis*, www.dsm5.org/Pages/Default. aspx, accessed 23 May 2012.

Avila, M., Thaker, G. and Adami, H. (2001) 'Genetic epidemiology and schizophrenia: a study of reproductive fitness', *Schizophrenia Research*, 47, 2, pp. 233–41.

Babiak, P. and Hare, R.D. (2006) *Snakes in Suits: When Psychopaths go to Work* (New York, HarperCollins).

BehaveNet (2012) *Psychotic Disorder due to a General Medical Condition*, http://behavenet. com/psychotic-disorder-due-general-medical-condition, accessed 28 October 2012.

(Continued)

(Continued)

Bentall, R. (2003) *Madness Explained: Psychosis and Human Nature* (London, Allen Lane).

Bentall, R. (2012) 'Researching psychotic complaint', *Psychologist*, 20, 5, pp. 193–5.

Birchwood, M. and Trower, P. (2006) 'The future of cognitive-behavioural therapy for psychosis: not a quasi-neuroleptic', *British Journal of Psychiatry*, 188, 2, p. 108.

Bola, J. and Mosher, O. (2003) 'Treatment of acute psychosis without neuroleptics: two-year outcomes from the Soteria Project', *The Journal of Nervous and Mental Disease*, 191, 4, pp. 219–29.

Boyle, M. (2002) *Schizophrenia – A Scientific Delusion?* (Hove, Routledge).

Boyle, M. (2012) 'The problem with diagnosis', *Psychologist*, 20, 5, pp. 290–2.

Bull, S. (2008) *Pre-natal Nutritional Deficiency and the Risk of Adult Schizophrenia*, www.ncbi.nlm.nih.gov/pmc/articles/PMC2632499//, accessed 20 May 2011.

Campbell, P. (2012) 'Hearing my voice', *Psychologist*, 20, 5, pp. 298–9.

Cardinal, R.N. and Bullmore, E.T. (2011) *The Diagnosis of Psychosis* (Cambridge, Cambridge University Press).

CARTA (2012) *Psychosis*, www.carta.anthropgeny.org>MOCA>Domains>MentalDisease, accessed 1 June 2012.

CASL (2010) *The Campaign for Abolition of Schizophrenia*, www.asylumonline.net/legacy/casl/htm, accessed 23 May 2012.

Chadwick, P.K. (2011) *Schizophrenia: The Positivist Perspective. Explorations at the Outer Reaches of Human Experiences*, Second Edition (London, Taylor and Francis).

Chadwick, P.K. and Birchwood, M. (1994) 'The omnipotence of voices. A cognitive approach to auditory hallucinations', *The British Journal of Psychiatry*, 164, 2, pp. 190–201.

Chadwick, P.K., Lees, S. and Birchwood, M. (2000) 'The revised beliefs about voices questionnaire', *British Journal of Psychiatry*, 177, 3 pp. 229–32.

Cooper, S.R., Mizrahi, R. and Li, M. (2005) 'From dopamine to salience to psychosis – linking biology, pharmacology and phenomenology of psychosis', *Schizophrenia Research*, 79, 1, pp. 59–68.

Craddock, N. O'Donovan, M. and Owen, M.J. (2006) 'The genetics of schizophrenia and bipolar disorder? Implications for psychiatric nosology', *Schizophrenia Bulletin*, 32, 1, pp. 9–16.

Cromby, J., Harper, D. and Reavey, P. (2012) 'Moving beyond diagnosis', *Psychologist*, 20, 5, p. 289.

Crow, T.J. (2008) 'The 'big bang' theory of the origin of psychosis and the faculty of language', *Schizophrenia Research*, 102, 1, pp. 31–52.

Dillon, J. (2006) 'A Personal History', paper given at the anniversary congress of the English National Hearing Voices Network, Manchester, 7 September.

Faulkner, A. and Lazell, S. (2000) *Strategies for Living: A Report for User-led Research into People's Strategies for Living with Mental Distress* (London, Mental Health Foundation).

Garety, P.A. (2003) 'The future of psychological therapies for psychosis', *World Psychiatry*, 2, 3, pp. 147–52.

Garety, P.A., Bebbingon, P., Fowler, D., Freeman, D. and Kuipers, E. (2007) 'Implications for neurological research of cognitive models of psychosis: a theoretical paper', *Psychological Medicine*, 37, pp. 1377–91.

Gelder, M. (2005) *Psychiatry* (Oxford, Oxford University Press).

Harper, D., Cromby, J., Reavey, P., Cooke, A. and Anderson, J. (2012) 'Don't jump ship!', *Psychologist*, 20, 5, pp. 302–04.

Hay, P. (2009) *Post-Partum Psychosis: Which Women are at Highest Risk?*, www.ncbl.nlm. nih.gov/pmc/articles/PMC2637919, accessed 28 May 2012.

Hercz, R.D. (2012) *Psychopaths Among Us*, www.hare.org/links/saturday.html, accessed 20 May 2012.

Hochman, K.M. and Lewine, R.R. (2004) 'Age of menarche and schizophrenia onset in women', *Schizophrenia Research*, 69, 2–3, pp. 183–8.

Howard, R. (2005) *Psychosis – in the Elderly* (London, Taylor and Francis).

International Mental Health Research Organization (2012) *Schizophrenia Facts and Statistics*, www/schizophrenia.com/szfacts.htm, accessed 28 May 2012.

Kaplan, V. and Sadock, B. (eds) (2008) *Concise Textbook of Clinical Psychiatry*, Tenth Edition (New York, New York University).

Kender, K.S., Kallagher, T.A., Abelsom, J.M. and Kessler, R.C. (2012) *Lifetime Prevalence, Demographic Risk Factors, and Diagnostic Validity of Nonaffective Psychosis as Assessed in a US Community Sample. The National Comorbidity Survey*, www.ncbi.nlm. nih.gov/pubmed/8911225, accessed 28 May 2012.

Kua, J.K. and Wong, E. (2003) 'A twenty-year follow-up study on schizophrenia', *Syngapore Acta Psychiatrica Scandinavica*, 108, 2, pp. 118–25.

Lefly, H.P. (1990) 'Rehabilitation in mental illness: insights from other cultures', *Psychosocial Rehabilitation Journal*, 14, 1, pp. 5–12.

Lesser, J.M. and Hughes, S. (2006) 'Psychosis-related disturbances. Psychosis, agitation, and disinhibition in Alzheimer's disease: definitions and treatment options', *Geriatrics*, 61, 12, pp. 14–30.

Lewethe, F.M. and Koethe, D. (2008) 'Cannabis and psychiatric disorders: it is not only addiction', *Addiction and Biology*, 13, 2, pp. 264–75.

May, R. (2000) 'Routes to recovery from psychosis: the roots of a clinical psychologist', *Clinical Psychology Forum*, 146, pp. 6–10.

May, R. (2012) 'Working outside the diagnostic frame', *Psychologist*, 20, 5, pp. 300–1.

McCabe, R. and Priebe, S. (2004) 'Explanatory models of illness in schizophrenia comparison of four ethnic groups', *British Journal of Psychiatry*, 185, 1, pp. 225–30.

MedicineNet (2012) *Brief Psychotic Disorder*, www.medicinenet.com/brief_psychotic_disorder/page2.htm, accessed 28 October 2012.

Moncrief, J. (2009) *The Myth of the Chemical Cure: A Critique of Psychiatric Drug Treatment* (Basingstoke, Palgrave).

Moncrieff, J. (2012) 'Diagnosis and drug treatment', *Psychologist,* 20, 5, pp. 296–7

Pantelis, C., Velakoulis, D., McGorry, P.D., Wood, S.J., Suckling, J., Phillips, L.J., Yung, A.R., Bullmore, E.T., Brewer, W., Soulsby, B., Desmond, P. and McGuire, P.K. (2003)

(Continued)

(Continued)

'Neuroanatomical abnormalities before and after onset of psychosis: a cross-sectional and longitudinal MRI comparison', *Lancet*, 25, 361, pp. 281–8.

Paul, F. and Morrison, A. (2004) *Early Detection and Cognitive Therapy for People at High Risk of Developing Psychosis* (Chichester, John Wiley and Sons).

Pitfield, M. and Openheim, A.N. (2006) 'Child rearing attitudes of mothers of psychotic children', *Journal of Child Psychology and Psychiatry*, 5, 1, pp. 51–7.

Read, J. (2008) 'Schizophrenia, drug companies and the internet', *Social Science and Medicine*, 66, 1, pp. 99–109.

Renn, P. (2007) *Relational Psychoanalytic Perspectives on Psychosis*, www/counselling-directory.org.uk/counselloradvice.1.html, accessed 20 May 2012.

Seeman, P., Scharz, J. and Chen, J. (2006) 'Psychosis pathways converge via D2High dopamine receptors', *Synapse*, 60, 30, pp. 319–46.

Segal, Z.V., Kennedy, S., Gemar, M., Hood, K., Pedersen, R. and Buis, T. (2006) 'Cognitive reactivity to sad mood provocation and the prediction of depressive relapse', *Archives of General Psychiatry*, 63, 7, pp. 749–55.

Startup, H., Freeman, D. and Garety, P.A. (2006) 'Persecutory delusions and catastrophic worry in psychosis: developing the understanding of delusion distress and persistence', *Behavioural Research and Therapy*, 45, 3, pp. 523–37.

Thara, R. (2004) 'Twenty-year course of schizophrenia: the Madras longitudinal study', *Canadian Journal of Psychiatry*, 49, 8, pp. 564–9.

Thornicroft, G., Rose, D., Kassam, D. and Sartorius, N. (2007) 'Stigma, ignorance, prejudice or discrimination', *British Journal of Psychiatry*, 190, pp. 192–3.

Versola-Russo, J.M. (2006) 'Cultural demographic factors of schizophrenia', *International Journal of Psychosocial Rehabilitation*, 10, 2, pp. 89–103.

Wilcox, R.A., To, T., Koukourou, A. and Frasca, J. (2008) 'Hashimoto's encephalopathy masquerading as acute psychosis', *Journal of Clinical Neuroscience*, 15, 11, pp. 1301–4.

Wiles, N.J., Zammit, S., Bebbington, B., Singleton, N., Meltzer, H. and Lewis, G. (2006) 'Self-reported psychotic symptoms in the general population: results from the longitudinal study of the British National Psychiatric Morbidity Survey', *British Journal of Psychiatry*, 188, pp. 519–26.

10

Somatoform Disorders

LEARNING OBJECTIVES FOR THIS CHAPTER

- Recognise signs of a somatoform disorder
- Gain theoretical perspectives
- Glean insights from research
- Understand that environmental and internal factors can impact on somatising

---

Somatising is when stress creates physical symptoms. Somatoform disorders are an extreme type of somatisation and create much distress, often long-term. Sufferers believe that their symptoms are not due to mental distress but to physical causes.

SOMATOFORM SIGNS

If individuals suffer from hypochondriasis, conversion disorder, body dysmorphia, or pain disorder, they can be categorised as having a somatoform disorder. Some examples of somatising are irregular periods, erectile dysfunction, headaches, back pain, chest and/or urinary discomfort. Individuals with such problems are not pretending and feel emotional about them, but medical tests into other causes are negative.

SOMATOFORM PREVALENCE

Speculation is that between 1 and 20 per cent of the population suffer from a somatoform disorder (Right Diagnosis, 2012).

SOMATOFORM INTERVENTION

Offering therapy for sufferers of somatoform disorders is not easy, because they usually reject the idea that mental stress causes their physical ailments. So how far to go with diagnostic tests is particularly challenging. Researchers Bateman and Tyrer (2004) systematically researched literature and found that when compared with other interventions, psychodynamic therapy was the most supportive. However, more research is necessary before such findings can be generalised, since the evidence they found was inadequate for making a recommendation. There is some support for the use of CBT for two of the somatoform disorders (hypochondriasis and body dysmorphia), but methodologically sound-enough research, which supports the use of CBT for treating conversion and pain disorders, is meagre (Allen and Woodfolk, 2010). Recently, the EMDR Institute conducted research using EMDR (eye movement desensitisation and reprocessing) with seven individuals who manifested with signs of a somatoform disorder and after three sessions, five of them did not fulfil the criteria for suffering with it (2012). Nevertheless, findings from such small studies are not to be generalised, however tempting. At the time of writing, NICE (2012) has yet to commission guidelines for somatoform problems.

SOMATOFORM EXPECTED OUTCOME

What is not good news is that often the problem is long-standing because sufferers are convinced that their problem is not rooted in mental distress. Interestingly, those suffering from one of the somatoform disorders also tend to have another mental health issue, for example depression, substance misuse or anxiety. In such cases, the good news is that dealing with the other mental health issue can help with the problem of somatising. Although medication need not play a large part in somatisation issues, it often does (for instance, in the form of painkillers), but if those who somatise accept that the root of their problem may be mental stress, then therapy can help.

DYSMORPHIA

This word originates from the ancient Greek, which when literally translated means 'not beautiful'. If individuals spend much time being concerned about a small physical defect that they may or may not have, which causes them distress, they suffer from body dysmorphic disorder (BDD).

BDD theory

There is a strong sociocultural theory speculating that societal pressure contributes to BDD via the media (da Costa and Nelson, 2007). This is criticised however, on the grounds that BDD was documented before mass media existed, as far back as the nineteenth century (Phillips, 2005). Another theory is that abuse, neglect and traumatic experiences as a child are the cause (Phillips, 2009).

BDD research

Investigations show that approximately 75 per cent of adult sufferers report childhood stressful experiences (Phillips, 2009). Further research results reveal that anti-depressant medication helps with BDD (ADAA, 2012).

BDD signs

Symptoms incorporate focusing, out of all proportion, on a minor physical defect or on a purported physical defect that nobody else can see. For instance, a person may think that they have a crooked tooth (which others cannot see) or a blemish on the face (which most would consider trivial). Nevertheless, the individual is so preoccupied with the purported defect that a great deal of time is spent looking in the mirror (perhaps smiling with a closed mouth, or wearing concealer make-up).

BDD may be confused with OCD due to, for instance, repeatedly looking in the mirror, but it is different and those suffering from BDD tend to have greater suicidal ideation when compared with OCD sufferers. BDD can only be diagnosed if preoccupation with a purported blemish disrupts daily functioning and or causes much distress.

BDD prevalence

The prevalence of those suffering from BDD is approximately 3 per cent of the population (Mind, 2012).

BDD intervention

CBT is often used (Institute of Psychiatry, 2012).

BDD expected outcome

For most BDD sufferers, there is reported improvement with CBT.

BDD in practice

When faced with a client with BDD, the use of mindfulness techniques, cognitive restructuring, behaviour response prevention, exposure, and behavioural experiments (as described in the case immediately below) either one-to-one or in a group, can be beneficial (Mind, 2012).

BDD CASE VIGNETTE

Amanda, who had had several facelifts, was deeply concerned with her appearance, believing that her face was blemished and ugly, despite her life-partner repeatedly telling her that she was beautiful. Amanda was very distressed about her belief, thinking that her partner was just saying what she wanted to hear, so she went for therapy. Her therapist collaborated with her and chose to use a CBT model, as follows.

He and Amanda created two theories regarding her looks.

Theory I: 'There is a problem with the way I [Amanda] look.' The therapist said, 'For many years your behaviour's been based on Theory I, that your appearance is problematic. Let's look at Theory II: that you have a problem with the way you see your physical image, with how you perceive what your face looks like. This may have developed because of your early experiences of being picked-on, teased about your appearance, and forced to try to look different by applying heavy make-up, as you explained to me earlier. Are you willing to live the next twelve weeks as if Theory II is true?'

Amanda agreed.

(Continued)

(Continued)

He then said, 'If Theory II were true, how would you behave differently and how would you feel?' Amanda gave profound thought and put in enormous emotional energy into considering a way that presumed the truth of Theory II – that she was not actually physically defective. She replied, 'I'd go out without make-up and feel good about myself'.

Amanda was open to the therapist's support, who incorporated the following techniques into her care programme (Mind, 2012):

- mindfulness (she became aware of the way she thought, felt and behaved, moment by moment)
- cognitive restructuring (she found alternative ways of thinking)
- behaviour response prevention (she stopped the practically continuous seeking of approval from her husband)
- exposure (she reduced the amount of make-up worn when going out to a public place)
- behavioural experiments (she eventually went out without make-up, repeatedly, to more and more public places, starting with visiting her sister but not using public transport. She used a step-wise process where each journey became more demanding, eventually managing to attend a friend's sixtieth birthday party after having a beauty-facial but not wearing make-up).

This liberated Amanda. She disclosed feeling good about herself, having the choice of whether to wear make-up or not, and realised that her looks were 'OK'. Amanda's self-esteem was boosted! Her symptoms disappeared, she stopped suffering from dysmorphia and is not planning more plastic surgery.

Many sufferers have surgery performed on them to look what they believe to be 'normal' in appearance; sometimes repeatedly. Since plastic surgery does not address the problem of BDD at its root, many are not satisfied with the end result of their operation/s. They might even move their attention to another part of their body, or they may become aggressive towards their surgeon, or become suicidal.

HYPOCHONDRIASIS

Sufferers of hypochondriasis are extremely preoccupied with their health. They tend to focus on a symptom, believing that they have a physical disease.

Hypochondriasis theory

There are four main theories:

1 normal body sensations are amplified
2 negative stress as a child causes hypochondriasis in the adult
3 hypochondriasis is learned behaviour
4 there is a genetic predisposition to it (H.A., 2012).

Hypochondriasis research

Researchers have yet to agree on definitive causes of hypochondriasis, but they do agree that the reasons for having it are complex (Maj and Akiskal, 2005).

Hypochondriasis signs

Symptoms include being very concerned that minor physical sensations mean that a serious physical illness is present, seeing medical doctors repeatedly and having many medical tests done or exploratory surgery where no problem is found, seeking the opinion of more than one doctor when the first one does not find a problem and either talking excessively with others about personally perceived health problems or not talking about them for fear of disbelief (Mayo Clinic, 2012).

Hypochondriasis prevalence

Hypochondriasis has been found to affect approximately 8 per cent of the general population (Levenson, Dimsdate and Soloman, 2011).

Hypochondriasis intervention

Recent research shows that a programme of group CBT in a psychiatric setting is an effective intervention (Hedman et al., 2010).

Hypochondriasis expected outcome

For those who complete a ten-week group CBT programme for hypochondriasis, the outcome is positively effective even after a six-month follow up (Hedman et al., 2010).

Hypochondriasis in practice

When seeing clients, mindfulness-based cognitive therapy does not exacerbate their condition and those who complete such a programme report benefits (Williams et al., 2011).

CONVERSION DISORDER

If individuals have neurological symptoms (for example, paralysis or blindness) that cannot be explained medically, then they may have conversion disorder (CD). Signs of CD usually emerge suddenly following a stressful life episode (Blais et al., 2008).

HYPOCHONDRIASIS CASE VIGNETTE

Marcus thought that he had a serious heart problem, believing that he had heart attacks. Medical tests did not reveal any problems and he was referred to a therapist.

The therapist used a CBT approach. She collaborated with Marcus to collect evidence (that might either back-up or refute his belief about the purported heart attacks) regarding two theories: A and B.

Theory A: 'I [Marcus] have a serious problem with heart attacks.' Evidence for Theory A: 'I have palpitations, tiredness and agitation.'

Theory B: 'I have a a a belief/worry (rather than a fact) that I [Marcus] have heart attacks.' Evidence for Theory B: 'When I feel stressed, palpitations occur. Concentrating on my symptoms makes me more tired. My agitation goes away when I am reassured.'

Next, the therapist used reframing, and as a result of collaborating with Marcus, the following reframes were established.

- Palpitations have many causes, such as tension, heat and anxiety.
- Tiredness can be because I use my energy focusing on my problem.
- Agitation is common when stressed and although I have had my symptoms for years, their seriousness has not increased.

It was a deeply moving experience for Marcus when he realised that it was his stress that he needed to manage, rather than be medicated for a heart problem that was not there.

Mainly due to attending a programme of stress management that included learning mindfulness techniques (in a group conducted by his therapist) Marcus's symptoms disappeared. He no longer suffers from hypochondriasis.

(A description of the CBT model explained here can be found in Salkovski and Bass (1997).)

CD signs

Symptoms of CD incorporate the loss of one or more bodily functions, for example speech, paralysis, numbness and/or blindness. After having diagnostic medical tests, no physical reasons are found for these signs (A.D.A.M., 2011).

CD prevalence

Approximately 0.3 per cent of the general population may suffer from CD (Brown and Lewis-Fernandez, 2011).

CD intervention

Although stress management can help, what is also necessary is accessing support from a primary health care practitioner (for example, to exercise any paralysed limb in order to prevent muscles being wasted) until the signs are no longer present (Blais et al., 2008).

CD expected outcome

This disorder usually disappears as suddenly as it arrives, but its debilitating effect can last for weeks (Brown and Lewis-Fernandez, 2011).

CD in practice

The main thing to keep in mind is that clients with CD are not making anything up and it is not 'all in the head'. In reality, they experience the symptoms they describe. To reduce the signs, training in stress management can be helpful (A.D.A.M., 2011).

CD CASE VIGNETTE

Emily suffered from dizziness each day at around 4 p.m. Five days a week she went to bed due to feeling nausea and faintness. At about 7 p.m., she felt well enough to get out of bed, watch TV for the rest of the evening and eat a take-away pizza with her husband. Then she slept at approximately midnight. Her husband was concerned about her symptoms and they visited the GP, who did not find any physical problem with Emily so he referred her for therapy. During therapy, she revealed that her husband expected her to do all the housekeeping, complained about any meals she would prepare and the state of the house. Her therapist noted that Emily's physical symptoms appeared just before the husband was due to come home after work. Consequently, the therapist suggested couple therapy, which she and her husband agreed to. Emily reported that she did not experience her husband as listening to her, saying that she felt like an unpaid slave because she thought he expected her to cook and clean up after him. The therapist urged her husband to listen to her, which he did. He took a more active role in cooking and they worked out a housekeeping rota. Emily's conversion disorder vanished. The couple stopped therapy after seven weeks.

PAIN DISORDER

Pain disorder is when an individual experiences chronic pain that is believed to have psychological rather than physical causes. Chronic pain related to an incurable disease (such as final stages of cancer) is not discussed here, since it is not categorised as a mental health disorder (Dersh, Polatin and Gatchel, 2002).

Pain disorder theory

Although a substantial amount of interest was shown during the twentieth and early twenty-first centuries in the relationship between psychopathology and pain, there is no one particular model that can adequately explain such a relationship (Dersh, Polatin and Gatchel, 2002). Indeed, we do not yet know whether it is pain or mental disorder that comes first.

Pain disorder research

New research from neuroscience, particularly the neuroimaging of pain processing, is revolutionising the remedying of pain disorder and chronic pain (Matthews, Honey and Bullmore, 2006). If pain causes loss of brain matter in certain areas, for example the dorsolateral prefrontal cortex with its important involvement in sensory circuitry (Zikopoulos and Barbas, 2006), and dealing with emotions can be effective as part of a pain-relief programme, then emotional circuitry has a greater role to play than sensory. What seems to be emerging from research as important is not only the amelioration of pain to reduce loss of brain matter, but also the uplifting of emotions while enhancing hope (Borsook et al., 2007).

Pain disorder signs

With pain disorder, pain warranting clinical attention is experienced, but no medical cause can be found. It disrupts important areas of functioning such as work and or social life.

Pain disorder prevalence

Approximately 8.1 per cent of the general population suffers from unexplained pain symptoms (Frohlich, Jacobi and Wittchen, 2006).

Pain disorder intervention

Intervening medically (perhaps with appropriate tests performed by medics to ensure no biological problem is the cause of pain), together with therapeutic interventions to help sufferers manage pain effectively and social support to ensure that they are not isolated, are relevant interventions (Moskowitz, 2009).

Pain disorder expected outcome

Since psychopathology (especially depressive disorder) plays a major role in chronic pain, a therapy programme without a mental health component may be unsuccessful (Dersh, Polatin and Gatchel, 2002). For successful outcomes, it may be necessary to touch on three areas of a person's life: social, biological and psychological.

Pain disorder in practice

When faced with a client possibly experiencing pain disorder, enquire about psychological, biological and social factors, as mentioned above.

PAIN DISORDER CASE VIGNETTE

A woman was seriously injured in war when her country was invaded. After recovering from injuries (her left arm was amputated), a severe and persistent pain developed in her right arm, distressing her and causing her to stop using it. Strong, medically prescribed painkillers had no effect. The pain lasted for two years up to the time of referral to a therapist. After the initial assessment, she had five CBT sessions.

Session 1: She learnt about the relationship between emotions and physical sensations. For homework, she practiced relaxation, monitored pain and scheduled activities.

Session 2: After reviewing the homework, her therapist explained cognitive errors and automatic thoughts. Homework was to keep a record of her automatic thoughts and do time-based paced activities.

Session 3: Her recorded automatic thoughts were evaluated, evidence was explored regarding whether they were factual and their helpfulness was discussed. The therapist also offered assertiveness training to manage anger and frustrations.

Session 4: Negative automatic thoughts continued to be identified and modified, and her core beliefs were pinpointed by using the downward-arrow technique (as in Briers, 2009).

Session 5: Learnt material was revised and the client formulated a plan for dealing with future stress or pain.

At a follow-up session six months after therapy ended, she was pain-free, no longer taking painkillers and coping well.

AGE

Somatoform disorders begin at any age.

GENDER

Women suffer from somatoform disorders more than men (Dersh, Polatin and Gatchel, 2002).

CULTURE

Cultural aspects such as beauty and image contribute to BDD. For instance, when the media depicts ideal men as being big-built with puffed-up muscles, this can cause men to develop BDD by obsessing about size and by over-exercising in an attempt to gain the body self-perceived as perfect. Overall, somatic presentation of psychological disorders can appear in any country, although research has found that the type of somatoform disorder that manifests varies between countries (Janca et al., 1995).

Points to ponder

- Since emotion is important in pain management, why is the issue of emotions still on the 'back-burner'?
- Overall, medical conditions have mental health issues linked to them.
- If emotions affect brain waves and brain waves affect muscles, for example by creating heart problems, as recent research (Lemaire et al., 2011) shows, then propagating emotional literacy is imperative.

Exercise

(Answers are embedded in this chapter.)

1 What are the main somatoform disorders?
2 State the signs of a somatoform disorder.
3 Is a person suffering from hypochondriasis pretending to be ill?
4 Which therapeutic approach seems to be effective for pain disorder?
5 How might body dysmorphia be caused?
6 Explain 'conversion disorder'.

CHAPTER SUMMARY

Hypochondriasis, conversion, dysmorphia and pain disorders are categorised under the somatoform disorders classification.

CBT tends to be favoured as a therapeutic approach for these disorders.

A somatoform disorder can manifest in different ways, depending on the culture the sufferer is embedded in, irrespective of age and gender.

LIST OF USEFUL RESOURCES

- Buhlman, U. (2011) 'Perceived ugliness an update on treatment-relevant aspects of body dismorphic disorder', *Current Psychiatry Represented*, 13, 4, pp. 283–8.
- ICON (2004) *Conversion Disorder – A Medical Dictionary, Bibliography, and Annotated Research Guide to Internet References* (San Diego, Health Publications).
- Rudd, B. (2010) *Relating* (game) (Milton Keynes, Speechmark).
- Schweitzer, P., Barberie, S., Skritskaya, N. and Fallon, B.A. (2010) *Help for Hypochondriasis: A Guide to Understanding, Treatment, and Resources* (New York, Columbia University Medical Center).

RELEVANT WEBSITES

http://allpsych.com/disorders/somatoform/hypochondriac.html

www.mayoclinic.com/health/conversion-disorder/DS00877

www.scribd.com/doc/11352/CBT-for-BDD

REFERENCES

ADAA (2012) *Medication*, www.adaa.org/finding-help/treatment/medication accessed, 13 June 2012.

A.D.A.M. (2011) *Conversion Disorder*, www.ncbi.nlm.nih.gov/pubmedhealth/PMHOOO1950/ accessed 08/06/2012

Allen, L. and Woodfolk, R. (2010) 'Cognitive therapy for somatoform disorders', *Psychiatric Clinic North America*, 33, 5, pp. 579–93.

APA (2002) *DSM-IV-TR® Diagnostic and Statistical Manual of Mental Disorders* (Fourth Edition, revised) (Vancouver, American Psychiatric Association).

Bateman, A. and Tyrer, P. (2004) 'Psychological treatment for personality disorders', *Advances in Psychiatric Treatment*, 10, 5, pp. 378–88.

Blais, M.A., Smallwood, P., Groves, J.E. and Rivas-Vazquez, R.A. (2008) 'Personality and personality disorders', in Stern, T.A., Rosenbaum, J.F. Fava, M., Bierderman, J. and Rauch, S.L. (eds) *Massachusetts General Hospital Comprehensive Clinical Psychiatry* (Philadelphia, Mosby Elsevier).

Borsook, D., Moulton, E.A., Schmidt, K.F. and Reccera, L.R. (2007) 'Neuroimaging revolutionizes therapeutic approaches to chronic pain', *Molecular Pain*, 3, 25, pp. 3–25.

Briers, S. (2009) *Brilliant CBT* (London, Hodder Education).

Brown, R.J. and Lewis-Fernandez, R. (2011) 'Culture and conversion disorder', *Psychiatry: Interpersonal and Biological Processes*, 74, 3, 187–206.

da Costa, D. and Nelson, T.M. (2007) 'A narrative approach to body dysmorphic disorder', *Journal of Mental Health Counseling*, 29, 1, pp. 67–80.

Dersch, J., Polatin, P.B. and Gatchel, R.J. (2002) 'Chronic pain and psychopathology: research findings and theoretical considerations', *Psychosomatic Medicine*, 64, 5, pp. 773–86.

EMDR Institute (2012) *Somatoform Disorder Studies*, www.emdr.com/general-information/somatoform-disorder-studies.html, accessed 28 October 2012.

Frohlich, C., Jacobi, F. and Wittchen, H.U. (2006) 'DSM-IV pain disorder in the general population. A exploration of the structure and threshold of medically unexplained pain symptoms', *European Archives of Psychiatry and Clinical Neuroscience*, 256, 3, pp. 187–96.

H.A. (2012) *It's All in the Head … Or Is It? The Workings of Hypochondriasis*, http://serendip.brynmawr.edu/biology/b103/f01/web3/aryani.html, accessed 13 June 2012.

(Continued)

(Continued)

Hedman, E., Brjann, A., Ruck, E., Andersson, C. and Nils, G.L. (2010) 'Effectiveness and cost offset analysis of group CBT for hypochondriasis delivered in a psychiatric setting: an open trial', *Cognitive Behaviour Therapy*, 39, 4, pp. 239–50, accessed 8 June 2012.

Institute of Psychiatry (2012) *Body Dismorphic Disorder*, www.psychology.iop.kcl.ac.uk/cadat/GPs/BDD.aspx, accessed 6 June 2012.

Janca, A., Isaac, M., Bennett, L.A. and Tacchini, G. (1995) 'Somatoform disorders in different cultures: a mail questionnaire survey', *Society Psychiatry and Psychiatric Epidemiology*, 30, 1, pp. 44–8.

Lemaire, J.B., Wallace, J.E, LeWin, A.M., de Grood, J. and Schaefer, J.P. (2011) 'The effect of a biofeedback-based stress management tool on physician stress: a randomized controlled clinical trial', *Open Medicine*, 5, 4, pp. 154–63.

Levenson, J., Dimsdate, J. and Solomon, D. (2011) *Hypochondriasis: Epidemiology, Clinical Presentation, Assessment, and Diagnosis*, www.uptodate.com/contents/hypochondriasis-epidemiology-clinical- presentation-assessment-and-diagnosis, accessed 7 June 2012.

Maj, M. and Akiskal, H.S. (2005) *Somatoform Disorders* (Chichester, Wiley).

Matthews, P.M., Honey, G.D. and Bullmore, E.T. (2006) 'Applications of fMRI in translational medicine and clinical practice', *Nature Reviews*, 7 pp. 732–44.

Mayo Clinic (2012) *Hypochondria*, www.mayoclinic.com/health/hypochondria/ds00841/dsection=symptoms, accessed 7 June 2012.

Mind (2012) *Body Dismorphic Condition*, www.mind.org.uk/help/diagnoses_and_conditions/body_dysmorphic_disorder, accessed 7 June 2012.

Moskowitz, M. (2009) *Pain is its Own Injury*, www.bayareapainmedical.com/page1/page9/page9.html, accessed 14 June 2012.

NICE (2012) *Published Clinical Guidelines*, www.nice.org.uk/guidance/index.jsp?action=byType&type=2&status=3, accessed 7 June 2012.

Phillips, K. (2005) *The Broken Mirror* (Oxford, Oxford University Press).

Phillips, K. (2009) *Understanding Body Dysmorphic Disorder* (Oxford, Oxford University Press).

Right Diagnosis (2012) *Prevalence and Incidence of Somatization Disorder*, www.rightdiagnosis.com/s/somatization_disorder/prevalence.htm, accessed 5 June 2012.

Salkovski, P. and Bass, C. (1997) 'Hypochondriasis' in Clark, D.N. and Fairburn, C.G. (eds), *The Science and Practice of Cognitive-Behaviour Therapy* (Oxford, Oxford University Press).

Williams, M., Muse, F., Williams, K. and Mark, G. (2011) 'Mindfulness-based cognitive therapy for severe health anxiety (hypochondriasis): an interpretative phenomenological analysis of patients' experiences', *British Journal of Clinical Psychology*, 50, 4, pp. 379–97.

Zikopoulos, B. and Barbas, H. (2006) 'Prefrontal projections to the thalamic reticular nucleus form a unique circuit for attentional mechanisms', *The Journal of Neuroscience*, 26, 28, pp. 7348–61.

11

Personality Disorders

LEARNING OBJECTIVES FOR THIS CHAPTER

- Know what personality disorders are
- Understand that personality disorders are clustered into different nests
- Be familiar with major theories on personality disorders
- Gain insight into related research
- Discuss key concepts of personality disorder

Deep and continuous difficulties with social relationships are at the core of personality disorders (PDs). DSM-IV-TR lists ten PDs (APA, 2002). As I write, five are planned for removal from the fifth DSM edition – narcissistic, paranoid, schizoid, dependent and histrionic – leaving schizotypal, obsessive compulsive, avoidant, anti-social and borderline. One reason for this is that many working within mental health believe that the diagnostic framework for the spectrum of PDs needs overhauling (Aldhous, 2011).

The ten PDs are clustered into three sections, A, B and C:

- Section A, odd behaviour: schizotypal (bizarre actions or peculiar thoughts), schizoid (not interested in social relationships) and paranoid (unreasonably suspicious and distrustful of others).
- Section B, dramatic behaviour: narcissistic (prevalent style of pompousness), histrionic (extensive attention-seeking actions coupled with superficial or over-blown emotions), borderline (very insecure) and anti-social (vast disrespect).
- Section C, anxious behaviour: obsessive compulsive (inflexible compliance to regimes, ethical codes or excessive systematising), dependent (generally relies on others) and avoidant (holds-back socially, feels deficient).

To cover all the nests that the PDs are clustered in, I respectively deliberate on one from each of the above sections; specifically, schizotypal, borderline and obsessive compulsive, in relative depth, and spotlight the other two PDs which will presumably remain in the DSM (avoidant and anti-social).

DIFFICULTIES IN CATEGORISING PERSONALITY DISORDER

PD is characterised by interpersonal stumbling blocks. Most of us have periods of experiencing problems with others, but it does not mean that we have a PD. This could be why it can take years before individuals who have ongoing difficulties interacting with others, find support and are identified as suffering from PD. They may binge eat, be depressed or try to kill themselves. All these factors add to the difficulty of identifying the PD. Some therapists do not accept clients with PD because they think that the condition is too difficult to work with. Therapists need to be highly skilled in how they relate to a client with PD, know and understand what relevant research offers when faced with the client, while being therapeutically sensitive. Therefore, reluctance to take on these clients is understandable, especially when working in independent practice, where support from other professionals within the building that the therapy room is in may be non-existent.

SCHIZOTYPAL PD

As a reminder, schizotypal personality disorder (SPD) is nested within Section A (odd behaviour). It is considered to be within the schizophrenic spectrum but, unlike schizophrenia, it is not a psychotic disorder; rather, as with schizoid, it is a PD. The major difference between schizoid and schizotypal is that schizoid PD sufferers do not tend to experience paranoia, illusions and perceptual distortions which are typical of those with SPD.

SPD theory

Although causes of SPD are unknown, one theory is that genes are involved, because this problem is most common in the relatives of those who suffer from schizophrenia (Widiger and Lowe, 2007). Another theory is that SPD is caused by social and environmental factors, since these influence thoughts, emotions and behaviour (Questa, Peralta and Zarzuela, 2001).

American psychologist, Millon, proposed two subtypes of SPD: insipid and timorous (Millon et al., 2004). He stated that those with insipid SPD were depressed and tended to be dependent, while those with timorous SPD were avoidant of people and negative in attitude. Millon also theorised that those with SPD embrace a mix of both subtypes, with one being dominant; and that a person with one pure subtype was rare (2012). There is more on Millon's work later.

SPD research

Although research cannot be found showing that a prerequisite to suffering from SPD is having a relative with schizophrenia, as the above-mentioned Widiger and Lowe's (2007) theory seems to imply, certain empirical evidence can be found to back up Questa, Perelta and Zarzuela's (2001) theory that inappropriate parenting or early trauma might lead to the development of schizotypal traits (Anglin, Cohen and Chen, 2008). This may be because abuse during childhood alters brain functioning (Mayo Clinic Staff, 2012).

SPD signs

These incorporate:

- obsessive ruminations
- 'flat' emotional expression
- avoidance of social relationships

- distorted ideas (they know are distinguishable from consensual reality)
- odd behaviour
- tending towards social isolation (WHO, 1992).

SPD prevalence

Approximately 3 per cent of the general population suffer from SPD (Giles, 2012).

SPD intervention

Some SPD sufferers have a certain capacity for emotional warmth and empathy; it is wise if therapists build a trusting therapeutic relationship with these clients, since they are the ones who fare better with this approach – particularly, according to Giles (2012), if the approach is psycho-dynamically rooted. This might be because attachment may develop within the therapeutic relationship that can be transposed onto other relationships.

CBT, which aims to identify and change thoughts, can be used, but before this a trusting relationship needs to be established so that some of the social anxiety that clients feel is reduced in order for them to be able to explore their thinking processes. Offering specific suggestions, for example, regarding personal hygiene, learning communication skills and using DVD-recorded feedback (so clients see their appearance and behaviour) may help.

Other models can also be utilised, such as interpersonal therapy, in which clients can stay relation-ally distant until they feel safe to trust enough in allowing themselves to develop the self-awareness necessary to perceiving their distorted thoughts so that new self-talk can be used to guide them into experiences based on consensual reality.

Group therapy can be useful too for clients to experience socialising and receiving feedback in a safe environment, although this is not recommended for those suffering from SPD who have severe paranoid behaviour or extreme eccentricity.

Additionally, there is couples or family therapy, but this is uncommon, although a therapist can focus on helping a couple with their communication skills, or individuals in a family to find ways of becoming more healthily involved with one another.

Further, some drugs, for example fluoxetine (Prozac), can diminish particular symptoms such as paranoid thoughts, feeling depressed and being anxious.

SPD expected outcome

Prognosis does not appear good for those whose ways of coping seem set in stone. Unfortunately, if members of a client's family are very depended on, it is easy for that person to become apathetic and isolated.

SPD in practice

Therapists have witnessed improvement in those mildly affected because these clients are able to change their ways of perceiving.

> **SPD CASE VIGNETTE**
>
> For years, thirty-five-year-old Peter was a loner. He found it difficult sticking to a job and drifted between work and unemployment. Peter reported that during his childhood, his parents were cold and distant towards him. As an adult, others experienced him as cold and distant. He believed that if he thought something, it would happen. His clothes were noticeably too big and he looked unclean. Peter felt anxious if faced with social situations. He liked using the internet and a few individuals in an online-group he belonged to urged him to seek therapy. He did, via telephone contact.
>
> The therapist persuaded Peter to meet face-to-face. She sensed that trying to change his personality might be futile, therefore she endeavoured to help him interact more effectively in relationships.
>
> Initially, Peter seemed extremely distant when relating with her, but eventually, as a result of of her empathy, training him in communication skills, and a few suggestions about his appearance, he engaged with her, improved his appearance, his communication with others and consequently, his job prospects.
>
> Peter's therapy started one year ago and is still in progress.

To prevent SPD, and because it seems to arise within a client's family, it is best for the client to be in an environment that expresses genuine care and emotional stimulation, and which is nurturing and loving.

BORDERLINE PD

As a reminder, an individual suffering from BPD is classified within Section B (dramatic personality disorders) of the PDs spectrum. If BPD is the problem, then the person's relationships, self-image, behaviour and identity are unstable (see Chapter 12 for links between BPD and inadequate emotional literacy). However, this diagnosis can be contentious because at some point in life many of us experience instability regarding what we do and our self-image – such experiences do not mean that we are dysfunctional. Although a controversial diagnosis, BPD is listed in the diagnostic manuals used widely by therapists, such as the ICD-10 (WHO, 1992) and the DSM (APA, 2002).

BPD theory

Several theories abound. Three major ones are Benjamin's (1996) interpersonal model, Westen's (1990, 1998) functional domain model, and Millon's (1990, 2012; Millon and Davis, 1996) evolutionary social-learning model..

According to Benjamin (1996), if individuals are angry because of experiencing another as neglecting or abandoning them, then they can be categorised as suffering from BPD. Those with BPD treat themselves in the same (negative) way that others have treated them; they also 'regurgitate' their previous experiences with important others – that is, they elicit from other people what they previously experienced. This, however, is only a fraction of Benjamin's theory. A brief overview of his model is offered later.

Using Westen's (1990) model, BPD can only be diagnosed if certain tensions are present. For example, if clients chronically worry about being abandoned, are somehow incapable of adapting, inept at impulse control, or emotionally immature, then BPD can be assumed (Westen, 1998). His comprehensive model is described simply, further down.

Millon's model (1990, 2012; Millon and Davis, 1996) is also comprehensive. Its BPD aspect is associated with a sceptical and negative state of mind. He theorises that BPD sufferers tend to be irritable and discontented (2012). A simplified overview of the model is presented below.

BPD research

Baird, therapist and research scientist at the University of Colorado, found that 'repeated mis-attunement in childhood, when the neural circuitry is developing, can result in personality traits, or, in more extreme situations personality disorders such as BPD' (2008: 31). Mounting research links the experience of childhood abuse to BPD (for example, Cowley, 2012). Findings such as Cowley's however, can be criticised for using self-reports rather than combining these with interviews. Nevertheless, such results challenge the long-held view that BPD is a result of genetics (Lieb et al., 2011).

BPD signs

According to the government's NICE (2009) guidelines, if individuals experience more than four of the following and they have a major impact on their lives, then they can be diagnosed with BPD:

- relationship difficulties (for example, ongoing problems making and maintaining friendships)
- labile emotions (for example, feeling confident and positive one day, then angry and full of despair the next)
- unstable self-image (for example, sensing being clever with one person and stupid with another)
- delusions (for example, hearing non-existent sounds)
- fear of rejection (for example, afraid of being abandoned or alone)
- self-harming (for example, thinking about and/or hurting oneself)
- risk-taking (for example, drinking and driving).

Co-morbidity with depression, substance abuse and eating disorders are high in those diagnosed with BPD. They feel suicidal and attempt suicide more than any other group of clients (Stanley, 2009).

BPD prevalence

Usually, a diagnosis of BPD is only given during adulthood. Among adults, approximately 6 per cent of the general population is diagnosed with BPD; this figure, published by the National Institute of Mental Health is based on the most recent and largest study of BPD (Grant, Chou and Goldstein, 2008). It challenges previous smaller investigations, which reported that approximately 1 per cent of the adult population suffers from BPD (for example, Merikangas et al., 2007).

BPD intervention

NICE have yet to stipulate a specific therapy for BPD, recommending further research into dialectical behaviour therapy (DBT) and mentalisation-based therapy (2009). Given the problems with emotional regulation manifested by sufferers of BPD, mentalisation treatment shows promising results, even when delivered by professionals who have a moderate amount of supervision and relatively limited additional training (Bateman and Fonagy, 2010).

BPD outcome

Research in the USA shows that dynamic deconstructive psychotherapy (which includes enabling BPD sufferers in recognising and naming their emotions) correlates with the majority of this client-group improving (Goldman and Gregory, 2010).

BPD in practice

When seeing clients with BPD, check and follow through regarding suicidal ideation. One customary way is by using the BDI (Beck, Steer and Brown, 1996) for checking any suicidal plans of action (cross-reference this with Chapter 2). If the client states that they will follow through with their suicidal ideation, then it is necessary for the therapist and client to collaboratively have a plan which involves the GP but if the client does not agree, it may be necessary to re-state the limits of confidentiality with such an at-risk client (this too can be cross-referenced with Chapter 2) and ensure that the client gets to a hospital where they can be attended to 24 hours a day. Teach emotional literacy to clients with signs of BPD. Be a role model for experiencing the here-and-now. Highlight the positive. These experiences can be an antidote to feeling distraught, especially if clients have a poor self-image, are lonely and unable to manage their emotions.

BPD CASE VIGNETTE

Jessica was twenty-five years old and lived with her partner who was deeply concerned about her fluctuating emotions, pessimism about the future, talk of killing herself, tendency to self-harm and repeated visits to her medical doctor. Eventually, after much pressure from her partner, she agreed to see a therapist.

Quickly, the therapist realised that Jessica's sense of self-worth was low, therefore he aimed at enhancing her self-esteem and existing strengths (Aviram et. al., 2004).

He also suggested group therapy so that Jessica could practice being in a social situation for the opportunity of making and maintaining social relationships, and receiving feedback about how others perceive her within a social situation. However, she dropped out of the group. Since the experience within group therapy was not successful, her therapist used DBT after being reminded by his supervisor that it was the first empirically supported approach used with clients suffering from BPD (Linehan and Koerner, 2000).

For Jessica, the therapist embraced the four modes typical of DBT:

1 Traditional one-to-one therapy.
2 Teaching Jessica new behavioural skills such as assertiveness, mindfulness, social skills, and helping her identify and regulate her emotional experiences (Holmes, Georgescu and Liles, 2005).
3 Helping Jessica transpose the skills learnt in therapy into her day-to-day living, which involved coaching her by telephone contact during out-of-office hours so that she could apply the skills to situations she was experiencing in-the-moment.
4 Consulting with a support-team (designed to support the therapist), which included his personal therapy and practice supervision, to help him from burnout and build on his existing compassion for Jessica.

Over three years of therapy, Jessica's suicidal ideation, self-injury and repeated visits to her medical doctor decreased substantially. She now has increased insight into herself and is more optimistic about her future.

BPD groundbreaking investigations

Behavioural economics research into game theory illustrates that when playing an investment game (for example, the Trust Game) brain activity on those diagnosed with BPD shows different patterns when compared with brain activity in healthy players (NIMH, 2008). Game theory uses a mathematical approach when studying social interactions and its researchers have found a new way of describing BPD: they state that sufferers are either unaware of norms which are socially acceptable, or their view of such norms are distorted therefore they may respond to others in a fashion that breaks up trust and disrupts co-operation (NIMH, 2008).

OBSESSIVE COMPULSIVE PD

As a reminder: if individuals suffer from OCPD, it means that they conform inflexibly to rules and ethical codes, and that they systematise excessively. OCPD is within Section C of the PDs spectrum, related to being anxious.

Importantly, OCPD must not be confused with OCD (obsessive compulsive disorder). There is much overlap, but those with OCPD believe that they are right whereas those with OCD have unwanted thoughts.

OCPD theory

Contemporary thought on OCPD can be traced to Freud, as he was the first to name the obsessive-compulsive personality as the 'anal character', identifying its main components as frugality, rigidness and orderliness (1908). Most theories focus on social (Kelly, 1963) or biological (Halmi, 2005) factors as causes of OCPD. One social theory states that if a child has much contact with a significant other who is controlling and inflexible, then that obsessiveness is learnt and copied (Villemarette-Pittman et al., 2004) (this can be cross-referenced with Chapter 3). Different research findings support both the social (van der Kolk and Pinoos, 2009) and biological (Joyce et al., 2003) theories.

OCPD research

Investigations backing up the biological theory show that individuals with a certain type of gene (a form of the dopa-responsive dystonia gene) are likely to develop depression and OCPD, especially if male; although this may not happen unless triggered by childhood trauma (Joyce et al., 2003). Other findings illustrate that the stress of childhood trauma can eventually lead to mental problems such as OCPD as an adult (van der Kolk and Pinoos, 2009) (this can be cross-referenced with Chapters 3 and 12).

OCPD signs

If over three of the following are present, OCPD can be diagnosed:

- a focus on detail (so loses sight of the 'big picture')
- a dedication to work (at the expense of spare time)
- a systematic approach (such as list-making or schedule-planning)
- inflexible beliefs (for example, 'I am right, you are wrong!')
- perfectionism (making task-completion extremely difficult)
- an unwillingness to delegate ('because only I can do it properly')
- having do things their way ('because no other way will do')
- stingyness (even if affluent).

OCPD prevalence

Approximately 1 per cent of the general population has been found to suffer from OCPD (Mental Health, 2012).

OCPD intervention

It is difficult to find a valid and reliable specific approach to OCPD, perhaps because a fuller understanding of this client group is called for. More research is needed for exploring optimum therapeutic options. However, one investigation suggests that cognitive analytic therapy is helpful (Protogerou, 2008).

OCPD expected outcome

Although medication is not recommended, it has successfully reduced anxiety in OCPD sufferers. Rarely do those with OCPD seek help because they believe that they are right, but of those who do, self-help seems to be the port of call which can be of use to them.

OCPD in practice

Therapists can suggest co-operation from family and self-help strategies such as journal writing.

OCPD CASE VIGNETTE

Philip sought a therapist because his wife said, 'Get therapy or I'll leave!'

Eventually, one therapist accepted him on the condition that when Philip felt that the therapist did something wrong, he stayed in therapy. This is because she knew that approximately 50 per cent of OCPD sufferers drop out of therapy due to feeling outraged that the therapist has made a mistake.

Indeed, a point in therapy did occur when Philip felt that his perfectionist standard was violated due to an unwitting mistake the therapist made. After a reminder of their initial agreement, he stayed in therapy. This was a turning point because Philip was enabled in learning how to manage conflict. Part of his therapy involved role-playing conflict resolutions. He experienced these role-plays as powerfully helpful, since there was good rapport between him and his therapist with communication flowing freely.

As he did not leave therapy prematurely, Philip eventually faced and appropriately dealt with his outrage at imperfection and was enabled to stop seeing things as only black and white, realising that there were other perspectives.

His marriage is intact, perhaps because he managed to change his rigid attitude during the therapeutic process.

ANTI-SOCIAL PD

Anti-social people are either against society or harmful towards it. This is different from not being sociable.

ASPD research and theory

Therapist and researcher Baird (2008) has found that repeated mis-attunement during childhood can result in ASPD during adulthood. Relevant literature, whether relating to theory or research, suggests that those with ASPD grew up with harsh parenting (see Knott, 2012). This does not mean that everyone who experiences harsh parenting develops ASPD!

ASPD signs

These incorporate:

- superficial charm
- rapid irritation
- impulsivity
- remorselessness
- callousness
- recklessness.

If individuals aged eighteen years or over have at least three of these and a history of conduct disorder before that age, they can be diagnosed with ASPD (Knott, 2012).

ASPD prevalence

Approximately 2 per cent of the adult population suffer from ASPD (Cooper, 2012).

ASPD intervention

Although therapy is at the heart of intervening with this client population, a single therapy intervention is not recommended and referral to psychiatric services is suggested, where support can be utilised from a multi-disciplinary team.

ASPD expected outcome

Previously thought of as a life-long PD, emerging evidence indicates that positive changes can be made (Knott, 2012).

ASPD in practice

Group therapy and CBT are most popular with this client group. Whatever approach is used though, clients' needs and preferences must be taken into account and they should be offered the opportunity of making an informed choice regarding decisions about their care. A team of professionals can work together to create a tailored management plan for use in avoiding crises and violence.

AVOIDANT PD

AvPD is sometimes known as anxious PD. Fearing social situations, low self-esteem and seeming to be a loner yet longing for intimacy and friendship describes an AvPD sufferer.

AvPD research and theory

Researchers do not know the cause of AvPD, but theories are plentiful. Main theoretical explanations are that it is passed via genes, that the behaviour is learned from a significant other, or that it began as a coping skill that helped the sufferer as a child who continues to behave in that way during adulthood (PsychCentral, 2012).

AvPD signs

The following characterise individuals with AvPD:

- a pre-occupation with how others see them (because they are afraid of not being liked)
- imagining (rather than actually having) satisfactory social relationships

- low self-esteem (therefore not taking career opportunities)
- spending much time alone
- reluctant to meet new people even though they want to (Westen, 1990, 1998).

AvPD prevalence

Approximately 1 per cent of the general population suffer from AvPD (PsychCentral, 2012).

AvPD intervention

Training in social skills have been found to help (Health.am, 2006).

AvPD expected outcome

Therapy can be helpful but more investigations are needed to ascertain whether a short-term positive outcome lasts in the long term.

AvPD in practice

If faced with clients who have AvPD, it is important remembering that this does not mean that they suffer from an illness or that something is wrong with their brain. The problem may be due to the way of thinking, feeling and behaving that they have learnt to use, even though this way of being does not currently serve them adequately.

MAJOR PD MODELS

There are three main models used to understand PDs: Benjamin's (1996), Westen's (1990) and Millon's (2012). Below is a skeletal explanation of each.

Benjamin's model

This important interpersonal model incorporates three main theoretical aspects:

1 actions directed towards another; for example, an abusive parent
2 the person's response to either actual or perceived actions; for example, recoiling from abusive parents or important others
3 self-action; for example, self-abuse (for instance, what began as criticism from parents ends up as self-criticism).

Each of these three aspects incorporates a quadrant with the following factors

i love
ii hate

iii differentiation

iv enmeshment.

Using Benjamin's model can diminish co-morbidity among PDs (1996). For example, although overall, inappropriate anger is a characteristic of PDs, it is the person's perception of the other who apparently caused the anger that can determine which category of PD may be the correct one. For instance, if on the one hand individuals are angry because they perceive others as neglectful of them or abandoning them, then these angry people can be categorised as suffering from a BPD. On the other hand, if individuals are angered because they perceive others as not giving them everything they want, or as being slighted, then the individuals can (currently) be categorised as suffering from narcissistic PD (Benjamin, 1996). When anger is aimed at controlling the other person while being detached and cold, then such individuals can be categorised as anti-social PD sufferers. In this way, it is not difficult to understand that one angry explosion from an individual with PD can be because that person is trying to distance him or herself from the other, to hurt the other, or to elicit the other to respond in a fashion which pulls them into the relationship again.

Westen's model

This model seems more comprehensive than Benjamin's as it is more of a model of the mind than a theory of PDs. Westen endeavours to portray and systematise the key features of personality that define a person's character by drawing on observation (i.e. practice-based evidence), psychoanalytic theory (for example, Brenner, 1982) and psychological research (for example, Damon and Hart, 1988). In this way, he aspires to map not only disturbed personality dynamics but also healthy ones. The model proposes that three questions (each having several subquestions) need answering to formulate a case:

1 What does the individual wish for?

2 What is the client's experience of the self?

3 What psychological resources does the person have?

When using this model, clients with specific PDs can be categorised by the clustering of distinct tensions and intentions. For example, if they are chronically worried about being abandoned, are somehow incapable of adapting, inept at impulse-control or emotionally immature, then BPD can be assumed. Westen's model is described in an extremely simplistic way here; nevertheless, even for those who do not have a PD, the three questions listed above can be used to describe their personality dynamics.

Millon's model

An evolutionary and social learning model Millon's original theory embraced three aspects (pleasure/pain, active/passive, and self/other) but after further investigations he incorporated a fourth: thinking/feeling, to reflect the extent that an individual relies on intuition or abstract thought (Millon, 1990; Millon and Davis, 1996; Millon et al., 2004). For example, clients with histrionic PD are poor abstract thinkers, seek pleasure, are very active and self-centred yet interpersonally engaged; by contrast, clients with schizoid PD lean on abstract thinking rather than intuition, do not experience much pleasure and have little involvement with other people. It is because of Millon's theory that there is a distinction in the third edition of the DSM between avoidant and schizoid PD (1990).

Millon's model is widely used. Indeed, the instrument he developed for classifying PDs, although theory-driven rather than research-based, is now in its third edition (MCM1-111, Millon and Davis, 1996). It has been used in hundreds of studies and to assess clients in clinical practice (Kristensen and Torgensen, 2001; Espelage et al., 2002).

PDS IN PRACTICE

A therapist can observe as well as interview a client in order to ascertain if a PD may be of concern and, if so, to identify which one.

PSYCHOPATHY AND DANGEROUS PEOPLE WITH SEVERE PERSONALITY DISORDER

The term 'psychopathy' is currently not used in the DSM-IV-TR (APA, 2002). Instead, the term 'anti-social personality disorder' (ASPD, discussed above) is used. (See Chapter 12 for links between sociopathy and inadequate emotional literacy.) The term 'dangerous people with severe personality disorder' (DSPD) is a term coined by the UK government, which is why such a diagnostic category is not found in any DSM (Corbin and Westwood, 2005). For this reason, therapists may experience a double-bind because of conflicting cues; one from government stating that people labelled with DSPD must be put into detention, and the other that clients have a right to be offered the 'fittest' healthcare therapy. Lecturers in health sciences, Corbin and Westwood, explain that 'UK healthcare professionals may therefore find themselves increasingly in a position of being instruments of a political agenda … They may become more subservient to administrative exigencies … within a politically motivated law of "detention without offence", whilst simultaneously trying to preserve the rights and therapeutic treatment of patients/clients' (2005: 131).

LATEST THOUGHTS ON MINDFULNESS

Although mindfulness is a form of meditation that has been used since ancient times, according to the Mental Health Foundation (2010), the latest thoughts are that using mindfulness is therapeutic for PDs (this can be cross-referenced with developmental trauma models in Chapter 3).

AGE, GENDER AND CULTURE

Overall, it seems that it is young adults aged between eighteen and thirty-five who suffer with PDs (NICE, 2009). However, superstitious beliefs and practices, as well as the specific context of an individual's culture, must be evaluated before PD is diagnosed. Regarding BPD, men and women suffer equally, according to the most recent national survey (Grant, Chou and Goldstein, 2008), although a few smaller studies such as Winkler's (2008) suggest that in the UK approximately 75 per cent of individuals with the diagnosis are women.

Points to ponder

- One of many different perspectives for perceiving individuals with certain types of human distress is to diagnose them as PD sufferers; but distress occurs in all and although the perspective is not bad, some may feel unheard and depersonalised or misrepresented, if categorised in this way.
- Since BPD is characterised by instability in mood, behaviour and relationships, might interactive activities such as the Rainbow board game (Rudd, 2011) and EQ card game (Rudd, 2009) that were designed to include experiencing co-operation, emotional management and building friendships, be helpful?
- How might strong, relational therapeutic processes create hope and meaning in the life of distressed individuals, irrespective of whether they can be diagnosed within the PDs categories?

Exercise

(Answers are embedded within this chapter.)

1 What is the hallmark of PDs?
2 Name ten PDs in the fourth edition of the DSM.
3 What are the difficulties in categorising PDs?

CHAPTER SUMMARY

Odd, dramatic and anxious are the three types of behaviours into which PDs can be categorised.

'Dangerous people with severe personality disorder' is a term coined by government.

Mindfulness can be used to promote mental health.

Game theory explains PD in a novel way.

The majority of PD sufferers are young adults.

LIST OF USEFUL RESOURCES

- Elliott, C.H. and Smith, L.L. (2009) *Borderline Personality Disorder for Dummies* (Singapore, Wiley).
- Mind (2008) *How to Restrain from Violent Impulses* (London, National Association for Mental Health).
- Mind (2006) *Stepping off the Map: A Project about Personality Disorder* (DVD) (London, National Association for Mental Health).
- Rudd, B. (2010) *Anger Management* (game) (Milton Keynes, Speechmark).

RELEVANT WEBSITES

www.nice.org.uk
www.personalitydisorder.org.uk
www.nhsdirect.nhs.uk

REFERENCES

Aldhous, P. (2011) 'Fix you', *New Scientist*, 27 August, pp. 47–9.

Anglin, D.M., Cohen, P.R. and Chen, H. (2008) 'Duration of early maternal separation and prediction of schizotypal symptoms from early adolescence to mid-life', *Schizophrenia Research*, 103, 1, pp. 143–50.

APA (2002) *DSM-IV-TR® Diagnostic and Statistical Manual of Mental Disorders* (Fourth Edition, revised) (Vancouver, American Psychiatric Association).

Aviram, R.B., Hellerstein, D.J., Gerson, J. and Stanley, B. (2004) 'Adapting supportive psychotherapy to individuals with borderline personality disorder with individuals who self-injure or attempt suicide', *Psychiatric Practice*, 10, 3, pp. 145–55.

Baird, L. (2008) 'Childhood trauma in the etiology of borderline personality disorder', *Hakomi Forum*, 19, 20–21, pp. 31–42.

Bateman, A. W. and Fonagy, P. (2006) *Mentalization-Based Treatment for Borderline Personality Disorder: A Practical Guide* (Oxford, Oxford University Press).

Bateman, A. and Fonagy, P. (2010) 'Mentalization based treatment for borderline disorder', *World Psychiatry*, 9, 1, pp. 11–15.

Beck, A.T., Steer, R.A. and Brown G.K. (1996) *Manual for Beck Depression Inventory II (BDI-II)* (San Antonio Texas, Psychology Corporation).

Benjamin, L.S. (1996) 'An interpersonal theory of personality disorders', in Clarkin, J.F. and Lenzenweger, M.F. (eds) *Major Theories of Personality Disorder* (New York, Guilford Press).

Brenner, C. (1982) *The Mind in Conflict* (New York, International Universities Press).

Cooper, A. (2012) *Anti-social Personality Disorder*, www.health.am/psy/antisocial-personality-disorder/, accessed 15 August 2012.

Corbin, K. and Westwood, T. (2005) 'Dangerous and severe personality disorder: a psychiatric manifesto for the risk society', *Critical Public Health*, 5, 2, pp. 121–33.

Cowley, D. (2012) 'Does childhood abuse cause borderline personality traits?', *Journal Watch Psychiatry*, http://psychiatry.jwatch.org/cgi/content/full/2012/723/2, accessed 7 August 2012.

Damon, W. and Hart, D.S. (1988) *Self-understanding in Childhood and Adolescence* (New York, Cambridge University Press).

Espelage, D., Mazzeo, S.E., Sherman, R. and Thompson, R. (2002) MCMI-II profiles of women with eating disorders: a cluster analytic investigation', *Journal of Personality Disorders*, 16, 5, pp. 453–63.

(Continued)

(Continued)

Freud, S. (1959, original work published 1908) 'Character and anal eroticism', in *The Standard Edition of the Complete Psychological Works of Sigmund Freud*, 9 (James Strachey, ed.) (London, Hogarth).

Giles, G. (2012) *Schizotypal Personality Disorder*, www.minddisorders.com/Py-Z/Schizotypal-personality-disorder.html#b, accessed 29 January 2013.

Goldman, G.A. and Gregory, R.J. (2010) 'Relationships between techniques and outcomes for borderline personality disorder', *American Journal of Psychotherapy*, 64, 4, pp. 359–72.

Grant, B.F. Chou, P.S. and Goldstein, R.B. (2008) 'Prevalence, correlates, disability, and comorbidity of DSM-IV borderline personality disorder: results from the wave 2 National Epidemiologic Survey on Alcohol and Related Conditions', *Journal of Clinical Psychiatry*, 69, 4, pp. 533–45.

Halmi (2005) 'Personality and eating disorders', in Hollander, E., Zohar, J. and Sirovatka, P.J. (eds) *Obsessive Compulsive Spectrum Disorders* (Arlington VA, American Psychiatric Publishing).

Health.am (2006) *Avoidant Personality Disorders Treatment Recommendations*, www.health.am/psy/more/apd_treatment_recommendations/, accessed 9 August 2012.

Holmes, P., Georgescu, S. and Liles, W. (2005) 'Further delineating the applicability of acceptance and change to private responses: the example of dialectical behavior therapy', *The Behavior Analyst Today*, 7, 3, pp. 301–15.

Joyce, P.R., Rogers, G.R., Miller, A.L., Mulder, R.T., Luty, S.E. and Kennedy, M.A. (2003) 'Polymorphisms of DRD4 and DRD3 and risk avoidant and obsessive personality traits and disorders', *Psychiatric Research*, 119, 1–2, pp. 1–20.

Kelly, G. (1963) *A Theory of Personality* (New York, Norton).

Knott, L. (2012) *Antisocial Personality Disorder*, www.patient.co.uk/doctor/Antisocial-Personality-Disorder.htm, accessed 8 August 2012.

Kristensen, H. and Torgensen, S. (2001) 'MCMI-II personality traits and symptom traits in parents of children with selective mutism: a case-control study', *Journal of Abnormal Psychology*, 110, 4, pp. 648–52.

Lenzenweger, M. (ed.) (2004) *Major Theories of Personality Disorder* (New York, Guilford).

Lieb, K., Zanarini, M.C., Schmahl, C., Linehan, M.M. and Bohus, M. (2011) 'Borderline personality disorder', *The Lancet*, 94, 2, pp. 453–61.

Linehan, M. and Koerner, K. (2000) 'Research on dialectical behavior therapy for patients with borderline personality disorder', *Psychiatric Clinic North America*, 23, 1, pp. 151–67.

Mayo Clinic Staff (2012) *Schizotypal Personality Disorder*, www.mayoclinic.com/health/schizotypal-personality-disorder/DS00830/DSECTION=causes, accessed 21 July 2012.

Mental Health (2012) *Obsessive-compulsive Personality Disorder*, www.mentalhealth.com/dis/p20-pe10.html, accessed 15 August 2012.

Mental Health Foundation (2010) *Mindfulness* (London, Mental Health Foundation).

Merikangas, K.R., Akiskal, H.S., Angst, J., Greenberg, P.E., Hirschfeld, R.M., Petukhova, M. and Kessler, R.C. (2007) 'Lifetime and 12-month prevalence of bipolar spectrum disorder in the National Comorbidity Survey replication', *Archives of General Psychiatry*, 64, 5, pp. 543–52.

Millon, T. (1990) 'The Millon Clinical Multiaxial Inventory (MCMI): a review', *Journal of Personality Assessment*, 55, 3–4, pp. 445–64.

Millon, T. (2012) *Personality Subtypes*, http://millon.net/taxonomy/summary.htm, accessed 21 July 2012.

Millon, T. and Davis, R.D. (1996) 'An evolutionary theory of personality disorders', in Clarkin, J., Foelsch, P.A. and Kernberg, O.F., 'Factor structure of borderline personality disorder criteria', *Journal of Personality Disorders*, 7, 137, p. 43.

Millon, T., Millon, C.M., Meagher, S. and Grossman, S. (2004) *Personality Disorders in Modern Life* (New Jersey, John Wiley and Sons).

NICE (2009) *Borderline Personality Disorder: Treatment and Management*, www.nice.org.uk/nicemedia/pdf/BorderlinePersonalityDisorderNICEGuidelineForConsultation.pdf, accessed 1 August 2012.

NIMH (2008) *Borderline Personality Disorder: Brain Differences to Disruptions in Cooperation in Relationships*, www.nimh.nih.gov/science-news/2008/borderline-personality-disorder-related-to-disruptions-in-cooperation-in-relationships.shtml, accessed 7 August 2012.

Protogerou, E.T., (2008) 'Evaluation of cognitive-analytic-therapy (CAT) outcome in patients with obsessive compulsive personality disorder', *Annals of General Psychiatry*, 7, 1, Section 109.

PsychCentral (2012) *Avoidant Personality Disorder*, http://psychcentral.com/disorders/sx8.htm, accessed 9 August 2012.

Questa, M. J., Peralta, V. and Zarzuela, A. (2001) 'Are personality traits associated with cognitive disturbance in psychosis?', *Schizophrenia Research*, 51, 2, pp. 109–19.

Rudd, B. (2009) *EQ* (card game) (Milton Keynes, Speechmark).

Rudd, B. (2011) *Rainbow* (board game) (Milton Keynes, Speechmark).

Stanley, B. (2009) *Preventing Suicide in Patients with Borderline Personality Disorder*, http://nyp.org/enews/preventing-suicide-bpd-patients.html, accessed 1 August 2012.

van der Kolk, B.A. and Pinoos, R.S. (2009) *Proposal to Include a Developmental Trauma Disorder Diagnosis for Children and Adolescents in DSM-V*, www.traumacenter.org/about/about_bessel.php, accessed 8 August 2012.

Villemarette-Pittman, N.R., Stanford, M., Greve, K., Houston, R. and Mathias, C. (2004) 'Obsessive-compulsive personality disorder and behavioral disinhibition', *The Journal of Psychology*, 138, 1, pp. 5–22.

Westen, D. (1990) 'Towards a revised theory of borderline object relations: contributions of empirical research', *International Journal of Psychoanalysis*, 71, pp. 661–93.

Westen, D. (1998) 'Case formulation and personality diagnosis: two processes or one?', in Barron, J. (ed.) *Making Diagnosis Meaningful* (Washington DC, American Psychological Association Press).

WHO (1992) *ICD-10: The ICD-10 Classification of Mental and Behavioural Disorders: Clinical Descriptions and Diagnostic Guidelines* (Copenhagen, World Health Organization).

Widiger, T.A. and Lowe, J.R. (2007) 'Five-factor model assessment of personality disorder', *Journal of Personality Assessment*, 89, 1, pp. 16–29.

Winkler, M. (2008) *Borderline (Emotionally Unstable) Personality Prevalence – Statistics on the Frequency*, http://web4health.info/en/answers/border-prevalence.htm, accessed 1 August 2012.

12

Psychopathology and Possible Future Avenues

LEARNING OBJECTIVES FOR THIS CHAPTER

- Discuss the concept of psychopathology
- Know the importance of emotions
- Understand the construct of a holistic approach
- Deliberate on future possibilities regarding mental health

Medical discourse continues to dominate the therapeutic community. This chapter offers a different perspective on 'psychopathology'. In possible future approaches to mental health I expect surprises because I do not know what is around the corner.

INTRODUCING PSYCHOPATHOLOGY

Psychopathology is a classification system developed from ancient Greek times and fine-tuned from the 1950s leading to our contemporary understanding of it. Using categories for classifying mental distress offers structure and direction (see Chapter 1 for more on this), however, many who are diagnosed under the same label do not have the same symptoms, perhaps due to how they have developed through life (lifespan developmental stages are not mentioned in the diagnostic manuals, but I deliberate on them in Chapter 3).

DIAGNOSIS IN SERVICES

The exercise of diagnosis in current health services is useful because the UK government offers recommendations for treating the symptoms of recognised mental disorders with medication and or therapy. Such knowledge is important for cross-professional discourse.

Unfortunately, however, classifying mental health conditions may be problematic because being labelled can set in motion a 'machine' of treatments and perhaps patient dependence on experts. In my opinion, the future can offer a more holistic, health-focused (rather than symptom-alleviating) approach to (mental) care. (See below.)

FORMULATION VERSUS DIAGNOSIS

In Chapter 2, formulation is introduced as an alternative to using the DSM for diagnosing, asking questions such as, 'How can you define normality?' and 'What about culture and causes, not just symptoms?' Current classifying within mental health does not look at the individual as a whole. Perhaps therapists who classify human suffering should ask themselves 'Are we controlling or empowering the client?' Psychologist Golsworthy (2004: 28) states, 'Clients of mental health services should at least have the opportunity to know what we can tell them about the assumptions that drive their care and treatment'.

EMOTIONAL WELLNESS

Emotional wellbeing is fundamental for good-enough mental health, and ideally starts with having empathic parents (Fonagy, Sharp and Goodyer, 2008; Panskepp and Biven, 2012). If parents are skilled in spotting and explaining the reasons behind emotions their children experience, especially during the first twelve months after birth, then, according to research findings, they will grow into children with the ability to 'own' their emotions (see for example, Parsons, Young and Murray, 2010); that is, feel, identify and talk about their emotions. This will develop through their teens and into adulthood, along with the understanding that others have minds of their own and, therefore, the knowledge that others can think and feel differently to the way they do (Gerhardt, 2011).

If parents cannot accept the emotional states within themselves and keep their own selves well balanced, how can they be open to their toddler's emotional tantrums, especially if they feel that they have to shut off their child's emotion? When parents stay in touch with their emotions while keeping their equilibrium, simultaneously understanding their toddler's feelings and having the foresight of knowing the outcome of their child's actions, then those parents are mentalising. Having the skill to mentalise is subtly different from empathising (feeling the other person's emotion). Both are needed for good-enough emotional literacy, which can buffer against mental distress (see Fonagy, Sharp and Goodyer, 2008).

It is logical to theorise therefore that those who perceive others as having the choice to think, feel and act differently from them are those who first had their own mental states acknowledged. What is steadily emerging from research is that a way of developing empathy and acceptable interpersonal skills in children is to deliberate on their emotions and help them in perceiving what others may be experiencing (see for example, Laible and Thompson, 2003) (this can be cross-referenced with Chapter 3).

ADULT MENTAL PROBLEMS

If a person grows without the opportunity of developing emotional literacy, and is, for instance, defensive, then he or she can be very self-absorbed, so much so that the individual has signs of narcissism (this can be cross-referenced with Chapter 11). Alternatively the person may use another inappropriate defensive strategy, such as projecting (individuals who project may believe that others have the identical emotion as they do, but rather than realise that the genesis of the emotion comes from the individuals themselves, they incorrectly pinpoint the emotion as originating from the others). Those with unsuitable defensiveness may display signs of what is classified as BPD; unfortunately, an individual may be so defensive that she or he has symptoms of sociopathy (this can be cross-referenced with Chapter 11).

FROM INFANT TO ADULT

Young people do not grow into adults who for no reason suddenly suffer from profound mental distress. There is a thread through one's years linking early experiences with how life's ups and downs are coped with later. Skills we use for defensiveness are useful in helping us steer clear of potentially harmful relationships, while we can let our defences down for healthy relationships (Kegan 1982). As years go by, our defences become more complex as we learn to navigate through life.

BEING DEFENSIVE

Many adults do not move on from their childhood ways of coping with defending themselves psychologically. Individuals can be stuck in a basic way of coping with relationships. The more basic the way of coping with psychological pain, the younger the individual is likely to have been who had to initially use this type of defence due to experiencing profound distress. A few defence mechanisms are listed below. Interestingly, the term 'defence mechanism' originated with Freud's psychoanalytic theory (1937).

1 Basic defence mechanisms

- Dissociation
- Projection
- Denial.

Having these at a developmentally very early stage in life can lead to narcissism in adulthood, as a result of which the individual does not perceive that others have needs and that it is wrong to blame innocent others (Dombeck, 2011). Many of us have met people who, for example, talk for hours about how they are, without once asking how we are. It may be possible to grow out of this by experiencing a nurturing relationship (this can be cross-referenced with Chapter 11).

2 Neither basic nor sophisticated defence mechanisms

- Repression
- Intellectualisation
- Rationalisation.

Having these at a relatively early life stage, such as during adolescence, can lead to putting most of one's energy into work as an adult as a way of numbing emotion. Many of us have met people who, for example, rationalise everything, without showing emotion. It is possible to outgrow this by experiencing a nurturing relationship.

3 Sophisticated defence mechanisms

- Sublimation
- Affiliation
- Assertiveness.

To achieve this sophisticated level of defence, being a good listener and communicating well helps. As adults, we can choose this level of defensive skill. Many of us have met people who, for example, are warm, wise and unruffled (Dombeck, 2011).

THEORY

Speculation as to the cause of psychopathology is double-pronged: one, we suffer psychopathologically because of our genes; two, we suffer due to our environment. These theoretical positions can be cross-referenced with previous chapters.

PRACTICE

Irrespective of psychopathology, in my practice, compassionately supporting clients minimises difficult behaviour; coupled with this, appropriate non-verbal communication is crucial. Yet there is a paucity of looking in-depth at these aspects during therapy training, which concerns me, bearing in mind that the most impactful communication is non-verbal (Rudd, 2000). I tend to meet clients at their level in the therapy sessions. For example, I may speak from the physical level of the client: if they crouch, I crouch; if they sit, I sit.

In future, non-verbal communication can be fully unpacked so that therapists increase their awareness of the unspoken yet powerful messages they communicate to their clients.

RESEARCH

Much abuse is non-verbal, such as via a tone of voice used, irrespective of the words spoken. Rates of anti-social behaviour, drug dependence, alcohol abuse and anxiety disorders over a lifetime are significantly higher in those who were abused as children, when compared with those who were not (Harriet, MacMillan and Fleming, 2001). Although the association between psychopathology and childhood abuse has been well documented with clinical populations (for example, see Brown and Anderson, 1991), not so many have investigated the association within a population-based community (see for example, Jumper, 1995).

CAN ABUSED CHILDREN BE HEALTHY AS ADULTS?

Having experienced childhood abuse does not mean that a lifetime of psychopathological suffering must be endured. Other factors, such as family and society, may have a confounding effect, leading to greater vulnerability of mental distress. It is therefore important not to jump to general conclusions such as if children are abused they become mentally dysfunctional adults. Many adults who have experienced abuse as children function in a mentally good-enough way. They neither suffer from anxiety disorders (see Chapter 4), cognitive disorders (see Chapter 5), mood problems (see Chapter 6), eating issues (see Chapter 7), nor psychotic problems, somatising or personality disorders (see Chapters 8, 9, 10 and 11, respectively).

GENO/ENVIRONMENTAL MODELS OF PSYCHOPATHOLOGY AND THEIR INFLUENCE ON INTERVENTIONS

Childhood environment and biological factors influence interventions. For example, if a biological factor is considered to be the root cause of psychopathology, then it is not uncommon for the intervention to be medication. If childhood environment is considered to be the root cause, then the intervention is likely to be therapy. Interventions used are dependent on the lens the therapist looks through. With BPD for instance, if some clients suffer from this and their therapist is up-to-date with research that shows that sufferers have low emotional intelligence, then that therapist may educate the client in emotional literacy (Gardner and Qualter, 2009). If however, the therapist believes that BPD is due to inherited genes, then a referral to a medic for a prescription may occur.

WELLNESS, ILLNESS AND PSYCHOPATHOLOGY

There is no clear boundary between 'wellness' and psychopathological 'illness', because these concepts are culturally defined. Within the western world, overall robustness signifies wellness, while having the symptoms of one or more of the disorders listed in a mental health diagnostic manual signifies a purported mental illness. When individuals are perceived as suffering from a psychiatric illness, they are viewed through the psychopathology lens.

FUTURE OF PSYCHOPATHOLOGY

One direction may be three-pronged, embracing emotional research that includes diagnostic imaging, cross-diagnostic studies (which cut across existing diagnosis concerns) and learning emotional literacy. This path can lead to earlier intervention by increasing emotional intelligence thereby decreasing mental health problems (King, 2010; Schore, 2012). If such an approach focuses on the whole person rather than pinpointing discreet psychological disorders, the concept of psychopathology may become unnecessary.

PSYCHOPATHOLOGY DECONSTRUCTED

One way of deconstructing psychopathology is to understand that it is within political, economic and social contexts that individuals' mental problems are focused on as 'disorders'. Another way is to realise that the idea of psychopathology has been constructed in the western world by following a philosophical thread from ancient Greek times to the present (see Chapter 1). Professor of Counselling, Prichard (2008), deconstructs psychopathology by offering a 'conspiracy theory': to benefit society by propagating capitalism, certain behaviours must be pathologised to support corporate profits and continue with the existing state of affairs regarding social or political issues, because the ones with power over society have a vested interest in maintaining the status quo. A holistic approach has no such hidden agenda.

HOLISTIC

A holistic lens looks beyond psychopathology by spotlighting the existing inter-relationship between mind, body and spirit. Why is the mind-body considered as two separate entities: mind and body? We can blame the split on Descartes (Sorrel, 2000; see Chapter 1 for an explanation). Indeed, it was not until the latter part of the twentieth century that a team of researchers headed by scientist Felton, discovered a hard-wired link between the central nervous system and the body's immune system. Felton's research results (1981) show that the brain sends signals to the cells of the immune system by, for example, thinking happy thoughts to boost immunity, enabling us to sense a harmonious experience. With this in mind, therapists are in a position to make major differences for themselves and their clients by generating coherence.

COHERENCE

Coherence can be a future approach to mental health, but what is it? It is the body and mind working together in a measurable, coherent way. When there is coherence, the whole is greater than its parts. For example, when listening to a complete coherent sentence, its meaning is greater than the meaning of the individual words in it. Areas as diverse as physiology, cosmology, quantum physics, brain and consciousness research embrace the concept of coherence, which is applicable to global affairs, human interactions and individuals' mental states (McCraty, 2011).

What is the relevance of coherence to therapists?

Therapists who tend towards being coherent have the emotional literacy to deal with stressful issues and to bounce back from adversity. They have increased perception, are psychologically resilient and emotionally stable. This can make them effective role models for their clients. The importance of emotional literacy for mental health has been well documented (for example, Schore, 2012 and Goleman, 2011).

Why is coherence relevant for therapists' clients?

If therapists can guide their clients towards increasing their emotional literacy and teach them how to be in a coherent state, clients can benefit from the consequences of being in such a state. Benefits incorporate:

- greater awareness
- stable and harmonious homeostasis
- stopping excessive distress
- recovery from challenging experiences
- self-regulation
- creating positive emotions
- building resilience.

It is not possible to experience distress and coherence simultaneously (McCraty, 2011).

According to psychologist Goleman (2011), a hallmark of good-enough emotional intelligence is psychological resilience. In order to stop excessive distress occurring and to recover from challenging experiences, a large amount of resilience is required. Perhaps in a future avenue, learning to build resilience by raising emotional intelligence, developing emotional literacy and understanding the role of positive emotions can be a part of training for therapists. Emotions are linked with the heart (Dossey, 2009): the heart's coherence and our enriching emotional experiences are entwined. When we use our mind to create coherence with our heart, love blossoms as distress withers, while perception, emotional stability and resilience are boosted (Panskepp and Biven, 2012).

HEART

By experiencing positive emotions such as care, love, forgiveness, compassion and appreciation, the heart and brain intercommunicate and coherence occurs (Lipton and Bhaerman, 2011). This affects those close to us because the heart produces a large electromagnetic field (influenced by our emotions) that expands several feet beyond our skin. Consequently, the field (emanating from the heart) affects those around us (Laszlo, 2008; Dossey, 2009).

At a local level, it is important that therapists are emotionally literate so that they are able to be in touch with their heart and transform their emotions positively to change the heart's electromagnetic field for the better, so that it impacts in a healing way on those near them. Even if their clients do not know why they feel better, they may intuit that it has something to do with the therapist's own being.

On a macro level, this shows how amazingly interconnected we are to one another; we are not hardwired to be competitive and at war, but to be caring and co-operative (Deyhle and McCraty, 2010; Braden, 2012). Bearing this in mind it is unremarkable that what unites diverse perspectives in different cultural and spiritual traditions across history is the thread of naming the heart as intuition's and love's source, suggesting that it is not only a life-supporting pump, but also an intuitive or spiritual organ, which throughout history is related to humans' 'inner voice'. Re-enforcing this is the

CASE VIGNETTE

Uma was in her late twenties. Her partner was concerned about her negativity and judgemental attitude so he said he would pay for her to have therapy. She felt that she was not the negative, judgemental person others perceived her as, and therefore found a therapist, telling him that she wanted to re-discover her 'true self'.

Shortly before Uma's therapy began, the therapist finished a CPD course on learning to be in a coherent state and how to pass on that information to clients.

He shared this with Uma by teaching her a particular type of breathing that she practised during her sessions. The breathing technique was coupled with specific heart-felt emotions in a sustainable way. She also practised this between sessions, daily, at home.

Soon, Uma, her partner and others noticed that rather than being judgemental, she generated compassionate love.

This was due to the breathing technique coupled with positive emotion (see Bernardi, Porta and Spicuzza, 2005; Childre and Rozman, 2005).

expanding number of people listening to their heart's intelligence for inner guidance; investigations reveal that coherence is significant for inner guidance or intuition (see McCraty, 2004).

I use these self-regulatory experiences on myself and with clients. Although I thought that the self-regulating skills seemed simple, they initially needed regular practice for sustained improvement.

HEART-BRAIN

Studies show significantly improved outcomes in clinical populations with PTSD (see Vanderbilt, Young and MacDonald, 2008), depression (see Siepmann, Aykac and Unterforfer, 2008) and anxiety and insomnia (see McLay and Spira, 2009) as a result of using the self-regulating skills. Although the greatest seminal work on heart-brain communications confirmed that cognitive activity was modulated by the heart's performance, there were inconsistent findings in later investigations; however, still later research results resolved the inconsistency, showing that interactions between heart and brain have a greater complexity than previously hypothesised (see Wolk and Velden, 1987; Lacey and Lacey, 2007).

AGE, GENDER AND CULTURE

Across diverse populations, irrespective of gender, chronological age, cultural background, education and socio-economic status, when individuals are in a coherent state, there is a significant rise in their experience of being content, caring, grateful, resilient and peaceful yet having vitality, while there is a fall in the measures of anxiety, hostility, fatigue, anger, burnout, depression and stress, coupled with a sense of being connected with one's heart intuition (for example, see McCraty, Atkinson and Lipsenthal, 2003; McCraty, Atkinson and Tiller, 2003). Lack of coherence in people, whoever they are, can result in individual and societal pathology, such as violence and terror, as well as disunity in families, neighbourhoods and countries (Bohm and Hiley, 1993). If people are coherent, then individuals, families, neighbourhoods and countries live harmoniously (Laszlo, 2008).

IMPRESSIVE DISCOVERIES

Empirical experiments reveal that 'people trained in achieving high states of heart coherence could facilitate coherence in other people in close proximity' (McCraty, 2011: 97). This finding is pregnant with hope for the future of therapy and its consequent knock-on effect. I dare say that, since we are an integral part of social webs on the earth, which is a segment of the universe, some may consider it unremarkable that our physiological rhythms and activities in the world occur at the same rate as solar and geomagnetic activity (see Halberg, Cornelissen and Otsuka, 2000). A relationship between individuals and the universe has been noted for eras.

Although several ancient cultures, such as the Egyptians, believed that the sun influenced human behaviour, there was no empirical evidence until a Russia scientist, Tchijevesky (1971), showed that the harshest World War I battles happened during peak sun-spot periods. Since then, scientific evidence has accumulated showing that major human events happen around the time of intense sun-spot activity and that although the media tends to focus on negative aspects such as death and crime, admirable human achievements happen during maximum sun-spot activities (Ertel, 1998). I mention sun-spots because our mental health may be influenced by other factors not to do with our genes or obvious environment. An Associate Professor of Environmental

Health, Cherry, for instance, has compelling evidence of the relationship between suicide rates and other problems, in Christchurch New Zealand, relating to sun-spot activities (2006). His research findings can be utilised practically. For example, future activities within the therapeutic arena can be conducted during peak sun-spot activity.

GLOBAL COHERENCE INITIATIVE

My example immediately above is not as outrageous as it sounds: the Global Coherence Initiative, a scientific organisation examining interactions between humans' and the earth's magnetic fields, has found substantial evidence of a measurable interaction between them (GCI, 2013). Currently, there is growing awareness that cosmic inflows of energy are a component of a natural occurring series of events with the capacity to benefit humankind (McCraty, 2011). Nevertheless, individuals have responsibility for their personal energy and how to utilise their power in order to develop fuller connections and greater interactive caring with others, including all living creatures and the world we live on. Some contend that a collective of humans intentionally producing similar positive emotional experiences can influence our planet's magnetic fields (for example, Deyhle and McCraty, 2010). In such a situation, if enough individuals generate heartfelt positive emotions, then social and economic oppression and inequalities that affect mental health, may be usefully unpacked with a successful outcome. In sum, when we are emotionally literate and learn emotional self-regulation, personal coherence blossoms, leading to sensing connection with our whole selves, others and the universe. Consequently, when our coherence is stable, it can be mirrored in our wellbeing, society and even the earth (see for example, Lipton and Bhaerman, 2011).

ONGOING PREVENTION

Right from the start of life, ongoing prevention is important, although it is never too late to start. Rather than giving ourselves negative messages that release stressful cortisol and adrenalin (Rokade, 2011), we can begin, for example, to open our hearts and send reassuring 'I like you' messages to ourselves for what psychologist Bloom (2011) calls the endorphin (popularly known as 'the happy hormone') effect to happen. We can 'endorphinate' regularly by asking ourselves 'What do I love?' and doing it. Here is part of my 'love-list', to show what I mean:

- snuggling into my duvet a little longer
- having a spa-day
- smelling an aromatic rose.

Different things appeal to different people.

TOOLS FOR LIFE

Bloom (2011) theorises (based on evidence from practice) that tools for life to keep distress at bay are:

- do anything (harmless) that you like
- move daily for twenty minutes

- smile inwardly
- rest
- connect to the natural world.

'Tools for life' is not a model to be found in the NICE guidelines or a choice that is offered to those seen as needing psychological care within the current IAPT remit. This is understandable because no randomised control trials (RCTs) have been conducted to either support or refute his speculation. From our own subjective experience, we understand that individuals who are mentally troubled can have their minds soothed by loving compassion, yet IAPT suppose that those who become better do so as a result of medical treatment as opposed to psychological reasons (since loving compassion and mentally caring change brain chemistry). Rather than perceiving a client in a holistic way, mental conditions are treated as separate disorders; therapy models are prescribed in the way medical drugs are, instead of floodlighting their commonalities and embracing person-to-person relationships (Seager, 2012). Clinical psychologist Seager deliberated with colleagues to agree on universal human needs; five were identified:

- to be loved (attachment)
- to be heard (empathy)
- to belong (home, family, identity)
- to achieve (fulfilment)
- to have belief in something and hope for the future (meaning).

'Carl Rogers, one of the fathers of counselling, originally identified the highly important triad of empathy, warmth and genuineness' (Seager, 2012:16). With this in mind, another possible future avenue for mental health is meeting these needs to buffer against psychological deterioration while therapists continue to communicate their empathy, warmth and genuineness to clients.

LOVE AND COMPASSION

Since a person's electromagnetic field generating from the heart influences others, therapists need to expand their personal awareness in order to develop their love and compassion more fully, so that in future clients can benefit as soon as they and the therapist make contact (as explained earlier). This statement and other information within my final chapter challenge the orthodox scientific community that embraces the current psychopathology belief system. Existing diagnostic manuals mention neither love nor compassion. When data is seen as not sitting consistently with previous data that the scientific community embrace, the community dislikes it. However, mainstream science can benefit by embracing a further, holistic construct that includes the importance of love and compassion, the centrality of relationship, and the concept of the non-locality of mind, and how crucial personal meaning is to individual wellness, not only in the future, but now.

DISCUSSION

Although research using RCTs is deemed the pinnacle within a scientific community and relevant theories put forward by those who are esteemed tend to be taken on-board, anecdotal evidence too has a place within the field of therapy (Seager, 2012). Having an open mind is important, even if the main professional community we are part of seems blinkered due to holding on to its frame of reference tightly. Remember, the scientific community believed in a flat world and the unconventional scientist who put forward the idea that it was a sphere was badly treated! What I desire is that our minds are open, that we do not cease to use our imaginations, to dream of possibilities, while being respectful of differences between speculation, leaping to conclusions and having preconceived notions based on valid and reliable evidence.

Much of what I have written in this chapter is so cutting-edge that it may be difficult for some to consider, but references can be followed up. My hope is that non-traditional views aiming towards a holistic perspective are at least thought-provoking. I have presented many others' research findings and theories. When offering my opinion, I make this clear. We are fallible beings so it is not difficult to misinterpret research or theory. My view is that everything is open to being investigated, that many of yesterday's scientific 'facts' will be tomorrow's 'untruths', that just because there is no evidence backing up a theory, we should or should not accept it and that more will be discovered than we have ever fantasised in our wildest dreams. Orthodox scientists have a great deal to contribute and in several years time, perhaps much of what they are currently strongly attached to will be held lightly, enabling future possibilities, with their promise of tapping into amazing potentialities, to be welcomed and embraced by the therapeutic community. The cutting-edge concepts I have presented here are well founded but not yet widely utilised. In the future, perhaps the therapy profession will embrace these concepts, to provide clients with an even better service. (In writing this book, it has been my intention to make the subject of psychopathology more accessible by using as little jargon as possible. Once you have a picture in your mind of the subject, there is of course plenty of jargon that can be used relating to psychopathology.)

In order to qualify as a therapist, therapists have had to receive their own therapy. What did that therapy do? In essence, I trust that it improved therapists' coherence and emotional literacy. As coherent practitioner individuals, we may be best placed to offer a healing relationship to our clients, now and in the future.

Points to ponder

- What exciting dreams for the future of mental health care do you have?
- Consider how loving compassion can be used in clinical practice.
- If the heart's electromagnetic field is so powerful that it affects others, what can a therapist do if feeling negative before a client arrives?

Exercise

(Answers are embedded in this chapter.)

1 When might it be useful to psychopathologise?
2 How can the endorphin effect be released?
3 Explain 'heart-coherence'.

CHAPTER SUMMARY

Psychopathology is one frame of reference for looking at mental difficulties.

Feeling positive heartfelt emotions build wellbeing (Schore, 2012).

Possible future approaches to mental health are spotlighted:

1 As a therapist, generate coherence.
2 Teach clients to be more coherent.
3 Include learning about non-verbal communication and how to build resilience, in therapy training programmes.
4 Be in touch with the heart's energy field, and the myriad of energy systems it connects with, so that challenging experiences can be aptly managed (McCraty, 2004).
5 Improve self-regulation by boosting emotional intelligence because having appropriate emotional literacy is healthy (Panskepp and Biven, 2012).
6 Intense sun-spot activities can influence mental health so be conscious of sun-spot activities and plan actions appropriately while being accountable for ourselves (Cherry, 2006).
7 Send reassuring messages to oneself and use 'tools for life' to keep distress at bay.
8 See that the 'five universal needs' are met (Seager, 2012).
9 Expand personal awareness for developing love and compassion thereby fuelling empathy (Gerhardt, 2011).

What is considered 'true' today may be perceived as 'not true' tomorrow, therefore hold scientific beliefs lightly while having a mind that is open to novel evidence.

LIST OF USEFUL RESOURCES

- Bradley, R.T., Murphy, G. and McCraty, R. (2011) 'Non-local intuition in entrepreneurs and non-entrepreneurs: results of two experiments using electrophysiological measures', *International Journal of Entrepreneurs and Small Business*, 12, 3, pp. 343–72.
- Ornish, D. (1997) *Love and Survival: The Scientific Basis for the Healing Power of Intimacy* (New York, Harper Collins).
- Pert, C. (1998) *Molecules of Emotion: Why You Feel the Way you Feel* (London, Simon and Schuster).
- Rudd, B. (2011) *The Rainbow Game: The Personal and Social Skills Development Game* (Milton Keynes, Speechmark).

RELEVANT WEBSITES

www.bhma.org/pages/holistic-health.php
www.emotionalliteracy.eu
www.glcoherence.org

REFERENCES

Bernardi, L., Porta, C. and Spicuzza, L. (2005) 'Cardiorespiratory interactions to external stimuli', *Archives Italiennes de Biologie*, 143, 3–4, pp. 215–21.

Bloom, W. (2011) *The Endorphin Effect* (London, Piatkus).

Bohm, D. and Hiley, B.J. (1993) *The Undivided Universe* (London, Routledge).

Braden, G. (2012) *Deep Truth* (London, Hay House).

Brown, G. R. and Anderson, B. (1991) 'Psychiatric morbidity in adult patients with childhood histories of sexual and physical abuse', *American Journal of Psychiatry*, 148, 1, pp. 55–6.

Cherry, N. (2006) 'Suicide and solar activity linked through the Schuman resonance signal', www.neilcherry.com, accessed 6 September 2012.

Childre, D. and Rozman, D. (2005) *Transforming Stress, The Heartmath Solution to Relieving Worry, Fatigue and Tension* (Oakland CA, New Harbinger Publications).

Deyhle, A. and McCraty, R. (2010) 'The global coherence initiative', *Energy Magazine*, December/January, pp. 7–10.

Dombeck, M. (2011) *Defense Mechanisms*, www.mentalhelp.net/poc/view_doc.php?type=doc&id=4054, accessed 25 August 2012

Dossey, L. (2009) *Healing Beyond the Mind* (London, Time Warner)

Ertel, S. (1998) 'Cosmophysical correlations of creative activity in cultural history', *Biophysics*, 43, 4, pp. 736–41.

Felton (1981) *The Mind-Body Connection: Granny was Right*, www.rochester.edu/pr/Review/V59N3/feature2.html, accessed 25 August 2012.

Fonagy, P., Sharp, C. and Goodyer, I. (2008) *Social Cognition and Developmental Psychopathology* (Oxford, Oxford University Press).

Freud, A. (1937) *The Ego and the Mechanisms of Defense* (London, Hogarth Press and Institute of Psychoanalysis).

Gardner, K. and Qualter, P. (2009) 'Emotional intelligence and borderline personality disorder', *Personality and Individual Differences*, 47, 2, pp. 94–8.

GC1 (2013) *Together in the heart* www.youtube.com/user/GlobalCoherenceInit, accessed 9 February 2013.

Gerhardt, S. (2011) *The Selfish Society, How We all Forgot to Love One Another and Made Money Instead* (London, Simon and Schuster).

Goleman, D. (2011) *The Brain and Emotional Intelligence: New Insights* (Northampton MA, More Than Sound LLC)

Golsworthy, R. (2004) 'Counselling psychology and psychiatric classification: clash or co-existence?', *Counselling Psychology Review*, 19, 3, p. 28.

Halberg, F., Cornelissen, G. and Otsuka, K. (2000) 'Cross-spectrally coherent -10.5- and 21-year biological and physical cycles, magnetic storms and myocardial infarctions', *Neuroendocrinology*, 21, 3, pp. 233–58.

Harriet, I., MacMillan, M. D. and Fleming, J. E. (2001) 'Childhood abuse and lifetime psychopathology in a community sample', *Journal of the American Psychiatric Association*, 158, 11, pp. 1878–83.

Jumper, S. A. (1995) 'A meta-analysis of the relationship of childhood sexual abuse to adult psychological adjustment', *Child Abuse Neglect*, 94, 3, pp. 298–307.

Kegan, R. (1982) *The Evolving Self* (Cambridge MA, Harvard University Press).

King, A.M. (2010) 'The future of emotion research in the study of psychopathology', *Emotion Review*, 2, 3, pp. 225–8.

Lacey, J.L. and Lacey, B.C. (2007) 'Some autonomic central-nervous nervous system interrelationships', in Black, P. (ed.) *Physiological Correlations of Emotion* (New York, Academic Press).

Laible, D. and Thompson, R. (2003) 'Mother-child discourse, attachment security, shared positive affect, and early conscience development', *Child Development*, 71, 5, pp. 1424–40.

Laszlo, E. (2008) *Quantum Shift in the Global Brain: How the New Scientific Reality can Change Us and Our World* (Rochester VT, Inner Traditions).

Lipton, B. and Bhaerman, S. (2011) *Spontaneous Evolution* (New York, Hay House).

McCraty, R. (2004) 'The energetic heart: bioelectromagnetic communication within and between people', in Rosch, P.J. and Markov, M.S. (eds) *Bioelectromagnetic Medicine* (New York, Marcel Dekker).

McCraty, R. (2011) 'Coherence: bridging personal, social and global health', *Activitas Nervosa Superior Rediviva*, 53, 3, pp. 85–102.

McCraty, R., Atkinson, M., and Lipsenthal L. (2003) *Impact of the Power to Change Performance, Program and Stress and Health Risks in Correctional* Officer, Report No. 03-014s (Boulder Creek, California, Heartmath Research Centre).

McCraty, R., Atkinson, M. and Tiller, W.A. (2003) 'Impact of a work-place stress reduction program on blood pressure and emotional health and hypertensive employees', *Journal of Alternative and Complementary Medicine*, 9, 3, pp. 355–69.

McLay, R.N. and Spira, J.L. (2009) 'Use of a portable biofeedback device to improve insomnia in a combat zone, a case report', *Applied Psychophysiology and Biofeedback*, 34, pp. 319–21.

Panskepp J. and Biven, L. (2012) *The Architecture of Mind* (New York, Norton).

Parsons, C. E., Young, K. S. and Murray, L. (2010) 'The functional neuroanatomy of evolving parent-infant relationship', *Progress in Neorobiology*, 91, 3, pp. 220–41.

Prichard, D. (2008) 'Deconstructing psychopathology', *Journal of Progressive Human Services*, 17, 2, pp. 5–26.

Rokade, P.B. (2011) *Release of Endorphin Hormone and its Effects on Our Body and Moods: A Review* http://psrcentre.org/images/extraimages/1211916.pdf, accessed 10 February, 2013.

Rudd, B. (2000) Cross-cultural Inter-personal Space in Assumed Counselling Relationships with Same and Opposite Sex Pairs, and Counsellors' Perspectives on Proxemics, PhD Thesis, London, City University.

Schore, A. (2012) *The Science of the Art Psychotherapy* (New York, Norton).

Seager, M. (2012) 'Bad science and good mental health', *Therapy Today*, 23, 7, pp. 12–16.

Siepmann, M., Aykac, V. and Unterforfer, J. (2008) 'A pilot study on the effects of heart rate variability biofeedback in patients with depression and in healthy subjects', *Applied Physiology and Biofeedback*, 33, 4, pp. 195–201.

Sorrel, T. (2000) *Descartes* (Oxford, Oxford University Press).

Tchijevsky, A.L. (1971) 'Physical factors of the historical process' (trans. de Smit, V.P.), *Cycles*, 22, 1–2, pp. 11–27.

Vanderbilt, B., Young, R. and MacDonald, H.Z. (2008) 'Asthma severity and PTSD symptoms among inner city children: a pilot study', *Journal of Trauma and Dissociation*, 9, 2, pp. 191–207.

Wolk. C. and Velden, M. (1987) 'Detection variability within the cardiac cycle: toward a revision of the "baroreceptor hypothesis"', *Journal of Psychophysiology*, 1, pp. 61–5.

Afterword

At some point in their lives, approximately one in four people in the UK suffer with mental health problems (Mind, 2012). Ideally, debilitating mental conditions will not exist in future, but within my lifetime, I think there will still be people suffering with mental states. My vision is elimination of these states. Steps towards that vision are possible and sympathetic to the government's mental health boost goal for 2015 (Centre for Mental Health, 2006):

- Teach emotional literacy in schools (see www.emotionalliteracy.eu for resources I created for this).
- Maximise the practice of heart-coherence in order to promote a coherent society and minimise the costs of mental health problems (in 2010 they exceeded £100 billion – Centre for Mental Health, 2010).
- Support parents so that they have time to spend with their young people.
- Assist employers to include daily exercise and heart-coherence sessions for all at the workplace.
- Ensure buildings are constructed in a way that full-spectrum light can be utilised.
- Enable people in understanding how they can take responsibility for their own health.
- Build a sense of community so that relationships are positive and no person is lonely.
- Offer befriending and regular (aromatherapy) massage with relaxing music to those living alone.
- Promote nutritious habits and clarify the air so that pollutants are not inhaled.
- Have green spaces such as parks in residential, corporate and educational areas.
- See to it that all live above the breadline, so that quality of life is not compromised.
- Propagate cultural activities, being creative cross-culturally and enabling all to learn something new.
- Promote laughing out loud and helping others compassionately.
- Learn from frontier science to rapidly activate reliable and valid research findings for health promotion.

I believe that the cutting-edge discovery of epigenetics (in which factors outside genes influence their behaviour; Lipton, 2011), holds much hope for the future of mental health, and trust that if government knows of appropriate evidence (for example, citations in this book) such a vision can be put into action.

USEFUL RESOURCES

- Lipton, B. (2013) *The Honeymoon Effect: The Science of Creating Heaven on Earth* (London, Hay House).
- Rudd, B. (2009) *EQ* (card game) (Milton Keynes, Speechmark).

RELEVANT WEBSITES

www.impact-the-world.org/projects/tanzania.htm
www.kingsfund.org.uk/document.rm?id=7665

REFERENCES

Centre for Mental Health (2010) *Cost of Mental Ill Health in England Exceeds £100 Billion, New Figures Show*, www.centreformentalhealth.org.uk/news/2010_cost_of_mental_ill_health.aspx, accessed 14 November 2012.

Centre for Mental Health (2006) *The Future of Mental Health: A Vision for 2015*, www.centreformentalhealth.org.uk/pdfs/mental_health_futures_policy_paper.pdf, accessed 14 November 2012.

Lipton, B. (2011) *The Biology of Belief* (London, Hay House).

Mind (2012), www.mind.org.uk/help/research_and_policy/statistics_1_how_common_is_mental_distress, accessed 15 September 2012.

Glossary

aetiology: cause

affect: emotion

antagonistic: drug interaction decreasing drug effect

applied behavioural analysis: adapting behaviour to fit in with society

Appropriate Attribution Technique: a relatively new intervention programme – a cognitive psycho-educational technique, helping survivors rid themselves of the distress stemming from originally attributed self-blame as a result of a critical reattribution process

assessment: evaluation

attention deficit hyperactivity disorder: low frustration and boredom thresholds, problems concentrating, impulsivity and moving too much

autism: the severe end of autistic spectrum disorders

autistic spectrum disorders: socially impaired and restricted and repetitive movements

automatic thoughts: spontaneous thoughts

behavioural: to do with actions

biological: relating to biology

bi-polar: extreme mood swings

chronic pain: pain lasting for a long time, generally longer than six weeks

cognitive: to do with how we perceive information

cognitive behaviour therapy: therapy based on the thoughts that affect actions and behaviour

coherence: being in a harmonious state

co-morbidity: two or more disorders existing simultaneously

conscience: an inner sense, guiding us to the rightness or wrongness of our actions

core beliefs: individuals' central tenets on which they lead their lives

cross-coherence: synchronisation

delta-9-tetrahydrocannabinol: the main active chemical in cannabis

developmental: the process of growth

developmental trauma disorde: chronically or repeatedly exposed to relational stress, with detrimental consequences dialectics: a formal reasoning system to arrive at the truth by exchanging logical arguments

dopa–responsive dystonia: an inheritable gene prevalent in obsessive compulsive personality disorder sufferers

downward arrow technique: a socratic method of finding core beliefs

drug interaction: when taking two substances simultaneously, one has an effect on the other

dyslexia: reading age is rated lower than overall IQ age

entrainment: falling into synchronism

epigenetics: factors outside the gene influencing its behaviour

fight or flight response: the physiology that occurs when we are faced with real or imaginary stressors

formulation: creating a particular mental 'formula' regarding the cause, choice of therapy model and consequent relief of mental distress, which can be used as an alternative to the concept of psychopathology

generalised anxiety disorder: feeling anxious most of the time without knowing why

magnesium–L–threonate: an easily absorbed and assimilated form of magnesium

mentalising: being aware that others have thoughts and feelings (which can be different to yours) and that these have an effect on behaviour

obsessive compulsive disorder: irrational thinking and repeated compulsive actions

panic attack: physiologically acting very stressed without appropriate stimulus

pedagogical: teaching

post traumatic stress disorder: re-experiencing a past traumatic event as if it was happening in the present

prognosis: expected outcome

psychopathology: the empirical study of mental disorders

refer: pass on

reliability: the extent to which someone/thing can be trusted

resonance: synchronised vibration

schema: a 'template' through which the outer world is perceived

stress: a stimulus beyond that which the organism can healthily tolerate

symptoms: signs

synergistic: drug interaction increases drug effect

valid: supportive of the intended claim

Index